From
Chaos
to
Calm

From Chaos to Calm

Effective Parenting of

Challenging Children

with ADHD and Other

Behavioral Problems

Janet E. Heininger, Ph.D., and
Sharon K. Weiss, M.Ed.

Foreword by Sam Goldstein, Ph.D.

A Perigee Book

Perigee Books
Published by The Berkley Publishing Group
A division of Penguin Putnam Inc.
375 Hudson Street
New York, New York 10014

First edition: May 2001

Published simultaneously in Canada.

The Penguin Putnam Inc. World Wide Web site address is
www.penguinputnam.com

Library of Congress Cataloging-in-Publication Data

Heininger, Janet E.
    From chaos to calm : effective parenting for challenging children with ADHD and
other behavioral problems / Janet E. Heininger, Sharon K. Weiss.
        p. cm.
    Includes bibliographical references and index.
    ISBN 0-399-52661-7
        1. Problem children—Behavior modification.   2. Behavior disorders in chil-
dren.   3. Child rearing.   4. Parenting.   I. Weiss, Sharon K.   II. Title.

HQ773.H383 2001
649'.64—dc21   00-051050

Printed in the United States of America

10   9   8   7

The names of individuals in examples in this book have been changed. So we wouldn't get bogged down in the awkward "he or she" phraseology or the sometimes confusing alternating use of male and female pronouns, for simplification, we have principally used male pronouns throughout the book. All material, however, applies equally to both genders. When reading the information and incidents, you should apply them to the children in your world.

To Jack, my best friend, constant support and my greatest joy in life.
To all the Theodores, but especially to this one.

To my *Theodore*

CONTENTS

FOREWORD

Last spring I watched with interest and awe as two tiny swallows built a nest of mud and sticks under the eve of the deck attached to the back of my home. Over a week's time they worked diligently and cooperatively to build a small but secure dwelling. In the following weeks I watched as they came and went. In the evenings while sitting on the deck I could hear them chirping, secure in their new home. A month or so later I discerned a different sound coming from the nest, the sound of baby hatchlings. I couldn't see them but I knew they were there. When I ventured near the deck, at least one of the swallows would chirp loudly and fly back and forth, hoping to intimidate me to move away. During the following weeks I watched as the swallows came and went, bringing nourishment to their brood. Once, I spied a small chick's head extending from the nest and then quickly disappearing as one of the parent's heads protruded. These were vigilant parents; parents instilled by instinct to nurture and care for their young, preparing them for their adult lives. Then one day, they were gone. The babies experimented with flight, mastered a skill that many men have dreamt of, and off they went. I don't suspect there were emotional good-byes or long farewells. The parents had done their job. The offspring were ready for independent life.

For these swallows, parenting was reduced to an exquisitely simple formula. Provide a safe, secure home, bring offspring into the world, then protect and nourish them until they are ready to fly off on their own. Though seemingly easy, great effort and time was involved. Over a number of months, these two swallows devoted themselves exclusively to their offspring. Unlike salmon and snakes born with sufficient instinct to survive independently, these young swallows required a few months of nurturing and parenting. As we move up the chain of species' complexity, each species requires increasingly more and more time. Bear cubs require at least one year with their parents; higher primates at least three or four; and human beings at least ten, although in our culture we have extended childhood to at least twenty. For nearly all species, parents play a critical role. They are, in a sense, futurists. A successful species must bring offspring into the world, nurture, support, and, most importantly, prepare those offspring to transition successfully into their adult lives. In an unending cycle they then bring their own offspring into the future world.

I expect it would be quite simple to parent today's children if we were provided with sufficient instinct to do so. But we are not. We have created a complex culture, one that compromises children's ability to transition successfully into their adult lives. In their quest for guidance and help, parents turn to experts. Experts have increasingly turned to the print media to provide guidance and assistance. A recent review of books in print yielded 2,929 books available about parenting children. Parenting advice has become big business. A recent survey completed at Colorado State University found that the cost of raising a child from birth through age seventeen is over $160,000. It should not surprise us that some of that money can be best spent helping parents learn effective strategies by providing resources, guidance, and ideas to help parents raise their children.

As complex and complicated as parenting may be, most parents are reasonably successful. However, all parents are ill prepared for the stress and emotional turmoil they face when their children experience learning, emotional, behavioral, or developmental problems. These problems affect one in five children. These problems make daily life in school or out on the playground difficult and stressful. Success in these settings shapes and nurtures the mind-set necessary for children to transition successfully into their adult lives. Fortunately the fields of medicine, mental health, and education have generated large volumes of valuable information over the past twenty years about these problems in childhood. Finally, this information is finding its way to those most in need; parents raising children with challenging problems.

From Chaos to Calm offers a unique look into the minds, hearts, and emotions of the Heininger/Reuter family. The unique style of this text allows the reader to experience not only the points of view of parents and professionals but also of children, primarily Theodore's. This is truly a child-centered work. From the very first to the very final page of this book we are provided with Theodore's thoughts, feelings, and observations about his behavior. From the very start, we learn of a child frustrated because he knows what needs to be done but somehow can't seem to do it. His words generate a foundation of empathy for a child who desperately seeks the self-discipline necessary to meet not only his expectations but those of his parents and teachers. We also read the thoughts and words of Theodore's mother. As a clinical psychologist, I have heard these words echoed time and time again by families who are raising challenging children. Jan's words provide a valuable foil, helping us understand how lack of effective strategies and interventions lead to frustration, anger, and, ultimately, family conflict.

This text would be of value if it simply echoed family words. These words set an emotional stage for empathy and understanding. But this text also includes the words and guidance of an experienced expert in behavior management for families. In this text Sharon Weiss introduces her concept of "planned parenting," a style of parenting that provides parents not only with strategies and resources but with a practical, logical framework to assess child and family problems and intervene successfully. Sharon also offers tips to help parents understand and troubleshoot when effective strategies don't seem to work.

From Chaos to Calm highlights Sharon's years of experience working with medical, mental health, and educational professionals. The text contains two of the best chapters available to guide parents through the process of seeking professional help and then, most importantly, to "sequence treatment." It would be easy for an experienced professional to resort to the clinical terms and labels so prevalent in books of this nature. Instead, Sharon avoids such jargon; she defines behavior in operational terms and observable means, getting down to the business of helping parents help their children. Unlike so many texts choosing to focus blame upon children for their problems, this book helps readers quickly understand that Theodore's challenge lies not within him but within his parents and teachers and their ability to effectively raise and educate this young man.

We are increasingly recognizing that successful transition into adult life requires our ability to help every child identify and develop strengths, capabilities, and a resilient mind-set. Although Theodore is a child with attention deficit/hyperactivity disorder, the true value of this text lies in the fact that it is generic. It is a fine work that will offer guidance and help to parents raising children with any type of challenge. This is a work that will allow parents to "even the playing field" at home. By setting in place suggestions and strategies offered in this text, parents can focus their energy to help their children develop empathy, self-discipline, communication, and problem solving: skills that we are increasingly aware are critical, like flight for the swallow, in helping children transition successfully into their adult lives. These are skills that parents struggle to develop in children when they present daily behavioral and emotional challenges.

This is a book I will turn to repeatedly for ideas and suggestions. *From Chaos to Calm* is an essential reference guide that parents can read, place on their bookshelves, and refer to time and time again.

—SAM GOLDSTEIN, PH.D.
Coauthor of *Raising Resilient Children*

ACKNOWLEDGMENTS

The writing of any book is not a solitary process. Some require more support than others. For us, the encouragement reaches back across decades. We recognize that ours is not just a collaboration between two but the amalgamation of the efforts and support of many and we are grateful to each and every one of them.

Sharon: Jan, my coauthor, who, after all the prompts and offers, was the one who made it happen. She broadened my concepts of writing and editing and helped clarify thoughts, with an eye to the mission we both wanted to achieve. I want to thank Jamie, Jan's other half, who was the patient reader, editor, and computer guru.

I am indebted to Sam Goldstein, who from the very beginning has taken a personal interest in this project. He has been there as reader, reviewer, critic, supporter, resource, and the consummate mentor. Special thanks to him for his shared wisdom on all fronts. Barbara Ingersoll and Judith Stern were generous of time and spirit in helping me understand the process of publishing and team writing. Harvey Parker said I would and should write a book and offered personal support and publication of the book. What more could someone ask? Dr. Ken Kaplan, willing reader of my section of the medication chapter, kept me from practicing medicine without a license. Dr. Karen Miller unselfishly gave her valuable time and expertise to review the entire medication chapter. By generously sharing their own material, Karen and Dr. Tim Wilens enriched our book.

I owe more than I can say to Robin Niederpruem, who, from the early days of typing from handwritten notes through the whole book-writing process, made it seem like this was just like all the other tasks. All this while holding down the fort while the book got written. What would I do without you?

Thanks indeed go to Barry and Eydie Greene: To Barry who is my personal gadfly (everyone should have one), friend, tormentor, and supporter—who is aggravatingly right and who always thought I should write a book. And to Eydie, who read the proposal, asked for updates (as if it was something really important to her), and gave all the personal interest and support a real friend can give. Karen Altman-Steinfield, friend and colleague, who read and gave input through the whole process of writing, and rallied and encouraged me. Allyson Newman, longtime friend who rushed in to provide much-needed computer support. I also have to thank George Goldman for his very special contribution to my professional growth. Then there is the Club—Sally Sibley, Trudy Bell, and Marie Withrow—professional colleagues and personal friends who listened and when I winced always made me feel it was worth the effort because I had something to give.

I owe much to my parents because, thanks to them, I am what I hope they wanted me to be. My family, Babs and Jim, Ned and Claudia and their kids, Kathy and Mildred, constants in my life who understand my work ethic, share my personal dreams, and still love me in spite of it all. And Jack, who really has been my strongest support and biggest fan through this process and through my whole adult life. He manages to understand how important my work is, all the while knowing how much more important he is.

Finally, I thank all the families—children and parents—from the Phillips School for Contemporary Education and private practice, who've helped me understand how huge every small accomplishment really is.

Jan and Sharon: We owe much to our agent, Jeff Kleinman, for his enthusiasm for the project from the start, his personal perspective along the way, and his unwavering support. And to Iris Krasnow, who got us to Jeff. Our thanks to our talented editor, Sheila Curry Oakes, who liked the concept, recognized its potential, and wanted to undertake the editing of our book. We are grateful as well to

Sheila Moody for her meticulous copyediting.

Simple thanks is insufficient for Kathleen Gilles Seidel. Kathy dedicated her novelist's eye (and ear) to improving our prose, fixed Jan's mixed metaphors and Sharon's occasional awkward phrasing, and constantly reminded Jan to "tell the story." She took time from her own writing to edit every word—and kept brushing off our thanks by claiming that as a writer, it was refreshing to have the opportunity to edit someone else's work. If that weren't enough, she even took one of Sharon's techniques, tried it with her own family, and shared how easily she was able to adapt it for her own family's particular situation. Her enthusiasm for the book helped keep us going through months of writing.

Jan: I undertook this book—far outside my academic and professional fields—because I had a story to tell about our less-easy child that could be useful to other families struggling daily to cope with a challenging child. I knew, however, that my story would be more relevant if I explained in detail what had made the most difference in life with Theodore. Calming our chaotic household had been largely due to Sharon. With my story, Theodore's insights, and Sharon's techniques, we had a book that could help many other families with challenging children.

Our family owes much to Sharon. Jamie and I saw her for a year and did whatever she told us to do. The result was a household with structures that worked, a child who was able to follow routines that kept us from yelling at him all the time, and a far happier family all around.

Writing is inherently a lonely process. Collaboration eases that even as it adds time to ensure all parties agree. While it certainly took more time to write this book as Sharon and I e-mailed multiple versions of each chapter back and forth, when we finished, we were immensely proud of what we had accomplished. That's a measure of an effective collaboration.

I owe thanks to many who provided advice and encouragement throughout. Fellow author and colleague Frank Bierlein liked my idea, read an early proposal, and encouraged me to move ahead. Parenting expert and college classmate Larry Kutner took time from his busy career to educate me about royalties, serial rights, and other such things, and then generously read the entire manuscript. My brother, Ken Heininger, provided legal advice at several key stages, for which I am duly grateful. I thank James Adams, former bureau chief of the *Sunday Times of London,* for repeatedly advising me to convey my ideas by writing about people. Finally, I couldn't have done this without the support and willing ears of my longtime friends Judy Kozlowski and Donna Webber.

Special thanks go to others who also helped improve the quality of Theodore's life. Perceptive teachers Ron Jacobus and Maria Grabowski first noticed that he might have ADHD, brought it to our attention, and later shared more of their insights about him before and after his diagnosis. Neuropsychologist Barry Ekdom, Ph.D., did a careful and thoughtful evaluation of Theodore and subsequently provided helpful guidance on what parents should look for when deciding who should assess or diagnose their child. Bruce Pfeffer, M.D., not only monitored Theodore's medication treatment but has been a fount of information on ADHD and enthusiastic about this book. Thanks also to Susan Glaub and Susan Douglass for their efforts on Theodore's behalf.

His middle school sixth-grade teachers, particularly Joan Smith, Susan Steinberg, and Marcia Churchill, challenged Theodore intellectually and convinced him he could succeed in public school after difficult years in elementary school. So too did head counselor Millie Lawson. Our greatest debt is to teacher extraordinaire Joyce Murray, who in fifth grade recognized and fostered the vast intellectual capability behind Theodore's attention deficit disorder. For the first time, in her rigorous and intellectually stimulating class, Theodore felt he was special, competent, and gifted—not just different. He is unlikely ever again to have a teacher who will do as much for him as she did.

By leading Stepping Stones, the social-skills training program we and Theodore attended for a year, Rebecca Fleischer, Ph.D., Libby Robbins, M.S.W., and Rho Silberglitt, L.C.S.W., provided the tools for Theodore to begin to interact socially more effectively. Cathi Cohen, L.C.S.W., the director of In Step, graciously gave us permission to adapt Stepping Stones materials for use in this book. Patricia C. Landi, L.C.S.W., who has counseled Theodore through thick and thin, wishes all her clients made as good use of her time as Theodore has. I am grateful to her for sharing her insights into Theodore and for being one of his biggest boosters.

Finally, I thank my husband, James A. Reuter, and my daughter, Caroline Reuter, for their willingness to make our private life public. Caroline hasn't always been thrilled by changes we've made in our household to accommodate Theodore, but she helpfully shared her thoughts for this book. Jamie has patiently endured my immersion in an extended writing process three times. Having edited every word of that first book, I would have understood if he'd passed this time. He didn't. I am grateful for his careful editing, but particularly for his willingness to let the whole world know how much yelling has gone on in our home.

INTRODUCTION

When it comes to kids, challenging or less easy is in the eye of the beholder. What one parent might find challenging may seem like a breeze to another. Some children are difficult, frustrating, and would stymie almost anyone's best efforts. But just as often, almost any child can fit someone's description of challenging. At any given moment, a child's behavior may outstrip a parent's ability to deal with the situation. The situation, the child, or both can be challenging. That doesn't mean the adult is a bad parent or even inept. It only means that in that particular situation, the parent may not be up to handling the child's behavior or what is happening.

You're reading this book because there is a behavior problem in your family. Your child may be suffering—he's bullied or feels left out or inept in social or play situations. He may be struggling in school. More likely, you or the school is suffering. At times, it is overwhelming. Your child is considered "a handful." He responds to situations with anger or frustration. He refuses to follow directions. You've tried everything you know to do and have run out of options. You're concerned, frustrated, and feeling guilty. You may be worried that your child will always have problems. Or you may be afraid that if you don't get a handle on the situation now, it could spiral out of control. You may be agonizing that your child's difficult behavior is a measure of your competency as a parent or person. Bad child equals bad parent.

Maybe only you feel that something is wrong. Perhaps your child's father (or mother) keeps saying: "You're making too big a deal out of this. There's no problem." Or "Whatever it is, it'll pass." Maybe your marriage is already under stress because of other problems. Even if it isn't, it's probably under stress because of the challenge this child presents. Maybe your child's other parent blames you. "It's your fault Junior is like this." "If you'd just handled Jennifer differently, there wouldn't be any problem."

You're frustrated because you've exhausted the "tricks" you know. You started by doing what comes naturally. When that didn't work, you tried suggestions from relatives, friends, and your pediatrician. You are surprised by how angry your child makes you. You may be concerned that your reactions might be damaging your child.

Maybe you're almost paralyzed by your child's behavior. Again and again, you hear yourself reacting in the same old way. You know it isn't going to work, but you don't know what else to do. So, sometimes, you do nothing. You let it go. You know that's not the answer, but you're afraid of making things worse. You find yourself "walking on eggshells." You may even stop going places as a family because you fear your child's disruptive behavior. If so, you're probably seething inside, furious with yourself and your child. So, much of the time, you just react—with high volume, over-the-top emotion. You go from feeling out of control to having no control.

That's when the guilt sets in. You can't believe you said or did that. You hate the parent you've become. Or maybe you're so frustrated with your inability to change your kid's behavior that you've started to dislike your own child. "Who," you moan, "dislikes their own child? What kind of a parent am I?"

We have written this book to reassure you that there are many parents out there just like you facing the same struggles and finding solutions for their situations. Our book is a guide for planned parenting, rather than the reactive parenting you so often find yourself doing. In this book we present both the personal and the professional perspective as well as insight into what the "less-easy" child is thinking about his situation. The book is told in the voices of a parent (Jan), a child (Theodore), and a behavior expert (Sharon). Although Theodore was eventually diagnosed with attention-deficit/hyperactivity disorder—more commonly known as attenion deficit disorder (ADHD), the advice in this book can be helpful to parents with kids who have no diagnosis or whose children are challenging by virtue of behavior that often comes with anxiety disorder, autism, Asperger's syndrome, obsessive-compulsive disorder, or just a difficult temperament.

It is, of course, a success story, when read from start to finish. But it can be a valuable resource when you go straight to a chapter that addresses those issues most crucial to you. For instance, use chapter 2 when you are deciding on which professional to consult. Or turn to chapter 8 when educational issues are your biggest concern. The Solution Finder is a user-friendly guide for locating what approaches to use when addressing specific problems.

I'm Sharon Weiss and I have been a behavior expert for more than twenty years. I work with parents and educators, helping them understand how to make changes in expectations and guidelines and restructure routines such as getting up, doing homework, and going to bed so that day-to-day life runs more smoothly. I worked with Jan and her husband, Jamie Reuter, for a year to help them learn better ways to deal with Theodore, an undeniably less-easy child.

I'm Jan Heininger, Theodore's mother. I'm a historian by training, a foreign policy expert, a former college professor, and currently a filmmaker and writer. All the training in the world didn't prepare me to deal effectively with my challenging child.

I'm Theodore Reuter. I'm now twelve years old, in seventh grade, and I was diagnosed with attention deficit disorder when I was in third grade. Life in our house was pretty difficult until my mom and dad learned better ways to help me deal with my life. It's a whole lot better now than it used to be.

We hope that the voices that make up this book will give you a clear picture of what your child is experiencing, what parents typically encounter, and what you can do to reduce the chaos in your own home.

—JANET E. HEININGER, PH.D., AND SHARON K. WEISS, M.ED.

1

Chaos Reigns

Theodore, the Less-Easy Child

Theodore: My name is Theodore Reuter. In second grade my mornings were awful. I didn't understand why it was so hard for me to get out of the house every morning. Until one of my parents came in and started yelling as if the world were about to explode, I usually didn't get anything done.

My mind kept saying: "Stop this. You know you're supposed to be doing something else, like getting dressed or making your bed." But I was never able to do what my mind told me. I stayed glued to whatever I was doing, which was much more fun than getting my shoes on or brushing my teeth. Only if they yelled loud enough would my brain snap to attention—though not for long—to make progress on what I was supposed to be doing. A good morning was getting to breakfast without them yelling at me. I didn't have many good mornings. The whole process made me feel stupid.

Jan: I'm Jan Heininger and I'm Theodore's beleaguered mother. Mornings with Theodore were miserable. They usually went something like this:

"Theodore, it's seven-thirty. It's time to get up." I turn on the light, shake Theodore, and walk out of the room, already late myself.

Ten minutes later, I stride down the hall and back into his room. No movement from the bed. In a louder voice, I say, "Theodore, get up. You're late."

Five minutes later, my husband, Jamie, finds there is still no movement from the bed, throws off the covers, and in a raised voice, says, "Theodore, get going now!" Out he goes and Theodore sleepily wanders into the bathroom, book in hand, uses the toilet, and wanders out without flushing. Back he goes into his room and is immediately sidetracked by a LEGOs project.

At 7:50, I discover Theodore playing, still in his nightshirt, bed unmade, and start yelling: *"Get going!"* Out I run, leaving Theodore to his own devices.

At 7:55, Jamie roars into Theodore's room, finds him still not dressed, bed not made, starts throwing clothes at him, and yells: *"Theodore! Take off your nightshirt"* (yank) *"Put on this T-shirt"* (pull, tug).

Startled, Theodore looks up, a deer caught in the headlights. His soft, brown eyes widen in alarm. Why is his father so angry?

"Get these pants on" (yank, tug) *"Where are your shoes?"*

"I don't know."

Jamie rummages around and finds shoes stuffed into the back of the closet.

"Put these on, get your bed made, and get out there to make your lunch."

Exit Jamie. Theodore starts to pull on a sock and notices a book open on the floor. Sock stays halfway on.

At 8:00, I race in, catch Theodore reading, and start in: "WHAT ARE YOU DOING? GET THOSE SOCKS AND SHOES ON NOW!!!"

Theodore collapses in tears: "Why are you always yelling at me?"

"WHY DO YOU ALWAYS MAKE ME YELL AT YOU?" I shriek. *"WHY WON'T YOU JUST GET UP AND GET DRESSED WITHOUT OUR HAVING TO YELL AT YOU EVERY MORNING?"*

This is a typical morning. We haven't even gotten to making Theodore's bed, preparing his lunch, eating breakfast, gathering school materials, coat, hat, gloves, brushing teeth, combing hair, or getting him out the door in time for the bus.

Daily life is chaotic and stressful from the time Theodore groggily wakes up (or doesn't wake up) until he finally goes to sleep. I don't understand why nearly every day is such a struggle.

Getting Theodore to bed on time—and getting him to stay there—is as difficult as getting him out of the house in the morning. Our evenings are a lot like mornings in reverse.

10:15 P.M. Forty-five minutes past his bedtime, delayed by dawdling, I finish reading to Theodore and kiss him goodnight. His door is open before I even get down the hall. "I have to go to the bathroom," he announces.

"Hurry up," I grump.

10:30 P.M. I go back to check. Theodore is sitting on the toilet reading a book.

I start yelling again. *"Get in bed right this minute!"*

He exits, hurriedly, toilet unflushed. I shut the door loudly.

10:45 P.M. Theodore wanders out and asks, "What's the tallest building in the United States?"

I roar: "I don't know and I don't care. *Get back in bed now!"*

11:00 P.M. Theodore wanders out again. "I'm hungry."

Jamie yells, "TOO BAD. YOU SHOULD HAVE EATEN A BETTER DINNER. DON'T GET OUT OF BED AGAIN!"

11:15 P.M. Theodore creeps out, again, his little blond head peeking around the corner. I hear this plaintive voice (with Jamie asleep in the chair): "I can't sleep."

Frustrated and angry that he will not go to bed and leave me alone, I bolt at him, spinning him down the hall to his room. *"JUST GO TO BED AND DO NOT, I REPEAT, DO NOT COME OUT AGAIN."*

I just did not know how to deal with this child. Why was every day so difficult?

Theodore: I didn't want to go to bed. I wasn't tired. Except for the questions, I had lots of good reasons for getting out of bed. I did get hungry. I did need to go to the bathroom. I did get thirsty. But the bottom line was that I wasn't ready to go to sleep. I always had lots of questions, but when I was lying there wide awake, there was nothing to distract me so I'd focus on needing to get answers *right then* to my questions

Evenings felt just like mornings. I hated being yelled at. Mornings were a bit harder for me because a bad morning usually meant a bad day. Evenings were hard because my brain was usually racing a mile a minute and they didn't understand that's what kept me up.

The Less-Easy Child

Jan: From the beginning, I resisted labeling Theodore as difficult—despite all evidence to the contrary. He just was "less easy" than his sister, Caroline, who is three years older than him. I tried to pin some of the differences on gender, but that didn't explain everything.

And difficult he was. Theodore was demanding, inflexible, stubborn, and emotionally volatile. He was picky—about food, clothes, everything. He wouldn't eat tomatoes, onions, celery, carrots, apples, or most of what we cooked, for that matter. He wouldn't wear any clothes that "itched," "scratched," or constricted his neck (forget turtlenecks), had buttons (pullover shirts only), or zippers (elastic waist jeans only). Theodore was argumentative, impatient, and whiny. He was distractible, oh, so distractible. And he was extremely persistent. He spoke so rapidly it was difficult to understand him.

The contrast with his easygoing sister made it harder to live with Theodore. Moreover, unlike Caroline, he was not a compliant child. Getting him to do anything we wanted took immense effort because everything distracted him from the task at hand.

DAWDLING AND DISTRACTIBILITY

"Theodore, come and set the table." No response. I knew he had to have heard me—he was just fifteen feet away in the living room. I'd raise my voice (does the pattern sound familiar?) and call again. No response. Irritated, I'd march into the living room, find Theodore intensely focused on following intricate diagrams to build a LEGO castle. Was he deliberately ignoring me or did he actually not hear me? Theodore could focus for hours on building a space station with his LEGOs, but couldn't manage to finish three simple household chores.

His unwillingness—or inability—to shift his attention, do what we asked of him, and keep focused on the tasks at hand, drove us nuts. Our household was in constant turmoil, not just from Theodore's unwillingness to shift gears, but from our response to his chronic—and, we believed, intentional—dawdling. Frustrated and irritated, we were *always* yelling. He'd dawdle, we'd yell. He'd dawdle, we'd yell louder.

Theodore: I didn't dawdle to be bad, I just was distracted by other things— like books, LEGOs, toys, or magazines, which were a lot more fun than what I was supposed to be doing. Sometimes, I'd ignore them when they called me, like when I was watching TV, but other times I really didn't hear them because I was so into what I was doing.

Besides, I always thought I had more time than I really did.

RESISTANCE TO CHANGE—DEALING WITH THE UNEXPECTED

Jan: Theodore's resistance to change didn't help. What was familiar was comfortable; what was new was not.

Theodore: I want things to be the way I like them to be. Whenever I think about doing something I haven't done before, I feel like I'm not going to like it. Well, what I'm really afraid of is that I'm not going to be good at it and I'll look foolish. So I won't try it. My fear of looking stupid often keeps me from trying new things like ice skating or bowling.

Jan: Even at the age of three, four, or five, Theodore had to have things done his way. We assumed he would move out of the "terrible twos" and life would revert to "normal." It never did. He simply could not deal with unexpected changes. We thought of our life as fairly routine, but errands did have to be run, things did come up, unexpected changes did have to be made.

Once he entered elementary school (which added homework to an already stressful relationship), even on good days, when I did not lose my temper over unfinished homework or missing items, Theodore would erupt when I announced that we had to make a short stop to get milk or to do this or that.

Theodore: I was regularly in a bad mood when I got picked up because I didn't like the after-school program. It was a bad place for me to be. It was too noisy to get homework done. Kids were mean to me, and the counselors couldn't make kids stop teasing me. So when I got picked up, even on good days, I expected to go home right away. It made me upset when we had to run errands first.

HOMEWORK

Jan: Homework was a minefield for which I was an unsatisfactory coach. Every day we fought over homework done, not done, or done wrong. Usually the amount of time it took caused the explosions. Invariably, the whole evening would be shot supervising his homework. I couldn't understand why it took him so long to copy ten spelling words, do twelve math problems, and read two pages of social studies. Mornings and bedtimes were already battlefields; homework just added to the chaos.

Theodore: Homework was a nightmare because my parents had no clue about how hard it was for me to focus. They thought I was just dawdling and would yell at me. That just made me feel even worse and take even longer to get it done.

PERSISTENCE CAN BE ANNOYING

Jan: Theodore's persistence also drove us nuts. He had to be the one to decide when he was finished with something. That kind of persistence interfered mightily when we needed him to do something else. Moreover, his dogged insistence on getting his numerous questions answered exasperated us. Theodore seldom asked anything once. He would ask a question, then ask it again, and again, and again.

Often we would not answer a question the first time around if we were busy—getting dinner, concentrating on driving, thinking, talking on the telephone, focused on something else. While we marveled at his curiosity, Theodore's incessant questioning could wear anyone out. Sometimes we just wanted him to stop, to leave us alone.

Theodore: I'm very curious about everything I don't know. If they'd just answer my question the first time I ask, I'd shut up. Well, maybe not.

RESPONDING (POORLY) TO EMOTIONAL VOLATILITY

Jan: Persistence was also the hallmark of Theodore's temper tantrums, which would go on forever. When he exploded, we tried diverting his attention, letting him cry, holding him tightly, and giving him a bath. None of it worked.

Theodore: The tantrums were rarely small ones. The reason I blew up so often was that I couldn't control my emotions. I would explode because I would get frustrated. Almost any small thing—like not being able to spell a word right, or not being able to get a picture I was drawing look exactly the way I wanted—would spark the flame inside of me and I would blow up. My emotions would just overwhelm me. I didn't feel silly that I'd had a tantrum—I always thought I had a good reason for it. What I really felt afterwards was just glad to get away from all the yelling.

Jan: It was a vicious cycle. The more Theodore threw temper tantrums, the more we yelled. I worried that our pattern of interaction would scar him for life. It was not just the yelling, it was also the raised voice just short of yelling, the note of irritation that was omnipresent.

Theodore: My parents would think I was deliberately being disobedient when I didn't do what they told me to do, so they'd yell at me. Whenever they did, sometimes I would ignore them, but too often, I would yell back. I would also break into tears because some loud noises, like yelling, hurt my ears. I wasn't trying to be bad—like, I wasn't dawdling deliberately—but I just couldn't stay focused on stuff that bored me, like getting dressed or doing chores. I wasn't trying to be bad, but they thought I was, and so they yelled at me all the time. All the yelling hurt my feelings and made me feel really low and bad about myself.

Rethinking Deficiencies as Strengths

Jan: We struggled to find more positive ways to deal with Theodore. I stumbled on a parenting book, *Raising Your Spirited Child: A Guide for Parents Whose Child Is More Intense, Sensitive, Perceptive, Persistent, Energetic* by Mary Sheedy Kurcinka, that helped us to think differently about some of Theodore's behavior patterns. The first step was recasting negative labels to see the positive aspects of his temperament. Instead of thinking of him as impatient, I recognized he was compelling. He was dramatic, not explosive; assertive, not stubborn. It helped when I realized that he was acutely perceptive, not distractible. He noticed everything going on around him.

Theodore: I notice every little detail because I'm curious and I love to learn. Sometimes people think I'm distracted but I'm able to do more than one thing at once. I can observe and listen at the same time. I can play LEGOs and watch TV at the same time. I can read and eat at the same time. But my parents don't think so. They keep yelling that I slow down when I try to do two things at once. So now there's the "no reading during breakfast" rule.

The bad part about my curiosity is that in school I can be looking around, reading, or doodling and the teachers think I'm not paying attention because I'm not looking at them. Then I get in trouble. Sometimes they call on me to see if I'm listening and I can see they're surprised when I give the right answer. They think I can't possibly be paying attention while I'm doing something else, but I really am.

Jan: Beginning to think of Theodore as "spirited" instead of difficult (I mean less-easy) helped us focus more on his strengths—particularly his intense intellectual curiosity, big heart, and surprising resilience. Somehow, despite all the yelling and the daily turmoil, he had an ability to roll with the punches that I envied. He didn't hold grudges and his bad moods certainly didn't last as long as mine.

Although reshaping my view of Theodore helped, our more serious problems weren't solved. By third grade, his life at school was deteriorating. When we went to our first parent-teacher conference that fall, we heard the words all parents dread: "We need to talk about your child." The school was also recognizing the behavior that made our home so chaotic.

The Chaotic Household

Sharon: A chaotic household is one in physical or emotional disarray. Physical disruption may come from the frantic rushing around and arguing every morning as you try to get your child (and yourself) up, dressed, and out the door. It may be the shouting when he won't go to bed and you're so tired you can't take one more minute of his behavior. Maybe it's the anguish you feel whenever you attempt one of those increasingly less-frequent public outings that culminate in raised voices, tears, and wailing. It's the knot in your stomach when the teacher telephones and you have to forcibly resist the impulse to just hang up instead of listen to one more complaint about your child's behavior. It's the exhaustion you feel when you're asked to "do something" about your child's behavior and you have to keep from screaming at a teacher or day-care provider, "What do you want me to do? What do you want me to say? You're supposed to be the expert!"

The emotional drain of a chaotic household also comes from hearing yourself barking directions, issuing ultimatums, and knowing in the pit of your stomach that your child is not going to do what you want anyway. Too often, there's a palpable tension in your household—a feeling that an explosion is waiting to happen. At times, you're overwhelmed by a sense of helplessness; other times resolved to "get a handle on" the situation or behavior. Your inability to do so exacerbates your frustration, which, in turn, adds to the chaos.

Chaos is not just the reality of having an unpredictable child. It's the emotional volatility—the frustration, depression, and anger—that accompanies effort upon fruitless effort to "fix" the child's behavior. Family functioning seems to be at the mercy of this child. Even if that isn't actually so, it certainly feels like it. If the child's behavior is negative and unpredictable, then the household is, by definition, in chaos.

Are You a Challenged Parent?

Much of what determines "challenging" is your own mood, time of day, and outside pressures. What you see as a challenge one day may not seem so bad the next. But if you don't know what to do about it, if it keeps happening day after day, despite your best efforts to change it, you are a challenged parent.

A challenging or less-easy child is any child whose behavior stymies parental attempts to change it. This is the kid who won't go to bed, won't stay in bed, and has to negotiate every request and argue every direction. This is the child who holds the family hostage to his negative behavior. His reactions and overreactions dictate where you go and don't go, how long you stay, and whether you can go back again. Some may eventually receive a clinical diagnosis such as anxiety disorder or obsessive-compulsive disorder (OCD), oppositional-defiant disorder (ODD) or conduct disorder (CD), depression or bipolar disorder, attention deficit/hyperactivity disorder (ADHD), or Tourette's syndrome. Some may already have been identified as having autism or one of the related disorders such as pervasive developmental disorder or Asperger's syndrome. Some carry a diagnosis of Fragile X syndrome. Many have accompanying learning issues or speech and language disorders. Frequently, sensory integration disorder is a part of the equation. *But a challenging child is not just the child with the label; it is any child who has simply outstripped your ability to parent.*

We use the terms *challenging* and *less-easy* child interchangeably because some children are challenging because their behavior has earned them a label, or diagnosis, that confirms that you have a tough kid by almost anyone's standards. Others, however, are challenging because they are less easy by comparison—with their siblings, other students in their class, or other children in the neighborhood. They may also be challenging, or less easy, because their temperament simply isn't a good match for your own. They aren't "bad" kids, nor are you a "bad" parent. You simply must learn different ways to deal with the challenges this child presents. No one incident or behavior means your child has a disorder. But overlooking patterns of behavior can delay getting the help you need to deal with him.

Jan and Jamie had a challenging—or, as they called him, a less-easy—child. They knew that even though they resisted labeling Theodore as difficult. Devoted, concerned, and caring parents, they felt helpless and frustrated at their inability to change the behavior in Theodore that was driving them nuts. As they talked to his teachers about his mounting school problems, they began to see that they weren't the only ones struggling to cope with him. They were moving toward the realization that he—and they—needed help.

If any of this sounds familiar, or you see yourself this way, before you get a major case of the guilts (which, by the way, won't help the situation) ask yourself a few questions.

- Why would you like a project at which you are repeatedly unsuccessful?

- Why would you enjoy a task that continuously makes you feel inept?

- If the next-door neighbor's child came into your home and acted the way your child was acting, how much would you like the next-door neighbor's child?

You wouldn't. Then don't be surprised at your reaction to this behavior in your child. It's far more difficult when it's your own child. These emotions only prove you're normal. You obviously love your child. And, although you may wish you didn't have to deal with her behavior and someone would take her off your hands, you are still committed to helping your child.

What This Book Can Do for You

This book isn't going to tell you *the* right way to parent. "*The* right way" to parent doesn't exist. "*The* right way" implies that there is only one kind of child. Anyone with more than one child knows that children don't just come in all sizes, shapes, and colors.

They also have a variety of temperaments and a vast array of skills and behaviors. Some behaviors are good; many are not so good.

So, if there's no *one* right way to parent and kids come in all shapes, sizes, and temperaments, the next best thing to a manual (or warranty) for each child is a resource that helps you know what to do. Our book will help you know what to do to prevent blowouts and tantrums and make daily life run more smoothly. It will suggest ways to structure situations so that certain problem behaviors don't occur. It will help you decide what you can change to make a real difference in your child's life.

- We can help you set realistic goals for change.

- We can help guide you through the process of getting professional help.

- We can help you understand issues surrounding medication for challenging children.

- We can help you understand the common traps parents fall into when they deal with a challenging child.

- We'll provide you with new ways to think about discipline—ways to get your child to stop stalling and overreacting and do more of what you want instead.

- We'll tell you how to make those new ways work in your household with your child.

- We'll give you a process to follow to make concrete changes in your child's behavior.

- We'll explain why incentives work better than punishment, and give you guidelines for effective punishment when incentives aren't enough.

- We'll help you understand why your child has to be taught the social skills the rest of us pick up by osmosis.

- We'll give you strategies for working in partnership with teachers and educators on your child's behalf.

- We'll show you how to get family dynamics back on track.

- We'll show you how, with only one set of rules—one approach to parenting—you can provide what both your typical and your challenging child need. (And why it's so much less work than developing "special" rules for your challenging child.)

- We'll help you bring calm into your chaotic household and then tell you what to do to maintain it.

This book will give you a framework for knowing that what you do—the way you respond as a parent—is good for your child. You will learn what to do in those situations when you're not sure what to do. And gain some confidence that what you did was, in fact, just fine.

Our book uses the story of Jan, Jamie, Theodore, and Caroline to illustrate what the next year or two may be like in your family's life if you follow our suggestions. We'll help you learn what to do to maintain positive changes. We cover the whole gamut of issues Theodore's family experienced so you can see how one family implemented this approach.

I advocate and teach *planned parenting* rather than reactive parenting. It isn't easy. It takes more work, more time, and more thought. It's a lifestyle, not a one-time effort. It can effect the most empowering change I have ever witnessed in a parent. The result is the freedom to see your child for what he is, instead of what he is not, and to value and build on his strengths.

GETTING BEYOND THE BLAME GAME

Any discussion of challenging children seems inevitably to lead to a discussion of fault. Having another child who has good skills and age-appropriate behavior is often still not enough to help parents understand that they are rarely the cause of the problem. They judge themselves or each other based on the more difficult child. Assigning blame is not only unproductive, it's counterproductive.

Blame and guilt can be so overwhelming as to bring on inertia—an inability to make change. It is irrelevant, in many cases, how the child got this way. The question is, what are you going to do about it now? Whether it is nature or nurture that resulted in your child being this way (and the scales are tipping increasingly toward nature), it's nurture that will affect the situation now.

Effective parenting can make a difference. It may, and in fact often does, require the support of others—mental health experts, educators, physicians—but it's the parent who must become the expert at establishing the structure these children so desperately need. While this book won't make you an expert, it will provide you with concrete tools you can use to become more effective parents.

If your child's behavior makes him unable to function appropriately or unwelcome in certain settings, *the behavior has to change*. If the attention he draws is negative and self-defeating, *the behavior has to change*. It doesn't matter if your child has a disorder or disability that impairs "normal functioning." You (and professionals who assist you) may not be able to "cure" the disorder, but you can—with the right techniques—help your child change his behavior.

Virtually all parents need help in determining what to work on first. When parents are overwhelmed by their child's behavior, it is often difficult for them to narrow their focus and be realistic about what can be expected in the way of change. It is hard for them to accept that they—and their child—can work on only one or two things at a time. They cannot work on everything at once and expect, realistically, to fix all the problems. This book can help parents set priorities. Then they need to stay with those few things and have a reasonable gauge by which to measure progress.

CHALLENGED PARENTS MUST PROVIDE STRUCTURE AND PREDICTABILITY

The needs of these less-easy children are extraordinary. Challenging children unfortunately don't come with a manual. If they did, it would stipulate that their need for structure exceeds that of their peers. Therefore, what a parent did with Sally at this age may give little or no insight as to what her challenging sister, Anna, may need. The challenging child's needs go far beyond what most people's basic parenting skills can handle. This child needs more. She needs clear limits, routines, and lots of feedback, especially positive. In short, she needs *structure* and *predictability*. We'll repeat those two words over and over in this book.

The children who make the most progress are those whose parents and teachers become involved and, in fact, become experts in structuring their child's life. You can help your child. Our book will help you learn how.

Parents don't want to be punitive. They don't want to live in a chaotic household. It takes a lot more emotional energy to punish than it does to structure and reinforce. Nothing gives a child a greater chance for success than living in a home with parents who can anticipate his needs and structure his life until he acquires the skills to do so for himself. It requires parents who aren't defeated by the inevitable setbacks and can respond rather than react. We're here to guide you through the process of bringing calm to your chaotic household by becoming more effective parents of your challenging child.

Theodore: I'm now in seventh grade and my life is a whole lot better now than it used to be. Mornings aren't so bad anymore. Mom hasn't yelled in three weeks and Dad's blood pressure is back to normal. Your life can be better too.

2

"Help!"

Getting the Right *Help and Knowing When to Use It*

Theodore: I thought I was really going to like third grade. I really liked the teachers. But third grade turned out to be worse than previous years. I had a really hard time.

Jan: It was during third grade that our illusion of Theodore as merely the "less-easy" child vanished. We thought a combined second- and third-grade class taught by two talented, creative teachers would be ideal. We expected it to be a good year, when Theodore would finally "show his stuff."

It turned out the room was too open, too loud, and too stimulating. We had forgotten Theodore's unhappy and unsuccessful experience at age four with Montessori education, where self-direction and lack of structure defined the learning environment.

Now he was coming home on edge, ready to fall apart. The all-too-unstructured after-school program compounded the overstimulation he experienced in his noisy classroom of fifty kids. In addition, he was being teased by a group of physical and rowdy boys.

Theodore: To start with, the class was much too large and it was too noisy. I wasn't able to accomplish anything in school and the homework room after school was just as loud.

I really liked my teachers because they were kind to me and they gave me more chances than some of my other teachers had. I thought they liked me a little bit because I was smart.

But I liked only a few of the kids. And only a few kids liked me. Very few. Kids teased me mainly because of the trouble I had, especially because I would talk too much and too fast. They teased me because I had glasses and called me a "nerd." One even called me "Theo*dork*," which really upset me. They also teased me because I was small. Most of those who teased me weren't all that good as students. Some were just plain bullies.

A lot of anger built up inside me but I didn't fight back because these guys were large, tough kids and it always seemed as if there were so many of them. At recess I would be so mad that when nobody was watching, I would throw rocks at the ground or down the hill. It was even worse in the after-school program. Counselors couldn't control the kids, so they really ganged up on me there. When I'd tell the person who was supposed to be watching, they'd just tell me to live with it or fix it myself. But I couldn't. I felt extremely alone.

When I came home, I was always mad because it took so long to get my homework done and there wasn't any time left for fun.

Jan: Homework was an ordeal that put additional stress on the entire family. Getting Theodore to focus meant one of us had to stand over him. Spelling homework was a good example of the frustration we experienced every week. It didn't matter how many times we went over the words, he'd miss the same ones over and over. "I can't! I feel stupid," he would cry.

Theodore: Whenever I would get stuck on something I wasn't able to do well, like spelling, I would refuse to switch to something else. I'd keep working on it, trying to do better, trying to get it right. Then, because I was so intent on that one thing, I would feel I was stupid and I wouldn't be able to see that I was good in other subjects.

Jan: At the fall parent-teacher conference, his teacher gingerly queried whether we had ever thought that perhaps Theodore might have attention deficit disorder. We were thunderstruck. *Attention deficit disorder?* Our admittedly ill-informed image of attention-deficit/hyperactivity disorder (ADHD) was of the uncontrollable child bouncing off the walls. That wasn't Theodore. He was not hyperactive. He'd sit and read forever; that was one of the problems. Besides, we countered, wasn't attention deficit disorder the faddish, overdiagnosed label applied mostly to describe fairly typical "boy" behavior? Didn't doctors dispense Ritalin like candy to solve teachers' problems with unruly kids?

To our surprise, his teacher agreed. He, too, thought attention deficit disorder was overdiagnosed and too readily used to label boys whose behavior didn't conform to the norm. However, in his entire teaching career, he had seen only four children that he believed truly had it—and Theodore was one of them.

Somewhat reassured that he wasn't making the suggestion lightly, we listened to what he and the coteacher had observed. For one thing, there was a marked discrepancy between Theodore's reading ability, which was way above grade, and his spelling, which was noticeably below grade. This suggested inattention to detail in learning spelling patterns or inability to recognize them. When coupled with Theodore's distractibility, his tendency to roam restlessly around the room, and his below-capability performance, his teachers recommended that we have Theodore tested.

Several years later, after I had learned much more about ADHD—and perhaps was more ready to hear about how difficult Theodore had been then, I talked again with his third-grade teachers. They told me more about what they had observed during that year. Theodore was unable to make eye contact with them. It wasn't from fear, but reflected his diminishing self-esteem and lack of social skills. They were well aware that he was floundering socially. Friendless, he didn't know where he fit in. He bickered with his peers, often from miscommunication and his failure to pick up on social cues. He dissolved into tears when he got frustrated. He had great difficulty with transitions—moving from one activity to another. Or he would be so wound up by a social interaction that he couldn't let go of it. He constantly retreated into books, reading during class to relieve stress or calm himself down. Finally, he had great difficulty focusing on the simplest of classroom tasks, particularly when they were of little interest to him.

Theodore: When third grade started, because that was the first big jump in schoolwork, it got harder and harder for me because I was slower to adapt to the change than most other kids.

Jan: Theodore's behavior patterns clearly hadn't blossomed overnight. In all likelihood, they were aggravated by the constellation of pressures that accompany third grade. In retrospect, Theodore's inattention, impulsivity, and particularly his extreme talkativeness and tendency to act before thinking in dealing with his peers, were the more important indicators of ADHD. Though not yet ready to accept the suggested label, we knew we needed a professional's perspective.

When to Get Professional Help

Sharon: Two essential issues that parents of challenging children must confront are *When do I need to get help?* and then *How do I get the help I need?* There are no right or wrong answers. Neither the when nor the how is chiseled in stone.

Every family's reason for deciding to seek help is highly individual. Few do it lightly. The decision is usually precipitated by family comments, subtle suggestions by friends, or a direct recommendation from a teacher. Sometimes it's all three. Astute, experienced teachers noticed Theodore's symptoms. That's not always the way it happens—for ADHD or anything else. For some, the failure to make or keep friends is the catalyst for seeking help. Or the child seems explosive or anxious. Any one of these does not necessarily require you to take action. But a pattern of comments or situations might. In Jan and Jamie's case, the teacher's observations rang a bell that fit with their own "Theodore experiences."

KEEP A WRITTEN LOG OF YOUR CHILD'S PROBLEM BEHAVIORS

If you are uncertain about whether to seek professional help, keep a log of situations or behaviors you find challenging. Yes, it's time-consuming and hard to remember to do, but written records like these—and any notes you make during teacher conferences or other notes you receive from school—are useful when you begin the process of getting help.

If one parent thinks the other is overreacting, a notebook may help the couple decide whether the problems are isolated events or a trend. Moreover, if you do end up seeking help, professionals will find this information useful. If nothing else, it's a great history of your child.

Quick Tip

Keep a record of comments or situations that indicate difficulty. Include date, comment made, by whom, and situational details.

OBSTACLES TO GETTING PROFESSIONAL HELP

If a parent is not ready to seek help, he or she will often rationalize or ignore comments and recommendations.

Guilt can be a major deterrent to seeking help. Some parents are hobbled by simply having waited so long. Fearing that they overlooked obvious signs and ignored others' warnings, they agonize over having used potentially damaging parenting techniques, worried that it is now too late. "If only we had responded sooner." Or "If only I had insisted when my spouse was reluctant to get outside help." Listen to your gut instinct. If you think the situation needs professional help, it probably does. At the very least, a professional perspective can provide direction. Don't let fear or guilt override your good judgment.

Some parents are so concerned that someone will blame them that they refuse to seek professional guidance. Instead, if they do anything at all, they read book after book on parenting difficult children, rather than *combining* this information with a professional's insights. Books can provide insight and information. A knowledgeable professional can guide you in using this information to help your child and family.

Some families get mired in the question of "how he got this way." "What did I (or my spouse) do to cause this?" is often the unspoken concern. It's as if, until they know for sure, one way or the other, they're stuck. Similarly, the fear that help will lead to the stigma of a label deters many families from turning to professionals. When the question of "why" sidetracks them or the issue of guilt or fault gets so big that a family can't get past it, individual or couples' counseling must be considered an essential part of the treatment package. You can't help your child until you help yourself.

"DIAGNOSES" AND LABELS

You may be leery of seeing a professional to "diagnose" your child. But don't kid yourself—everyone is diagnosing your child. You are, your mother-in-law is, and so is your child's teacher. Everyone's trying to figure out what is "wrong" with your challenging child. (Or what's wrong with you.) A diagnosis is a label, and a label can be a very scary thing. But whether a label gets attached to your child is not really the issue. It doesn't change the difficulty your child is having just getting through his daily life. If much of life is a struggle for you or for him, advice from a professional with relevant education and experience may be just what you need.

How to Get the Help You Need

Jan: Jamie and I decided on private testing, rather than having it done by the school. We wanted the opportunity to weigh the results before deciding what, if anything, to share with the school. The implications of a "label" concerned us. (See chapter 8 for a more detailed discussion of working with your child's school.) But if we weren't going to have him tested by his school, then by whom?

Forays onto the Internet did not prove helpful. When I talked to the director of a local university's learning services center she directed me to some books and possible avenues for testing and diagnosis. I didn't find directories or lists of professionals in our area

who could test for attention deficit disorder. That meant I needed
to do a more detailed search for recommendations on who should
test Theodore. (See box on p. 29 for further information on how
to find the right professional.)

One book clarified that ADHD was a problem of brain chemistry. To me, it made sense to find out whether Theodore's brain

WHEN TO SEEK PROFESSIONAL HELP

It's time to seek *professional* help when:

- Your child does not achieve developmental milestones
  on time according to standard measures.

- Your child's behavior results in his calling negative attention to himself on a regular basis. His behavior requires special attention from adults to ensure his or
  others' safety. Peers avoid your child.

- Your child's behavior results in his exclusion from a situation or program that he wants to participate in and
  is a good match for his skills and/or interests.

- Your child consistently behaves or talks angrily; he is
  reactive.

- Parenting this child is an overwhelming, exhausting,
  and sometimes painful experience that leaves you
  wondering, "Is it him or is it me?"

- Other adults with a frame of reference (frequent contact with the child, experience with other children the
  same age, expertise in child development or child behavior) suggest it.

- Any potentially harmful or life-threatening behaviors
  occur. These warrant immediate professional advice.

was wired differently. I could deal with "different." This seemed more scientific (and accurate) than merely counting his behavioral symptoms of inattention, impulsivity, and hyperactivity to see if he reached a magic number for an ADHD label.

I called several recommended centers, but they used a protocol or set procedure of "Come see us, fill out some forms, get a teacher evaluation, and we'll talk to you about your child and his behavioral symptoms." That wasn't enough to give me confidence in whatever diagnosis they'd make.

Theodore's usual pediatrician was not an ADHD expert, and that's what we wanted. We started looking for an ADHD specialist, maybe a psychologist, psychiatrist, or neurologist. I concluded that I would only have confidence in the diagnosis if someone tested how Theodore's brain worked.

Theodore: Until the time my parents told me about the testing and all the appointments they had made, I had absolutely no clue about everything they were doing. I knew my life was difficult, but I never gave any thought to why. I thought either I was just difficult or the entire world was against me. The thought never came to my mind that I was born with something that made me like this. At school, things were going from bad to worse because we were doing things that were especially hard for me, like spelling, cursive writing, and English.

EDUCATION AND RESEARCH

Sharon: Talk to your pediatrician. Although Jan and Jamie didn't go this route, it's often the first place to start. Some doctors may minimize the problem and a few too quickly resort to medication, but most are highly knowledgeable and will have good ideas about how to proceed. Because pediatricians have seen many challenging children, they are often an excellent first resource and may be part of an initial evaluation. They may suggest reading material or direct you to other professionals. You should also talk to teachers—not just your child's current teacher, but last year's, too. Talk to friends who are educators. All of these are potential resources for professional referrals.

Before getting an evaluation, and certainly before starting any recommended therapies or services, educate yourself as much as possible. You are about to become your child's case manager. You're going to decide which stranger to trust. You have to determine which of many options are right for you, your child, and your family.

READ! Read books whose titles seem to capture your child's traits. Check some of the books we recommend in our Resources section at the back of this book. Follow the suggestions in other books for further reading. Ask a librarian where to find books that might be relevant for your child's problems. While some do not give specific solutions, most provide direction regarding professional consultation. They can help clarify what information you need to know before proceeding. In addition, most help give parents perspective on the situation—and perspective is important.

INTERNET RESEARCH

Do some research on the Internet. If your child has been recommended for testing for something like ADHD, or depression, anxiety, or autism, search the Internet by typing in a keyword, such as autism, and check out the sites that crop up. Bookmark whatever looks like it could be useful because you may want to go back to those sites after the testing has been done. Be sure to use multiple search engines to ensure broad coverage of the Internet's resources. The best sites provide linkages to other sites for further information. Many also provide lists of recommended books, some of which have ratings that may or may not be useful for your situation. Often a keyword search will lead you to organizations or support associations for parents of children with behavior problems. These can be very useful.

Internet sites come and go so don't rely solely on the following list. Try www.conductdisorders.com for conduct disorder (CD) and obsessive-compulsive disorder (OCD). Try www.autism.org for autism. Government sites, located by typing in "National Institute for Mental Health," can provide information on behavior disorders, current research, and sources for further help. The site for the National Depressive and Manic Depressive Association (www.ndmda.org) can provide information on childhood depression and bipolar disorder. Try www.chadd.com, the site for Children and Adults with Attention-Deficit/Hyperactivity Disorder.

The information you gather in this early phase will help define the problem. Equally important, it will help you develop a list of questions to ask a professional, such as the following:

- Does this behavior warrant a diagnosis?

- How will this affect my child at school?

- What types of services have proved successful?

- Who can best deliver these services?

- What steps do I take first?

Often it helps to draw up a list of questions even before you begin your research and revise it according to what you learn. Sometimes, once you begin the process, there's so much new information you can't figure out what you need to know. A list of questions keeps you focused on the kind of information you originally thought important. As you read and speak to others, you can modify the list.

Choosing Whom to See

Jan: More than anything, I wanted to ensure we had the "right" person to do the testing. I didn't want to end up skeptical about the validity of any diagnosis.

After six weeks of gathering recommendations, I called the parent of another child in my daughter's class. Her son had ADHD. I wished I'd called her sooner. It was a relief to talk to a parent who was further along in this process. She gave me the names of the psychologist who had tested her son as well as a therapist her son was seeing.

> **SEEKING OTHER PARENTS WITH CHILDREN LIKE YOURS**
>
> ■ Ask teachers for names of parents you might talk with.
>   (They might want to get that parent's permission first.)
>
> ■ Ask neighbors or relatives for more names.
>
> ■ Find a local support group where parents can share
>   their experiences dealing with their challenging child.

Since we were increasingly concerned about Theodore's eroding self-esteem, I called the therapist. She strongly urged that we get testing results first to better understand what we were dealing with. Only after that should we bring him to see her.

This was my introduction to the concept of "sequencing interventions." Sequencing interventions means doing treatments or getting professional assistance in a sequence instead of all together. If you do everything at once, you won't know what's working and what isn't. Gradually I learned how important this is for using professional assistance wisely—and not overwhelming either my child or my pocketbook.

We narrowed the names I'd received down to a highly recommended neuropsychologist. When I called him, I reached him directly and had the chance to ask questions about how he tested for attention deficit disorder. Reputation, sterling recommendations from more than one person, and direct contact were the important factors in my decision. Then my gut instinct took over. I felt I could trust that this person knew what he was doing.

GETTING A FORMAL ASSESSMENT OR EVALUATION

Sharon: When you reach the point where you want professional help, think in terms of getting a formal "assessment" or evaluation to help you understand what is happening with your child. Many people can administer tests; fewer have the ability to interpret the scores using their experience to understand your child. While technicians may be adequate for administering a test, the best assessors learn as much from talking with the child, family, and teachers, and by observing how a child "gets" to the answer, as they do from the scores themselves.

The trick is finding the "right" professional to evaluate your child—the one in whom you'll have confidence that their evaluation of your child rings true. To find that person (or persons), you have to do research and gather recommendations. (See box titled "How to Find the Right Professional," p. 29.) It's a good sign when you get the same name from several, disparate sources. Interview qualified candidates for a comfortable fit. That doesn't necessarily mean you'll agree with everything they tell you—or that you'll like the conclusions they'll reach. The important thing is to find someone whose experience and judgment will help you better understand your child.

To find the professional who is right for you, some of the questions you should ask include:

- What is your particular area of expertise?

- What are your qualifications?

- What are you licensed to do?

- Do you specialize in evaluating children?

- What's involved in an evaluation?

- Do you provide specific recommendations as part of your evaluation?

- How many sessions will it take?

- What is the cost?

In addition to these questions about qualifications, costs, etc., you should also prepare a list of questions about what they—or any other expert you may see—might be able to do for you and your child.

- Will your services result in a diagnosis?

- Are you able to attend meetings to discuss the findings and make recommendations to educators?

- Will the evaluation highlight my child's learning style and strengths as well as any disabilities?

- Do you recommend additional services?

- Do you provide any of the therapeutic services that may be necessary?

- What can we expect to see in the way of change as a result of these services?

Once you are in someone's office, it's easy to become side-tracked and leave without asking important questions. Make sure whomever you see sets aside enough time to address all of your concerns. That often means forwarding your list of questions before the meeting.

Jan: Once we had decided who to see, we told Theodore that we were going to have his brain tested to see if it worked differently from other people's. If it did, we said, that might explain why his life was so hard.

Theodore: My parents told me that they were going to take me to do some testing to see if I had something called attention deficit disorder. When they told me that, we then got into a long conversation about what ADHD was. After that conversation, I got a bit nervous about whether they were going to give me shots or do blood tests. Even though they said that they were just going to do some tests, like hand-eye coordination, memory, engineering skills, and other things, I still was afraid that they were going to do something that might hurt. I don't like to go to any doctor, dentist, or orthodontist for that very reason. I just focused on what they were going to do, not on whether they were going to find out something that explained why my life was so difficult.

Jan: It took several visits to complete the testing. Some of the tests were done on the computer, some with pencil and paper, and some through interviews with us and with Theodore. Three months after that critical parent-teacher conference, in early January 1997, we discussed the results with the neuropsychologist. The testing clearly demonstrated that Theodore had attention deficit/hyperactivity disorder, inattentive type. The discrepancy between his

HOW TO FIND THE RIGHT PROFESSIONAL

- Consult your pediatrician.

- Call support group(s). Locate support groups on the Internet; then look for a local chapter in the telephone book. Or call the national organization for recommendations in your area.

- Call local mental health agencies. Start with your city or county health service. Ask them for names of private agencies as well.

- Do research—read books; seek information on the Internet.

- Survey professionals. Look for overlapping referrals:
  - From your pediatrician
  - From school
  - From friends and knowledgeable acquaintances

- Interview professionals you might want to use.

- Trust your gut instincts. The professional (or professionals) you choose has to "feel right" or you may not have confidence that the diagnosis is correct, especially if you don't like it. If it doesn't feel right, you will be far less likely to follow the specialist's recommendations for treatment.

spelling and reading ability, which had started all this, was due, in part, to a word retrieval problem associated with his ADHD. Theodore could visualize a word's correct letters, but had difficulty retrieving them in the right order.

Sharon: Any diagnosis should be the result of a thorough evaluation, not a judgment or pronouncement at the end of a single appointment. It's a process, based on a great deal of information supplied by the child and parent, and gathered by the specialist(s). The evaluation process results in a *differential diagnosis*, that is, a determination not only of what your child's diagnosis is, but, just as importantly, what it is not. Through an extensive review of information, combined with parent and child interviews and observations, an experienced professional makes an *assessment*, or diagnosis. It is this *thorough* process that drives decisions regarding treatment. If one professional doesn't handle all aspects of a complete evaluation, seek referrals for those who can augment what has been done. It can be lengthy and inconvenient but it is invaluable.

Assessment or Evaluation Components

COMPONENT	REASON
Family evaluation (with a social worker or other specialist)	To determine what family dynamics, if any, may be contributing to the child's problem; suggest having a family behavioral modification therapist involved in case
Psychosocial and school assessment (teacher or guidance counselor contact)	To assess child's peer functioning; determine academic and behavioral performance at school
Psychological testing (with a psychologist)	A broad group of tests that assess the child's emotional and cognitive (thinking) functioning
Neuropsychological testing (with a psychologist)	Extensive and specific tests to evaluate a child's thinking or information-processing abilities
Structured parent interviews	Detailed questions about your child's history

COMPONENT	REASON
Medical assessment (pediatrician)	Physical examination and laboratory studies as indicated; suggested prior to using medications and when there are concerns about a medical contribution to the child's problem
Medication evaluation	Thorough history of the child and his or her current and past emotional and behavioral problems; review of above

This table represents potential assessments for children with behavioral and emotional disorders. The evaluation process varies greatly dependent on the region of the country, the type of practice, and the circumstances of the child.

Adapted from "Table 2. Elements of the Psychopharmacology Evaluation Process," in *Straight Talk about Psychiatric Medications for Kids* by Timothy E. Wilens, M.D. (New York: Guilford Press, 1999), p. 56.

As important as the evaluation and diagnosis are, they are the beginning, not the end, of the process. Armed with this information, parents still need to understand what it means to have pervasive developmental disorder (PDD) or an anxiety disorder, or any of the other names given to the problems children may have. What does this label tell you about your child's needs? What can you expect in your child's future development? What services are available to help you address your child's needs? How can you locate those services? How can you evaluate the service and the person who delivers it when you do find it? While having received a diagnosis may feel like a stopping point, it is the time to take action— whether your child has a formal diagnosis or not.

Jan: As part of Theodore's assessment, we received a number of recommendations:

Home and Social Environment
1. Have a physician evaluate Theodore as a candidate for medication therapy.

2. See a behavior specialist to help us with daily life.

3. Theodore should see an educational specialist to improve his organizational skills.

4. He should remain deeply involved in athletics to provide a setting for increased social skills and to address any confidence issues that might arise.

5. He should learn some type of martial arts. The training in self-control is excellent for those with attention deficit disorder.

School

1. As a quick learner who is easily bored, Theodore should have increased intellectual stimulation and enriched educational curriculum to improve his motivation and engagement.

2. Since mild processing difficulties would limit the speed of his writing, teachers should allow extra time on writing assignments including tests that involve writing or they would not be an accurate reflection of his knowledge relative to others. Eliminate unnecessary copying requirements. Similarly, he might require adaptations (the use of a laptop or a tape recorder), since copying from the board and taking in-class notes might be difficult for him.

3. His teachers should understand that he might require extra efforts to facilitate his written language development.

4. He might require increased clarification of expectations and more detailed instructions than others might. It might not be sufficient just to repeat directions; they may have to be reworded.

5. He should do as much of his work on the computer as possible.

Theodore: Once we found out that I had ADHD, I was relieved that we had a piece of paper that explained why I was different. It proved I was not strange or weird—just that my brain worked differently. On the other hand, I didn't like it because I felt I was the only person who had it and I felt different from everybody. I didn't tell anybody because it was very personal. It took a long time before I told anybody.

Sequencing Professional Help

Jan: With a firm diagnosis, we had to figure out what to do first. That wasn't easy. The neuropsychologist gave us the names of different experts to consult: a pediatrician to determine whether medication might be beneficial, a behavior specialist, a social-skills expert, and an educational consultant. Clearly, this was going to be both expensive and time-consuming.

Naturally, we wanted to do *everything* right away, so we called them all. The first one we could see was the education specialist, so we embarked on weekly visits to get Theodore's school-related problems sorted out. The physician, a pediatrician considered one of the best in the area for treatment of ADHD kids, however, was not taking any new patients. We finally got an appointment— though it was six long weeks away. It also took time to get in to see Sharon, the behavior specialist. Because third graders at Theodore's school were already learning keyboarding, we put off enrolling him in after-school computer classes until the following fall. We also enrolled him in a tae kwon do studio, where he progressed rapidly.

MORE ON EDUCATION AND RESEARCH

Sharon: Parents must educate themselves. Read as much as you can to better understand your child's problems and explore likely treatment options. In the Resources section I've listed a number of books I've found particularly useful, but there are others just as good.

There is a vast array of fringe treatments being offered. The use of high doses of vitamins and minerals to treat attention deficit/hyperactivity disorder is one such example. Since a more complete analysis of such treatments is beyond the scope of this book, *Attention Deficit Disorder and Learning Disabilities: Realities, Myths and Controversial Treatments* by Ingersoll and Goldstein is a particularly good source of information. In many cases, there's little or no medical basis for such treatments and no research substantiating their effectiveness. You may hear individual stories of how this treatment or that vitamin was helpful. Often there is no data supporting their claims. Unfortunately, there are no miracle cures. Dealing with your child's problems will take hard work, energy, and time. Listen to a professional you trust who can tell you about the proven, documented-as-effective treatments *before* you spend a lot of time and money on something that may have no real benefit. Unsubstantiated "treatments" can be harmful if they delay giving your child what he really needs.

Just as it's important for parents to educate themselves, it is equally important to educate children about their situation. I often recommend one or more of the books listed in the Resources section (and videos when appropriate) for parents to share with their children. I further recommend that parents talk to their pediatrician or teacher to find others who may be struggling with the same issues. Though they will need to obtain permission from the other families before passing on their names to you, it is worth the wait and the effort. Contact with another child who has successfully come to grips with the situation is invaluable. Understanding that they are not alone, that they are not the only ones with this condition, makes children less anxious and less likely to feel stigmatized.

Theodore: My parents gave me a couple of books about ADHD kids. They were about how ADHD affected those kids' lives and how they were able to learn to live with it. They helped me understand that I wasn't the only ADHD kid in the world. My parents also gave my sister Caroline a book about how a sibling feels about having a brother or sister with ADHD. When I'm feeling blue or down, I sometimes reread one of these books to help remind me that I'm not the only one like this. These books also give me comfort that I can be successful even though I have ADHD.

SETTING PRIORITIES AND SEQUENCING PROFESSIONAL HELP

Jan: By the time we saw Sharon, who had been highly recommended by the neuropsychologist, we had a fairly good understanding of the areas of Theodore's life that needed attention. We had identified the people we wanted to work with. Armed with all this information, we were ready to fix everything at once. Sharon quickly disabused us of that notion.

"If you try to fix everything at once, how do you know what's working?" she asked. We naively believed—and probably still do to some extent—that if we just got Theodore all the help he needed from the *right* experts, he would be "fixed" and everything could be "normal."

We had the right person to prescribe medication; the right person to fix his behavior; and someone to teach him organizational skills for school. We'd finally located a place for social-skills training and we even had a counselor so he could talk about things that bothered him. So why couldn't we fix everything at once?

Sharon: In wanting to fix everything at once, Jan and Jamie are not unlike other parents with challenging children. Once they've gotten a diagnosis, they want to get on with it and fix everything they can. While expediency is important, challenging children rarely have only one issue. Theodore has only one primary diagnosis: ADHD. But think about the range of issues confronting him: schoolwork and learning skills; making and keeping friends; learning how to cope with teasing; and getting himself out of bed and ready for school without driving his parents nuts. Each of these required a different type of treatment or therapy.

Like it or not, you can't fix everything at once. Taking on too much is confusing for your child, tough on your schedule, and exceedingly hard on your wallet. Your child didn't get this way overnight. You aren't going to fix his life overnight either.

When you begin to consider professional services, you must prioritize your child's needs. You have to figure out what kinds of assistance your child may need and determine what can be done to help him with those problems. Determining what is available for your child's needs takes research. Numerous good services are available. But will they help *your* child? You need to answer the following questions:

- What problems does my child have that could benefit from professional help?

- What kinds of help are available?

- Do these services specifically address my child's issues?

- Finally, in what order should we tackle these problems and with what professional services?

There are three primary benefits from sequencing various treatments. First, you won't confuse the child by bombarding him with too many new ideas. Imagine what it would be like for a child who attends social-skills training on Monday, learns strategies for doing homework on Tuesday, goes to a therapist for low self-esteem on Wednesday, and then finishes up the week with a visit to his pediatrician to see if his medication needs adjustment. What kind of life is that, for him or for you? How's he going to get to all those appointments? What happens to the rest of the family while all this is going on?

Second, too many services can give your child a sense that he's broken. Whatever the problem, it's been going on long enough that your child knows something's amiss. He's just not the same as others his age. He may not think it's a problem, but he does know he's different and different is not always good. Too many doctors, therapies, and services confirm that there's a serious problem requiring immediate and significant attention. Though this is sometimes the case, be careful not to burden your child with an unwarranted sense of urgency.

The third reason for sequencing services is that it clarifies for you what works and what doesn't. If you start three services at once and your child improves, how do you know which helped? If he has difficulties later, to which service would you return to address the problem? Was it medication that made Sally less depressed or the talk therapy? Was it social-skills training or medication that helped Johnny make friends?

It takes a lot of research and networking to decide how best to proceed. It takes the books you read, the support groups you call, and the specialists you contact.

In sequencing treatments for your child, there are some obvious things to consider. The most important one is to *deal with any issue regarding you or your child's physical safety and well-being first.* Nothing takes priority over these. If you have any concerns that your child might harm himself or others, is losing touch with reality, or experiencing an abrupt halt in development (sudden loss of language, for example) you must get help *immediately.* Start with your family doctor or pediatrician. Your child may need immediate professional treatment, even hospitalization.

The stress and strain of daily life compounded by coping with a challenging child may make you a threat to your child's health, safety, and well-being. If so, you may need immediate help. Call your family doctor for a referral to a mental health professional; see if your community has a hot line for child abuse prevention and call it. Talk to a friend, a member of the clergy, or a relative. You must get relief—-have someone else care for your child temporarily. Get out of the house. Do anything it takes so that you do not harm your child. Challenging children can push you to the limit but you can't help your child if *you* lose control.

After dealing with any safety issues, an evaluation for medication should be your next consideration. Though it may not result in a prescription, the process can shed light on when and on what basis you should consider medication in the future. Medication may bring relief from some significant symptoms for children with bipolar disorder, obsessive-compulsive disorder, or ADHD in particular. In many instances, it simply doesn't make sense to try such things as social-skills training, therapy, or educational counseling if these treatments have to bash their way through a wall of disabling symptoms. I'm not recommending that everyone try medication. On the contrary. An evaluation to determine if medication is warranted may help clarify what other therapies should be pursued first.

Then address those few behaviors that truly drive you crazy. When it goes on day after day, it's wearing. Although every child and situation is different, behaviors that affect daily routines can be exceedingly disruptive to everyone's quality of life—yours as well as your child's. Because they may be eminently fixable, tackle these before such things as floundering in school or peer-relationship problems. Getting a handle on behavior can help family dynamics. Find a professional who can tell you what to do

SEQUENCING PROFESSIONAL HELP

In general, the following sequence should help you make decisions about who to see first:

1. Deal immediately with serious worries about your child's life, safety, and control of your own behavior. Ask yourself:

   - Am I afraid my child may hurt himself or others? If so, get help *now*.
   - Is my child losing touch with reality, seeing or hearing things that aren't there, or experiencing an abrupt halt in development (such as sudden loss of language, sudden appearance of head-banging, etc.)?
   - Am I afraid I may harm my child?

2. If you receive a recommendation that medication might help, investigate that next.

3. Focus on behaviors that drive you crazy—specifically those that adversely affect daily routines. If things have deteriorated too far, family or individual therapy may be necessary.

4. Consider auxiliary services recommended such as occupational therapy, speech and language services, or physical therapies.

5. Depending on the child's need and family priorities, consider family or individual therapy, social-skills training, couples therapy, and educational counseling. Evaluate each child on an individual basis.

about getting your child out the door in the morning. Locate someone who can give you tools to address his name-calling and meltdowns. Find someone who knows behavior who will tell you what to do to help your child act in a different way.

When evaluating and selecting among other treatment options, including individual therapy and family therapy, social-skills training, education/organizational-skill training, and so on, consider your child's needs. What are his other problems? What remains after you've addressed the principal issues?

Jan: One of the first things Sharon did was help us sort out what to do and when to do it. She knew we'd located an excellent group of experts, but we had to decide in what sequence to tackle things. We were prepared to start medication, continue with the educational consultant, enroll Theodore in social-skills training, and do whatever she recommended to restructure our household and his daily life. It was too much, too fast, and in some cases, too soon.

We made our first priority getting Theodore on an effective dose of medication. We stopped seeing the educational consultant, while recognizing that we might come back to her later. We deferred enrolling Theodore in social-skills training for at least six months. Sharon suggested waiting until he had gone to sleep-away camp that summer where he would have a chance to interact with a new group of kids. Finally, we embarked, at much the same time as Theodore was undergoing a medication trial, on restructuring our household and Theodore's daily life according to Sharon's suggestions. In retrospect, we believe that this process, described in detail in chapter 4, was significantly helped by Theodore's initial, positive response to medication.

THE IMPORTANCE OF TEAMWORK

Sharon: Once you've done research, determined what help your child needs, found the right people, and figured out in what order to do things, you have to get the experts to work together as a team. That might be five people or two. Or it might be just one person you need to communicate with at your child's school.

While it can take a little more work, for both you and your professionals, insist that they work as a team. If there are multiple service providers, such as pediatricians, mental health counselors, educational consultants, or others, they need to communicate with each other, as well as with you as the parents.

Unless the team concept becomes the norm, the labor-intensive task of raising a challenging child is made much more complex. It also helps you, the parents, evaluate information you're getting to judge what works and what doesn't. If they don't, or won't, work as a team, you'll have to become an expert (or at least be conversant) in many different areas. If you're doing all the coordination yourself, it will overwhelm you. It's help you need, not another job. As the parent you will be the ultimate judge and evaluator of what is happening with your child; however, all communication lines must be open so you and others know what is going on.

Jan: One of the chief reasons Theodore has made so much progress is that from the beginning we developed a real team working together for Theodore's best interests and all members of the team communicated with one another. Through careful research, we chose experts who knew each other and respected each other's work. Equally important, we liked, respected, and trusted each of them. We had confidence they knew what they were doing. We knew they would (and did) talk to each other as issues arose that affected another's area of expertise. Working as a team saved us time, money, and energy. We never had to worry about one of them contradicting another. If they recommended different things, we'd tell them to talk to each other and agree on how to proceed. We kept everyone informed, but they communicated regularly as well.

Quick Tip

Encourage professionals to communicate. Sign a release of information form (professionals each have their own) and suggest that all of them exchange information so they can truly function as a team.

Sharon: The process of evaluation and diagnosis is exhausting, more emotionally than physically. It is easy to become overwhelmed or mired in misinformation. Educate yourself. An initial investment of time and energy can result in a partnership with professionals who will be there, if needed, as supportive resources for a lifetime.

Theodore: When we started seeing people, it helped a lot. I started feeling better about myself. It helped me understand why I was the way I was and what could be done to learn better ways to deal with the problems. It also helped me because I knew that somebody else was on my side and that we were on the way to make a better life for me.

3

The Power of the Pill

Neither Curse nor Cure

Theodore: In the beginning, I thought medicine was going to fix everything. It didn't. Then for a while I didn't appreciate the medicine, but when my parents told me about the effects that they and my teachers were seeing in me, I changed my thoughts about it. Now I don't mind taking it. Even though it won't fix all my problems, it does help them.

Sharon: More than one parent (and too many educators) think stimulant medications are magic bullets that will radically change a challenging child like Theodore into a responsive, compliant, focused, accommodating individual who is happy and has great self-esteem.

Many parents are averse to medicating challenging children. Because there is no blood test for emotional distress or X ray that shows an imbalance in brain chemistry that may be affecting their child, they are unsure if medication is really needed. These same parents do not hesitate to use medication to treat bacterial infections or insulin to treat juvenile onset diabetes, but they do—and should—have serious reservations about giving their child medication for a condition that is not easily quantified. However, you cannot allow media hype, your own emotions, and pressure from well-meaning but ill-informed family members and educators to make the decision for you.

Medication is generally suggested for two reasons. The first is for short-term use to help a child get through a traumatic situation, such as depression because of a death in the family. In these cases, the child has no underlying chemical imbalance and stops taking the medication when he has recovered. More relevant for parents of challenging children, however, is that medication is often recommended when someone, hopefully someone who's knowledgeable in the field, thinks there is an imbalance in the child's brain chemistry. Some disorders like ADHD or obsessive-compulsive disorder are rooted in the brain's chemistry. In these instances medication is used to reestablish a delicate chemical balance, thus enabling the child to function better in daily life.

Naturally, parents want to ensure that medication is warranted. Responsible professionals feel the same way. They gather a great deal of information before writing a prescription for medication that affects behavior or emotions. Some challenging children, however, are not good candidates for medication. For example, medication cannot correct or even improve most learning disabilities. In other cases, the condition itself does not respond to medication.

The issue of appropriate use of medications is extremely complex. This book should not be considered a primary resource on types or dosages of medication. Nor do we mean to provide a detailed analysis of medication options for different problems, or medication side effects. Other books, such as *Straight Talk about Psychiatric Medications for Kids* by Timothy E. Wilens, M.D., better address the finer points of psychopharmacology.

Instead, we focus on issues that arise any time such medications are being considered, hassles parents encounter, and problems kids experience. We include recommendations for making the process more productive and less onerous. We focus on Jan and Jamie's decision to use medication therapy, Theodore's feelings about medication, and his opinion of the results.

This last point deserves special mention. As emotional as this topic may be for you, the parent, think how difficult it is for your child. A very young child will generally accept what you and the doctor say. Eventually, however, many will challenge it. "Why do I have to take this stuff?" "I'm tired of taking these pills." "None of my friends has to take medicine every day." By the time he is older, the social stigma and the need to be "normal" can significantly affect a child's feelings about taking medication. In addition, you may be making the process more difficult for him by telegraphing your own concerns.

Be proactive rather than reactive. The prescribing physician can tell you what concerns your child may have about medication and suggest ways to handle them. Talk to other parents whose children are on medication. Find out if other children your child's age (or a little older) are available to talk with your child. Teens will listen to their peers long before they will listen to you. A peer "medication mentor" can be ideal for an adolescent. Education is the key— both for you *and* for your child. There are excellent books written for children that also make wonderful resources for you. Those listed in the Resources section include several that may be helpful. Reading these before medication treatment starts will better enable you to predict and respond to your child's concerns.

Quick Tip

A peer "medication mentor" can help your child, particularly in adolescence, handle the inevitable concerns that arise about medication.

Any decision to introduce medication into a child's system is a serious one and should not be made lightly. Whatever the decision, it should be an informed one, not just an emotional one. Because there is so much information and misinformation, it is especially important that parents do their homework and not rely on word-of-mouth, possibly uninformed opinions. Jan and Jamie were touched by the emotionality and aware of the hype, but they also did their homework. This better prepared them for the roller coaster ride of helping to manage Theodore's medication treatment.

INITIAL REACTION: *"OH, NO! YOU'RE NOT GOING TO DRUG MY KID!"*

Jan: My reaction when Theodore's third grade teacher suggested that he might have attention deficit disorder was the thought, *Oh, no. Not Ritalin!* Ritalin and ADHD were inextricably linked in my mind and it wasn't favorably. I'm not opposed to medications per se. Giving hyperactive kids stimulant medication just made little sense. How could stimulant drugs calm down a hyperactive kid? Or make him less distractible? Or less impulsive? I wasn't comfortable with "drugging" an eight-year-old, though I had no problems with the drugs his sister, Caroline, took to prevent sinus infections. Somehow Ritalin was different.

The more I read, the more I understood how stimulant medications (used for ADHD) worked. Since ADHD is a problem of congenital *under*stimulation of parts of the brain that regulate attention, impulsivity, and activity, then medications that stimulate those parts of the brain to work more effectively made sense to me. The more I understood about the potential benefits, the more open I became to the idea of medication for Theodore.

GETTING GOING: FROM THE DOCTOR'S OFFICE TO THEODORE'S MOUTH

We found a pediatrician with a developmental background and an exceptional understanding of ADHD. Between the extensive questionnaire his office sent us to complete and the testing information we provided, the doctor had a lot of information about Theodore before he even saw him. We all liked him immediately. He felt confident that Theodore was a good candidate for medication and would likely benefit from it. He said that we should start seeing the effects almost immediately—within a day or two, although he cautioned that it would take some time to determine the optimal dose.

He started Theodore on Ritalin (its generic name is methylphenidate), which is short acting—lasting roughly three to five hours, though four hours is the average. He recommended we follow his usual practice, which was to begin with the lowest dose possible, seven days a week, and add to it until everyone felt it was effective. He told us that Ritalin's effect on Theodore was more likely to be seen first at school. Initially, he timed the doses to get Theodore through the school day, suggesting he not take it too late in the day to avoid sleep disturbances. We discovered that Theodore didn't fit the norm and we soon added a small, early-evening dose.

Theodore started on five milligrams of Ritalin three times a day—at breakfast, at lunch, and at 4:00 P.M. We hoped the Ritalin would last through the after-school program and help him get homework done. We agreed it was important to keep Theodore on this schedule on weekends as well as school days. If he needed Ritalin to focus his attention, to reduce distractibility and impulsivity at school, he needed it at home and in social situations too. More important, Theodore's desire to do better at home and with friends reinforced the doctor's recommendation of weekend medication. We also felt it was important, as did the doctor, to keep him on medication during the summer.

MEDICATION REALITIES AND SCHOOL POLICY COLLIDE

Not surprisingly, having Theodore take medication at school entailed numerous problems. Because they are subject to abuse, stimulant medications like Ritalin, Adderall, or Dexedrine are classified as controlled substances. This means that there are additional controls on their prescription and use. Physicians cannot call a prescription in to the pharmacy and may not authorize refills. They must write a new prescription every time and cannot fax the original to a pharmacy. If your doctor is willing, he can save you time by mailing the prescription directly to the pharmacy.

School systems have rigid rules for dispensing such medications, which add another layer of inconvenience. Theodore's school required a signed form from the doctor, which could be faxed to the school nurse, authorizing the school to give Theodore the medication. Other safeguards included use of original prescription bottles and new forms and new bottles when dosages changed. The process was time-consuming and frustrating.

It was especially onerous whenever Theodore's medication or dosage changed. Since his medication was altered only because the existing dose or medication wasn't effective, quick action was necessary. All the rules, however, meant that he suffered unduly when a simple change took so long. I learned to keep the pediatrician supplied with extra school forms and stamped, addressed envelopes so we could change doses with the least hassle.

Quick Tip

For a child on stimulant medication, supply the doctor with self-addressed, stamped envelopes and school medication-authorization forms to speed up the process for medication refills or changes. You may save time if the doctor is willing to mail the prescription directly to the pharmacy.

Finally, before Theodore started on the medication, we met with his teachers and school nurse so they would know what to expect. In addition, we set up a system for regular communication with his teachers (weekly telephone calls, supplemented by occasional notes and brief face-to-face meetings) for the first few weeks to help get Theodore's dosage right.

Although we didn't have a written checklist for Theodore, we had a mental one that we covered in each conversation. Was Theodore interacting more appropriately with his peers? Was he less emotionally volatile in class? Did he seem less easily frustrated? Was he able to concentrate for longer periods of time on his schoolwork—especially when it was of little interest to him? Was he interrupting less often? Was he less easily distracted? Was he better able to contribute to group discussions without blurting out or interrupting? Did he seem less restless? Most important, was the quality of his academic work improving?

Quick Tip

Provide the teacher with a written checklist of behaviors that can indicate whether the medication is working. This is especially helpful when starting medication or after dosage or medication changes.

WOW! IT WORKS!

Inconveniences aside, the Ritalin worked. We saw changes in Theodore almost immediately. He seemed less "wired" the first or second day. His teachers reported that he was far more focused, less distractible, and not as emotional or sensitive to slights. After only one month, the change was like night and day: his academic performance soared. Although his speech remained rapid (as in faster than a speeding bullet), he could share more of his thoughts with his classmates. He interrupted less often, withdrew less often into books, and participated better in groups. At home, though homework was still no picnic, he did it with fewer distractions. He was calmer and a little more focused.

Initially, we scheduled his after-school dose at 4:00 P.M. so the doses would be evenly spaced throughout the day. However, Theodore's after-school program was not vigilant in ensuring he got his medication and, not surprisingly, he didn't often remember on his own. We realized he didn't like to take medication at school because it made him feel stigmatized—"different." Eventually we developed a routine for Theodore to go to the nurse for his last dose when school was over on his way to the after-school program.

Theodore: I thought there was something wrong with me because I never fit in with other kids. I felt even worse when I learned that I had ADHD. When I found out I had a brain problem I felt like some kind of an outcast. I thought that nobody else had ADHD and nobody else took Ritalin.

At first I never liked to take my medication because I had to raise my hand, wait for the teacher to call on me, and then ask in front of everybody if I could go and get my medicine. I didn't like that. Other kids knew I took medicine, even though I didn't have asthma or strep throat or something. I felt like they thought I had some weird physical or mental problem. When I started taking my medicine on the way to lunch and right after school, I felt better because I could casually walk away from the group and go get it.

When I first started taking medication, I was afraid other kids would make fun of me, but they never did. Now I don't feel so bad about it. No one notices. Besides, I've found out a lot of other kids take medication for ADHD too. Plus, I know that it helps me pay attention and stay focused in school.

REASONABLE EXPECTATIONS FOR WHAT MEDICATION CAN DO

Sharon: Medication is often an essential component in the treatment of some disorders. Schizophrenia, for example, can't be effectively treated without medication. Though the media would have you believe that treatment with stimulant medication is controversial, it is, in fact, carefully studied and its benefits well documented by the research. It can make an enormous difference in the ability of a child with ADHD to focus and reduce impulsive behaviors. Other types of medication can even modify the more extreme behaviors associated with disorders such as bipolar or anxiety disorder.

However, medication cannot enable a child to demonstrate behaviors or skills he does not have. Medication may lift a depressed child's black moods but it won't necessarily enable him to make friends—the lack of which may have contributed to the depression. Similarly, if a child's behavior is a function of poor impulse control or inability to focus, then stimulant medication may be beneficial. However, if a child's mechanism for expressing anger is to deck someone, the only change stimulants may produce is that he will check to see if anyone's looking before he decks someone. Stimulant medication will not teach a child a better way to express anger. It may only give him the impulse control to delay his instinctive response. Medication alone is unlikely to be the magic bullet or, more to the point, the magic pill.

Medicating doesn't mean you're taking the easy way out. Your child's need for medication does not signify failure as a parent. Ideally, it means you've made an informed decision and understand what medications can and cannot do. A dogmatic stance in either camp—opposition to or insistence on medication—will not serve your child well.

Sometimes medication may be what your child needs. For some children, it enables them to better benefit from other treatments. It may make a child more receptive to learning new ways of doing things. An older child or adolescent may be more cooperative in group or individual counseling. It may reduce impulsivity so that a child with ADHD can benefit from social-skills training.

Discussions of medication tend to focus on fears and cures, both of which are exaggerated. Your first obligation is to educate yourself. Ask questions about why your child needs this. Ask what the medication is supposed to accomplish. Ask what you can expect as signs the medication is working. Ask how long it will take to see these signs. Ask about side effects. Your child's use of medication requires vigilant monitoring. As emotional as the topic may be, education and vigilance can reduce the stress.

MEDICATION DOESN'T FIX EVERYTHING

Jan: It took a long time—probably three months—to get Theodore's Ritalin dose to a fully effective level. Close monitoring, by us at home and by Theodore's teachers, helped determine when he reached an optimal dosage.

It took even longer to figure out what the Ritalin could and couldn't do. Ritalin allowed Theodore to control himself better. It allowed him to concentrate better in class and follow the routines we were trying to establish at home. It didn't, however, enable him to make friends, slow down his speech, or suddenly give him the maturity and capabilities of an older child. He still forgot things, lost stuff, and got distracted, although less than previously.

Although we hoped that Ritalin would help Theodore become more organized, the biggest changes at home were achieved when we restructured household routines. That enabled us to appreciate the improvement in Theodore's ability to get through his chores and homework—which *was* due to the Ritalin.

Adjusting the time of his morning dose also made a difference. By giving half of the dose when we woke him up, he was better able to get through his morning routine. Getting the rest just before he left home helped get him through the school morning.

Theodore: When I started taking medication, I really didn't feel any different. Medication didn't make me feel weird or strange. But it also didn't make me feel calmer or better able to focus. On the other hand, I can tell when I need to take it because I get fidgety, restless, and pumped up. It's hard to describe. Once I've taken my medication, I don't feel "changed," but I'm able to perform better physically and mentally. Even though other people told me my behavior was changing, I didn't see it. In looking back, I realize that my parents were yelling at me less, but I didn't notice at the time.

Jan: Theodore's doctor warned us that since most kids feel normal and cannot tell when the medication is working, we should not rely on Theodore's report as to how well it was working or whether it was helping him. Usually the first thing they can tell is how they are when they forget a dose or when it wears off. They might say things such as "I get the squirmies around one thirty" or "I start getting loud again."

Medication was supposed to make Theodore less impulsive. It did, to a point. But the chief manifestations of his impulsivity were extreme talkativeness and a tendency to act before thinking in dealing with his peers. Unfortunately, the medication really didn't affect these traits.

LEARNING TO RECOGNIZE WHEN MEDICATION ISN'T WORKING

For a long time, I clung to the belief that the medication would work every day, every dose, without fail, and that was mostly the case. Occasionally, Theodore would get up on the wrong side of the brain (biochemically) and the medication just wouldn't work. Or, one dose out of his daily three or four didn't work. While Theodore was never hyperactive, he was indeed restless. One of the first indicators that his Ritalin dosage wasn't working was that he seemed "wired." I had to accept that occasionally—rarely, actually—Theodore's medication just didn't work. Even then, it usually only affected a single dose.

MONITORING MEDICATION'S EFFECTS ON YOUR CHILD

Sharon: Whether the medication is for depression, anxiety, ADHD, or anything else, one of your responsibilities as a parent is to monitor the effect it has on your child. Including your child in the assessment and monitoring process reinforces this as a team effort, not something done to "fix" him. Moreover, it may increase his awareness of the benefits of medication so he is better able to judge its effectiveness himself.

Here is a list of questions you should ask when your child begins medication therapy, changes dosage, or starts taking a different medication.

- Is the medication having a positive impact on your child's mood and/or behavior?

- Do you think the dosage or medication is working?

- Does your child think the dosage or medication is working?

- Does the dose need to be increased or decreased?

- What was the change in a specific behavior or set of behaviors that caused you to conclude that the medication needed to be evaluated?

- Is your child experiencing any side effects (e.g., headaches, stomachaches, fatigue or sleeplessness, dry mouth, etc.)?

- What is the likelihood those side effects will last? (Ask your doctor.)

- Do any lasting side effects (if any) outweigh the medication's benefits?

- Do you or your child think a medication or dosage level has stopped working?

Pointer for Effective Parenting

Alert the doctor about any changes in your child's emotional, behavioral, or physical well-being. Don't make changes in medication or dosage on your own.

You need to sort out whether the positive and negative changes you see are a function of the medication. To do so, you need a clear understanding of what behaviors and/or moods to monitor to help decide whether a medication is working. Sometimes it's a matter of what to look for in assessing changes the medication produced. It's also important to know which behaviors might change.

To start, get a baseline or measure of one or more behaviors *before* treatment begins. You're looking for improvement but improvement in what? A child's behavior may be different in various situations. If you and your child's teachers complete a behavior rating scale or symptom checklist before starting medication, and repeat the process at intervals throughout treatment, it can provide a more objective measure of change at home and at school. Be specific. Tailor a checklist for behaviors that are relevant measures for your child. (See Sample Behavior/Symptom Checklist.)

Checklist data, combined with your general impressions, will help your doctor make necessary medication changes. The goal is to determine what produced the improvement (or deterioration) in your child's behavior. Is the change really the result of the medication? Are you attributing too much of any change in attitude or behavior to the medication? What else could be responsible?

You also have to consider typical changes in temperament most children experience. You have to recognize that the onset of an adolescent "attitude" may be just that, and not a medication issue. Where once you had a questioning child, now you have a balking adolescent. Does that mean the medication isn't working anymore? The key is whether the medication is doing what *it* is supposed to do, not what you, the parent, thought or wanted it to do.

Sample Behavior/Symptom Checklist

Date:

Check the box that best describes this child compared with other children of the same gender and age.

	NEVER	SOME-TIMES	OFTEN	VERY OFTEN
Loses things necessary for tasks or activities				
Leaves seat in classroom or other situations when expected to remain seated				
Has difficulty getting along with other children				
Seems sad, moody, depressed, or discouraged				
Worries about or avoids activities previously enjoyed				

Adapted from Castellanos, F. Xavier, and Karen J. Miller, "Attention Deficit Hyperactivity Disorders," *Pediatrics in Review* 19, no. 11 (Nov. 1998): 373–84.

The latter is wish fulfillment and not a valid measure of a medication's impact.

NECESSITY FOR VIGILANT MONITORING

Jan: If Theodore's medication wasn't working on more than just an occasional basis the signs were subtle, and they often appeared at school before we saw them at home. We gradually learned to distinguish between when an occasional dosage or the medication itself was no longer working for Theodore.

Ritalin worked for nearly two years. However, in fifth grade, Ritalin stopped working almost entirely. Theodore's grades began to slip. Though projects were never his long suit, Theodore was particularly unable to stay focused, plan, or do anything without exceedingly close supervision on a big project. It was as difficult as

STEPS FOR MONITORING MEDICATIONS

1. Keep a written record or log of all medications (including dosage changes) prescribed for your child (see Sample Medication Log). Record impressions by you, teachers, Scout leaders, grandparents, and anyone else he regularly sees of the effect the medication has on him.

2. Write down anything the doctor says about potential side effects and changes you can expect to see in your child because of the medication. *Don't rely on your memory.*

3. Share that information with your child's teacher and other interested adults because signs of medication (in)effectiveness may not show up first at home.

4. Establish a schedule for regular communication with your child's teacher and other interested adults. Adhere to it.

5. Use a simple written checklist of behaviors to monitor (see Sample Symptom Checklist). This is helpful for you and for teachers. It provides a consistent measure of change (if any) and assures that everyone is looking at the same things.

6. Consult your child's doctor if you see behavior changes that suggest the medication may not be working.

it had been before his diagnosis. By the end of a weekend of yelling and screaming, we began to wonder if the Ritalin simply wasn't working anymore. His teacher reported that he was constantly interrupting, bothering his neighbors, and having a hard time sitting still.

It wasn't clear that we could just increase the Ritalin dosage as in the past, because it was now nearly at the maximum level. We could try one last increase, which probably wouldn't work, or switch him to a different medication. Adderall usually lasts longer than Ritalin (generally 5½ to 6½ hours) and might last him throughout the school day as it does for some children. However, we didn't know how long it might take to find the most effective dose. We reluctantly opted for one more Ritalin increase, but rapidly concluded that it no longer worked. So, with some trepidation but no real choice, we switched him to Adderall. To our—and Theodore's—relief, it worked immediately. However, since Theodore metabolizes medication quickly, we weren't surprised that he needed a lunch dose.

This lengthy process meant that Theodore had been undermedicated for too long. If we had been keeping a medication log or a data sheet that recorded specific behavioral changes at home and at school (see Sample Medication Log), we might have shortened the time it took to adjust Theodore's medication. Knowing what to look for would have helped us spot changes far more quickly.

Sample Medication Log

START DATE/ END DATE	MEDICATION	DAILY DOSE	RESPONSE	SIDE EFFECTS	COMMENTS

Adapted from "Medication Log," in *Straight Talk about Psychiatric Medications for Kids* by Timothy E. Wilens, M.D. (New York: Guilford Press, 1999), p. 249.

This wasn't our first adjustment in Theodore's medications, and it obviously won't be the last. Although we didn't keep a daily medication log, we did keep a log of his medication changes. (See Theodore's Changes in Medication Log.) Monitoring and adjusting Theodore's medications is an ongoing task. Theodore took medication daily; the chart below shows each change since he began.

THEODORE'S CHANGES IN MEDICATION LOG

DATE	MEDICATION	DOSAGE (IN PILLS) AND TIME
Third Grade		
2-17-97	Ritalin 5 mg	1 at breakfast, 1 at lunch, ½ late afternoon
3-12-97	Ritalin 5 mg	1½ at breakfast, 1½ at lunch, 1 after school
4-14-97	Ritalin 5 mg	added ½ early evening
4-28-97	Ritalin 5 mg	2 at breakfast, 2 at lunch, 1 after school, 1 evening
Fourth Grade		
11-17-97	Ritalin 5 mg	2 at breakfast, 2 at lunch, 2 at 3:30, 1 at 7:30 P.M.
3-23-98	Ritalin 5 mg	2½ at breakfast, 2½ at lunch, 2 at 3:30, 1 at 7:30 P.M.
4-20-98	Ritalin 5 mg	3 at breakfast, 3 at lunch, 2½ at 3:30, 1½ at 7:30 P.M.
Fifth Grade		
10-8-98	Ritalin 5 mg	3 at breakfast, 3 at lunch, 2½ at 3:30, ½ at 7:30 P.M.
11-29-98	Ritalin 5 mg	3 at breakfast, 3½ at lunch, 3 at 3:30, 2½ at 7:30 P.M.

DATE	MEDICATION	DOSAGE (IN PILLS) AND TIME
Fifth Grade (continued)		
12-16-98	Adderall 10 mg	1 at breakfast, 1 at lunch, ½ at 5:30 P.M.
2-6-99	Adderall 10 mg	1½ at breakfast, 1½ at lunch, ½ at 5:30 P.M.
4-15-99	Adderall 10 mg	1½ at breakfast, 1½ at lunch, ¾ at 5:30 P.M.
5-10-99	Adderall 10 mg	continued as before; added:
	Wellbutrin 75 mg	1 at breakfast, 1 at 4:00 P.M.
Sixth Grade		
9-15-99	Adderall 10 mg	1½ at breakfast, 1½ at lunch 1 at 5:00 P.M.
	Wellbutrin 75 mg	no change
9-27-99	Adderall 10 mg	2 at breakfast, 1½ at lunch, 1 at 4:30 P.M.
	Wellbutrin 75 mg	1 at breakfast, 1 at 4:30 P.M.
12-23-99	Adderall 10 mg	2 at breakfast, 1½ at lunch, 1½ at 4:30 P.M.
	Wellbutrin 75 mg	1 at breakfast, 1 at 4:30 P.M.
2-8-00	Adderall 10 mg	2 at breakfast, 1½ at lunch, 1½ at 4:30 P.M.
	Wellbutrin 100 mg	1 at breakfast, 1 at 4:30 P.M.
2-14-00	Adderall 10 mg	2 at breakfast, 1½ at lunch, 1½ at 4:30 P.M.
	Wellbutrin 100 mg	1 at breakfast
	Wellbutrin 75mg	1 at 4:30 P.M.

In fourth grade, we went through several months when Theodore's dosage during school hours became seriously inadequate, but having let regular communication with his teacher lapse, we didn't know about it until he got nailed on his report card. That episode taught us how essential it was to educate his teachers about signs that medication might not be working and their need to communicate with us when they suspected that might be the case.

We should have given his teacher a behavior/symptom checklist (see page 54) to help her know what to look for. Then she might have recognized that his deteriorating behavior and grades were symptoms of medication ineffectiveness rather than simply poor performance. We would have become aware of the situation before seeing a poor report card. Those unhappy months reminded us of the necessity for regular (not occasional) contact with Theodore's teachers.

Vigilant monitoring of stimulant medication is essential not only to ensure that it's working, but also to catch other problems that need attention. While we were alert to the occasional need to tinker with his Adderall dose, we completely missed new symptoms of borderline depression. In fifth grade, we discovered a serious episode of bullying Theodore had tried to cope with alone. I was dismayed I hadn't spotted it sooner. Even worse, I had missed signs of depression—his increasing withdrawal and not wanting to go to school.

I took Theodore to see a counselor who concluded he was on the verge of depression from the stress of this bullying. In addition to initiating weekly therapy with Theodore, she recommended that his doctor reassess his medications. He did so and then prescribed Wellbutrin, which helped elevate and stabilize Theodore's mood. Since it has worked well, Theodore has stayed on it. This episode was another painful reminder that we cannot go to sleep at the switch when it comes to Theodore's medication—and that kids can develop the need for another medication even if they are successfully being treated with another. It also reminded us that medication isn't all that Theodore needs. In this case, bringing in a counselor when depression became an issue was critical to getting him back on track.

Theodore: I talk fast because I'm curious about all sorts of things and have so many ideas I want to share. People are always asking me to slow down. I try, but my non-fast speech doesn't last long. The Ritalin or Adderall [stimulants] haven't helped me with my speech, but since I started taking Wellbutrin [antidepressant], I've been more aware of my fast speech. I've tried to slow it down, but it hasn't helped all that much.

Sharon: As should be clear from Jan and Jamie's experiences, as a parent, you need to become familiar with this complex field. You will have to sort out often-conflicting information. You may have to answer your child's questions regarding medication. And you must deal with your own and others' frustration when medication does not prove to be a magic bullet.

Jan: Although we haven't had to change Theodore's medication recently, slowly, I have understood that no matter how much I want it to be so, medication for Theodore isn't ever going to be something that we finally "get right." What is right today may not be right tomorrow. Theodore's medication therapy needs frequent modification, with changes in dosage or the drugs themselves as he undergoes developmental spurts, as different needs arise or diminish, or as side effects wax and wane.

Most of the medication concerns I had initially haven't materialized. It hasn't changed who Theodore is, impaired his creativity, or turned him into a zombie. Side effects have been minor and manageable. Most important, the medication has done what it is supposed to do. I just wish that what worked today would work forever. I no longer vacillate between wishing that medication was a cure-all and preferring he could do without it. Well, that isn't exactly true. I still wish he could take a pill every day that would magically make his ADHD disappear.

4

Getting Up, Going to Bed, and Other Routines

How to Restructure Daily Life
So It Isn't Pure Hell

Sharon: In any household with children the following phrases are frequently heard:

"When are you going to learn?"
"Why do you make me yell at you?"
"Why can't you just get up?"
"Why do I have to tell you to do the same things every single day?"

However, the challenging child can't benefit from this litany of complaints. While most kids perceive it as nagging (because they heard what you said and may already know what to do), the challenging child often doesn't understand all that is expected of him.

The challenging child handles his world the best way he knows how. His best way generally entails overreliance on adult support to get anything done. His parents moan: "All I want him to do is take responsibility for his own behavior." He never has to because his parents have already taken responsibility for his behavior. They tell him when to get up, repeat directions over and over, and stay with it until he's finally out of bed. Then they talk him through getting washed and dressed. Then they talk or yell him through pulling things together and getting out the door. The result is a child totally dependent on that level of support to get through his daily life.

Establishing Routines

One of the first steps in reducing household chaos is to establish routines. That means determining what situations occur regularly and then establishing a structure or sequence to be repeated every single day. Routines mean repetition and repetition means practice. Practice allows a child to become proficient (or at least better) at completing the basic requirements by himself. This is helpful to all children, essential for some.

The process for establishing a routine or changing a specific behavior requires answers to three questions: *What do I want the child to do instead of what he is doing? How can I put it in a visual format so he doesn't have to rely on me telling him what to do? What will make it worth his while?*

Quick Tip

To establish routines or change behaviors, answer these questions:

- What do I want him to do instead of what he is doing?

- How can I put it in a visual format so he doesn't have to rely on me telling him what to do?

- What will make it worth his while?

Without an answer to all three questions you will have failed to clarify your expectations in a way that allows your child to check what you wanted and double-check his progress toward those expectations. A visual format gives him the ability to do that without you reminding him. Moreover, it provides the necessary incentive to keep him going.

Since Theodore's inability to get out of the house in the morning without major hassles drove Jan and Jamie crazy, we worked on that first.

Morning Routines

Jan: We knew there had to be a better way to do things. We recognized that Theodore was not just being difficult. With his diagnosis of attention deficit disorder, we understood there was a reason for his being "less easy" than his sister. We had done our homework, read books, gathered our list of experts, met with them all, and, we hoped, gotten the right help. We had sorted, selected, and sequenced how we were going to tackle Theodore's ADHD. We had researched, soul-searched, and started Theodore on Ritalin.

OK. So far, so good. The Ritalin really was making a difference. We saw some changes at home, but more important, his third-grade teachers reported major changes in the classroom. He was more focused, he interrupted far less, and his comments were relevant and interesting.

So, why wasn't everything all fixed? Why was it still such a struggle to get him out of the house in the morning? Why did bedtime remain such a battleground?

Theodore: I thought Ritalin was going to fix everything. But it didn't stop all their yelling, especially in the mornings.

Jan: One of the first issues we raised with Sharon was how to prevent the daily morning havoc. We, of course, blamed Theodore. He never got himself up. He slept right through the radio alarm, then right through the alarm buzzer. One of us would have to go in his room, wake him up, leave, and then go back ten minutes later to find he was still in bed. Sometimes we'd have to go in four times.

"*THEODORE!! GET UP THIS INSTANT! I'VE HAD IT*

WITH YOU. WHY DO YOU ALWAYS MAKE ME YELL AT YOU?"

Theodore would either yell back or start the day in tears. Unfortunately this bad beginning would set the tone for how everything else was likely to go. I would yell at Jamie if he was yelling too much at Theodore and Jamie would yell at me to go take care of it if I had any better ideas. Theodore, by this time, was scrambling to stay out of sight.

Getting him out of bed, however, was easier than what came next. Everything distracted him from what he was supposed to be doing, which was getting dressed, making his bed, coming out to the kitchen, making his lunch, getting and eating his breakfast, cleaning up his dishes, brushing his teeth, combing his hair, stuffing everything in his backpack, tying his shoes, tugging his coat on, getting good-bye kisses from Jamie and me, and flying out the door in time to catch the school bus.

Was this so unreasonable? we asked ourselves. We told him what he was supposed to do. Why wouldn't he do it? Occasionally there were days when he seemed more focused and did it all, but we couldn't rely on him to do his morning activities. We always seemed to have the responsibility and the only way we could get him to do anything was to yell. Why did we have to go through this e-v-e-r-y single day? I got myself up, dressed, fed, and out the door every morning; so did Jamie; and so, for the most part, did Caroline. Why wouldn't Theodore?

Theodore: It was hard for me to stay focused. I couldn't remember all those things I was supposed to do. Mom or Dad would come in and stand over me until I did one of them. Usually, they were mad and yelling at me. Then they'd leave and expect me to do the rest. Every time I'd move to another step, there would be something to distract me. For example, my bookshelf is right next to my clothes shelf. I would see a book I'd want to read, sit down, with my shirt or pants halfway on, and read until they came in yelling at me to get going. Each time they came in, they'd be madder than the time before. On and on this went, them yelling and leaving, me trying to do something, me getting distracted. Sometimes, they'd get so mad, they'd sit in my room until I was all done. I didn't look forward to mornings.

Sharon: One of Jan and Jamie's problems was that they had too many expectations—and no way to remind Theodore about what he was supposed to be doing except by their physical presence and raised voices. They were the only reminders of what to do next. Yet they were surprised and annoyed when Theodore waited for their reminders to complete standard daily activities. While their "technique" may have worked, it frazzled everyone's nerves and didn't make Theodore responsible for getting himself out the door every morning. They needed to develop a routine that Theodore could accomplish by himself with some other form of reminder—a visual cue—to tell him to "get back on track." They had to stop being the cues that said "get going."

Even in the most frantic of households there are only three things that your child must perform daily, but may have trouble doing consistently: get up and get dressed; eat; and go to sleep. If only these three events go more smoothly, you'd have a far calmer household.

Fortunately, you can devise routines to help your child accomplish these things. By routine, I mean a sequence of tasks your child can do every day in the same order. Most people establish routines by doing the same tasks regularly until the pattern becomes established. This learning by osmosis does not work for all children. They need a specific structure set up by someone else (you) that they can practice with reminders or prompts that do not include Mom or Dad standing over or yelling at them.

Steps Toward Establishing A Routine

STEP 1: DECIDE WHAT TASKS MUST BE DONE

To establish a routine you first have to agree on what tasks are truly important—not your idealized vision of what your child ought to do. What absolutely must be included as a part of the daily routine? The school will allow any child to attend whether or not he has made his bed, but a teacher will frown on children arriving buck-naked. Decide what tasks are necessary and in what sequence you want them to be done. If your child is over four, try

> ## STEPS TOWARD ESTABLISHING A ROUTINE
>
> 1. Decide what tasks must be done.
>
>   - Separate the desirable from the truly essential. Ignore the unessential—you can expand the routine once your child has fully mastered the essential tasks.
>   - Prioritize the important tasks.
>
> 2. Develop a written checklist and post it where your child will see it every time he needs to use it.
>
> 3. Reinforce routines with incentives for performance.

to include him in the decision making process. What does *he* think is important? Ask how much time he thinks he needs to get ready in the morning. Seek your child's input but keep in mind that very young children have no concept of time, and many challenging children have no inner clock; therefore they have no accurate sense of time passing. Furthermore, they may never develop one. Now is the time to teach them to rely on watches and timers. (See page 84 for ideas on how to use timers.)

Quick Tip

Make decisions about routines with your child's input, especially older children and adolescents. They can better adhere to a routine they have helped develop.

Ask how many reminders your child thinks he needs to get out of bed. An adolescent will often say "none" and accede to one. Agree on a sequence, prioritize what's really important, develop a checklist, and post it.

The checklist becomes the standard, so that both you and your child use it as a reference point. Place the checklist where your child will see it every time he needs to use it or give him a new copy to use every day.

Quick Tip

For any new routine, develop a written checklist and post it where your child will see it every time he needs to use it.

Let's review what Jan and Jamie expected Theodore to do every morning.

1. Wake up; get out of bed on his own when the alarm goes off at 7:30.

2. Get dressed (underwear, shirt, pants, and socks).

3. Make bed.

4. Put away pajamas.

5. Come out to kitchen and make lunch.

6. Fix breakfast.

7. Eat breakfast.

8. Put away clean silverware from yesterday. Load breakfast dishes in dishwasher. Put away cereal. Put away milk.

9. Brush teeth.

10. Comb hair.

11. Place everything for school into backpack.

12. Stash lunch box in backpack.

13. Remember to take trumpet on Mondays, soccer shoes and

shin guards on Tuesdays and Thursdays, and tennis racket on Fridays.

14. Put on sweatshirt/coat/hat/gloves.

15. Put on shoes.

16. Get good-bye kisses.

17. Get out the door in time to make it to the school bus.

Theodore can't do all that!

Hey, *I* couldn't do everything on that list and make it out the door by noon. The problem is not just the length of the list; it's the complexity. Do certain things on some days and not on others. If you're not a morning person it's enough to remember where the bathroom is, let alone which day it is and what equipment you need that day.

Some of Theodore's tasks aren't essential to the morning routine. After all, the goal is that Theodore get up and get ready for school and out the door on time—without his parents having to nag him. Remember the minimum standard is what the school accepts as "ready" when he walks in the door. As long as Theodore is awake, dressed, and relatively clean, he's acceptable, whether the bed is made or not. He's allowed into his classroom even if his family's dishwasher remains loaded with clean silverware. The morning routine has to include getting up, washed, and dressed and eating breakfast by a certain time.

I suggested that the night before, Theodore should organize any equipment he needed the next day. He should put instruments, sports equipment, or things to show friends downstairs the night before. He should also load his backpack the night before with homework, field trip permission slips, and so on and put it by the front door.

Some children benefit from a short checklist attached with Velcro to their backpack. The list includes things like homework, assignment book, forms, and lunch money, which the child checks off as he fills the backpack. To help a child learn to use the list, the parent's responsibility is to reward the child for using it.

Parents need to establish a rule that "if it's not in the backpack and down by the door, it doesn't go to school." For the child to make the connection and take responsibility, he may have to bear the consequences a few times of having forgotten to put his homework in the backpack.

Quick Tip

Get the backpack prepared and down by the door the night before. In some cases, a short checklist of necessities can be attached with Velcro to the flap. The rule is: If it's not there the night before, it doesn't go to school.

Theodore hadn't figured out how to get himself out the door in the morning and relied on his parents to ensure he did so. He wasn't trying to drive them crazy. He just had difficulty keeping *their* agenda in *his* head without *their* help. If you give your child instructions and walk out the door, the child has nothing to keep him on track. You've become the walking, talking prompt for getting up and getting dressed. You've become the visual reminder.

Routines are necessary for everyone. But, with their brains whirring a mile a minute and their attention distracted by whatever interesting toy, book, or view out the window that catches their eye, most challenging children do not perceive the pattern that constitutes a routine. Nor do they feel any need to develop routines on their own. A momentary distraction blows huge holes in any plans they might set up for themselves—or that have been imposed on them by others.

Routines also keep adults honest, so that we don't change our expectations. On different days adults can have different expectations for the exact same situation. If you're running late or have an appointment, you're going to expect your child to get ready more quickly and with fewer reminders—because *you're* late! However, he's no more efficient today than he was yesterday when you gave him fifteen reminders and lots of support. Today, because you don't have the time, he gets fewer reminders to accomplish the same thing with greater efficiency. It is unreasonable to expect your child to hurry up just because you are in a hurry. *He's* not in a hurry and your rush is of no importance to him—except that you're now yelling that *he's* making you late.

To make matters worse, parents have a tendency to move the goalposts when it comes to expectations for their child's behavior—especially with challenging children who all too often don't meet expectations anyway. Moreover, their definition of what's appropriate can change with their mood. What was acceptable yesterday falls short today. Every day is a new opportunity to raise the bar and expect more from your child. Adults are often guilty of what I call the "You didn't comb your hair" syndrome. You beg, plead, cajole your child to be up, washed, dressed, and downstairs by 7:30 A.M. You repeat daily: "I need you to get up, get washed, dressed, and be downstairs by seven thirty." Finally, miraculously, one day the child is up, washed, dressed, and downstairs by 7:30. Then you look at him and say, "But you didn't comb your hair." If you keep moving the goal line, your child never gets to score a touchdown.

Adults need to state in positive terms what they want the child to do and limit comments to what is on that checklist. In every situation, they need to ask: "What do I want my child to do instead of what he is doing?" If you can't answer that question, there's no chance your child can. Parents must make sure that their expectations are realistic and reasonable. "Realistic" means that the child actually has the skills to perform those behaviors on his own. "Reasonable" means that parents are not asking too much. Can they reasonably expect their child to complete all that's being asked? Even with parental or external prompts, however, they cannot count on perfection. They can expect, given a limited number of tasks, that with practice, the child will be able to get through the list. Therefore, an *effective* checklist should not be more than three to eight items long, depending on age and ability to follow through on things.

Jan and Jamie first needed to determine which of the seventeen items on their list Theodore really had to do in those fifty-five minutes between the alarm clock ringing and running for the school bus.

Jan: Jamie and I had never looked at it that way before. Our first step, therefore, was to review the full list to see what wasn't really necessary, what could be done at another time, and what simply had to be accomplished. That process forced us to rethink whether we were overloading Theodore. We discovered that not only were our expectations excessive, they were also inconsistent. Theodore could not internalize and remember an exceedingly long list of tasks that varied daily.

We needed to do four things to help Theodore establish a routine he could follow by himself. We had to:

1. Give him fewer tasks

2. Create a written list of tasks that didn't vary from day to day

3. Provide incentives for completing the tasks successfully

4. Get off his back so he had to take the responsibility himself

Somewhat to our surprise, it was not hard to shorten the list. At Sharon's suggestion, we had Theodore make lunch the night before, which turned it from a ten-minute to a two-minute task since he was more focused at night. It also stopped our daily harassment of him: "Hurry up; you're going to be late. Where's your fruit? No, you can't have two desserts. Yes, you must have a decent lunch, so put that yogurt in your lunch box."

Also at Sharon's suggestion, we had him get his backpack, coat, hat, gloves, shoes, trumpet, and anything else (such as permission slips, homework, tennis racket, library books to be returned) ready the night before. He had to collect everything and pile it by the front door. Theodore was less likely to walk out without his tennis racket if it was next to his backpack. Shifting these two tasks to the night before eliminated the time-consuming struggle of harrying Theodore to do this, do that, finish this, hurry up, get going, get ready to go. With everything prepared the night before, there was no need to waste time hunting for soccer shoes. They were by the front door. No need to figure out where the math homework had been left; it was in his backpack by the front door. We were amazed at how much these two changes eased everyone's morning. Theodore, not a morning person, was better able to successfully complete these things the night before, when there wasn't additional pressure to get out the door.

Having the backpack ready by the front door, the night before, forced Theodore to organize himself ahead of time. It eliminated that frantic cramming of the backpack in the morning, the search for missing homework, and made him responsible for what went into it—or what didn't, such as homework or a signed permission slip. It was harder for me to remember to sign the permission slips in a timely fashion, put them on top of his backpack, and not respond to the occasional frantic phone calls from school.—*"Mom, I forgot my social studies homework. It's on my desk. Can you bring it to me?"*

GET READY THE NIGHT BEFORE

1. Have your child pack his backpack (according to a list) the night before.

2. Place it by the front door. (VERY IMPORTANT)

3. All homework, schoolbooks, paper, pencils, permission slips must be in backpack the night before.

4. Reward the child for completing all aspects of the routine with minimum of support.

   Rule: If the item is not in there the night before, it doesn't go to school.
   Rule: If it's not in there, Mom or Dad won't bring it to school.

Theodore: I used to hate to pack my backpack in the morning because I was always in a rush. I'd usually forget something. Right when I was about to run out the door, my parents would say, "Do you have so and so?" If I didn't, I'd have to run around and try to find it—usually I couldn't—and they'd come stomping back to my room and find it in two seconds. Having missed the bus, they'd drive me to school yelling all the way and I'd arrive in a crabby mood. Now that I pack it the night before it's much easier and I don't get yelled at.

Jan: Pared down to essentials, the following tasks remained:

1. Get up
2. Get dressed
3. Make bed
4. Get breakfast
5. Eat breakfast
6. Clean up breakfast dishes (and help empty dishwasher if necessary)
7. Brush teeth
8. Comb hair
9. Kisses
10. Depart for school bus

Sharon still thought the list was too long, but it worked for Theodore. Several years later, at a new school with an earlier starting time, we pared it down further to more of what Sharon thought were the true essentials: Get up, get dressed, make bed, eat and clean up breakfast dishes, brush teeth. (She still thinks it's too long.)

STEP 2: DEVELOP A WRITTEN CHECKLIST AND POST IT

That initial list didn't look too bad. However, it was still too much for Theodore to remember every single day. The solution: a written list.

When Sharon suggested this, I asked: "Why does he need it on a list? It's the same tasks every day." She responded: "He needs a visual reminder. How do you remember what you need to do, particularly when you have a large number of things to keep straight?"

I'm an inveterate list maker. I make lists for everything. I always have a running grocery list; turn voice mail messages into a list of phone calls to be returned; and clutter my purse with more lists of errands than I care to count. I remember to do things by writing them down. That simple act helps to imprint the tasks on my brain. Sometimes I don't need to refer to the list again; creating the visual format is enough. List making to help Theodore stay focused made sense.

Even more important, having a list to follow shifted the burden of responsibility from Mom and Dad, who weren't very good at mornings anyway, onto Theodore, who, after all, was the one who had to get up, eat, get dressed, and get out of the house.

Theodore: My parents taped my morning list to my wardrobe since I have to take my clothes out of there. They put another one on the bathroom mirror. I also have a bunch of lists in the kitchen to help me deal with my breakfast tasks and remember to put the finished list in the jar. When I have other things I have to do—like cleaning up my room or my homework—they make lists on yellow Post-it Notes.

Checklists

Sharon: A short written list of two to six items not only establishes the steps of a routine, but conveys expectations and criteria for performance as well. The list's length depends on the child's age, as well as his level of distractibility. Limit lists for younger children to one to three items; three to six items for adolescents. Often parents send children to their rooms with the direction "Clean up your room." A challenging child can't break down this complex task into its component parts. To him it is overwhelming and he either "can't do it" or says, "I need your help." Remember too that for any child—not just challenging ones—the concept of cleaning differs substantially from yours. Yours is akin to *House Beautiful* and his is that he moves his socks. There's a big gap there.

A list clarifies expectations in clear, observable terms so that both parent and child know when the task is completed.

1. Trash in the trash can
2. Toys (books and papers) on the shelf and/or in toy box or milk crates
3. Dirty clothes in the hamper
4. Clean clothes in drawers and/or hung up

Write the list on an erasable white board, post it on a bulletin board in the bedroom, or put it on a Post-it Note that you stick on your child's door. Whatever you do, put the list where your child can't miss it. Remind him to check off each task as it is completed. Use picture cues for very young children. When your child says he's finished, you both survey the results as compared to the list. Acknowledge successful completion of each step. Call your child's attention to items still incomplete *before* he moves on to another activity. This way, the list defines "finished," not you.

Theodore: I like yellow Post-it Notes because they catch my attention and make it easier for me to find them around the house. That way I have a reminder in the places I need them of what I'm supposed to do.

Sharon: A list can also lay out a schedule. An afternoon checklist might be:

1. Snack
2. Homework
3. TV/free time
4. Dinner

If your child asks to watch TV, refer him to the schedule. That way, the list—not you—reminds him that the policy is homework before TV. Similarly, allow adolescents to decide which three of six chores they'll do by noon on Saturday and which three they'll complete before they go out Saturday night or Sunday afternoon. Implicit in this is that they must do all six before the weekend is over. In fact, they have to do them all before they earn the privilege of socializing on Saturday night or Sunday afternoon.

Picture Checklists for Younger Children

A younger child can work from a picture list or schedule. Have the child use a camera to take pictures that show "out of bed," "wash," "dress," "eat breakfast," etc. (Take an extra set. Your child may have photographed his toes.) Arrange the pictures in sequence on a Velcro strip. After he completes each step, he pulls a picture off and places it in an envelope. When he finishes the sequence, he brings you the envelope.

Checklists + Schedules = Predictability = Fewer Meltdowns

Schedules visually demonstrate sequence to a child, thus making his world more predictable. A child enters a situation with a preconceived notion about what the outcome will be. Often, some of the worst meltdowns occur when a child's concept of outcome does not match reality. Some children have particular difficulty making transitions. Knowing what will happen, as well as what will not happen, helps prevent those meltdowns.

Adults generally know what's on the agenda. They know the stops they intend to make (or don't intend to make) when they're running errands. It's not a state secret. But we generally don't share our agenda until the child demands to stop for fast food. ("We can't, we don't have time. It's not on our schedule." "What schedule?" the kid wails.) Or when your teen thinks a trip to the mall was to buy her Nikes. Try not to take this personally, but your children are not interested in going to the linen store. It isn't on their schedule. A list of intended errands that the child can check off or the teen can review to see that the shoe store is only *one* of the stops reduces fallout. Errand lists are especially successful if you include child-friendly stops, contingent on their behavior at other stops.

STEP 3: REINFORCE ROUTINES WITH INCENTIVES FOR PERFORMANCE

Jan and Jamie weren't done yet. They'd done steps 1 and 2. The third step is to increase the child's role. Theodore had to take it on as his responsibility. Or in other words, Jan and Jamie had to ask themselves, "What's in it for Theodore? Why would he want to do it? What's the reinforcer?"

In most families, the reinforcer offered the child is the absence of parental wrath. "If you do this, I won't scream and yell at you." As any experienced parent knows, that doesn't always work. The list reminds the child what he's expected to do. Now the challenge is to find something to associate with it that is so important to the child that he will use the list on a daily basis. What works as a reward may change and needs to be reviewed on a regular basis. Determining what is an effective reinforcer is key.

Jan: What incentive did Theodore have to follow his morning list? The immediate gratification of playing with LEGOs and reading books still afforded greater pleasure than did following a routine and getting out of the house, even if the new routine had reduced the volume of sound emanating from Mom and Dad. We decided that money was the incentive Theodore needed. We realized, however, that the list was too long for one reward to keep Theodore focused. At Sharon's suggestion, we split the list in half. If Theodore finished the first half by 8:00 A.M., he would receive ten cents. If he completed the second half by 8:20, he received another ten cents.

A little experience resulted in a refinement. The delay and then "hurry up and finish" syndrome particularly affected the second half of the list, so we redesigned the incentive. If he finished after the deadline, but before 8:25, he didn't get the second ten cents but he didn't lose anything either. But if he took until after 8:25, and we had to hustle him out the door by collecting his lunch box, combing his hair, etc., then he had to pay us ten cents.

Accounting for completion of the routine was the final step. I printed up multiple copies of his morning list on the computer. He kept them next to his alarm clock in his bedroom. When he finished the list, he stuffed that copy of it in an old mayonnaise jar on the kitchen counter. Every Sunday night, we added up what he had earned and that became part of his allowance. Although some children need the more immediate feedback of allowance money paid daily, for Theodore, watching the lists accumulate in the jar and getting paid on Sundays was sufficient.

The list—with monetary rewards—proved to be a surprisingly effective tool. The reward was an incentive, not a bribe. As Sharon reminded us, a bribe is payment for doing something wrong or outside the law. In this case, the incentive got him to do what *we* wanted, which was something he had trouble doing on his own. For the most part, we stopped nagging and yelling, and he assumed responsibility (mostly) for getting himself out the door in the morning. As the months went by, we continued tinkering with the list until it looked like this:

THEODORE'S MORNING LIST

1. Make bed.

2. Get dressed, with socks.

   10 cents if done by 8:00 A.M.

3. Eat breakfast.

4. Clean up breakfast dishes.

5. Brush teeth for 3 minutes (orthodontist's orders).

6. Comb hair.

   10 cents if done by 8:20 A.M.

7. Put on shoes, jacket, backpack and out the door by 8:25 A.M.

Theodore: At first, I felt like I ought to be able to do mornings without all this stuff. When I started using lists, I felt like a baby that I needed all these reminders. The reward at first made me feel even more like a baby because I needed something to encourage me. Now I understand that the lists are there to help me. They really do make my mornings go much better. The incentive gives me something to work for. It keeps me focused instead of being distracted. Now I get money instead of yelling.

Sharon: For more distractible, oppositional, or younger children, it's often advisable to prioritize the list even further by giving larger incentives for the more important items (getting up and dressed) and smaller rewards for lower-priority items (making bed, cleaning dishes). Make some things optional. Require your child to do everything on the basic list first and allow him to earn bonuses for completing optional items.

When you establish reasonable and achievable routines, you are adapting household procedures, not creating a new set of rules to fix a broken child. It sends a completely different message to everyone in the family when you establish a new policy than when you set out to change a child. Besides, it is far easier to parent all children the same way than develop a different strategy for each child in each situation. In Jan and Jamie's case, it meant developing a morning list for Caroline as well as one for Theodore. Changing a policy, however, does not necessarily guarantee it will be welcomed by all—and it wasn't by Caroline.

Caroline: I unconsciously do the things required on the morning list, so I don't really understand why I have to do something for a reason that doesn't affect me.

Jan: Since we began to restructure our routines, there has been a sea change in mornings, both for Theodore and for us. He has the routine down pat. No longer are mornings the opening salvo of a battle that does not end until he is asleep at night. Not only has the yelling stopped, Theodore has assumed the responsibility for getting himself out the door in the morning. Not every day is perfect. It certainly isn't for me either. But now that we have stopped taking responsibility for his behavior and no longer harass him every five to ten minutes, he's in control. He decides whether he wants the reward badly enough to get things done expeditiously. For the most part, he does. Without the nagging, he is cheerful and enjoyable to be around.

Other Tools to Help Establish Routines

Sharon: Jan and Jamie made excellent use of a morning list—a visual cue for their expectations for Theodore every school day. Visual cues are essential to establishing routines, teaching the use of

---

SUMMARY OF PROCESS FOR ESTABLISHING ROUTINES

- Include the child in discussions whenever possible.

- Identify situations that occur on a frequent basis.

- *What do I want him to do instead of what he's doing?*

  - Determine one to five things (depending on child's age) that need to be accomplished as part of that routine.
  - Discuss and decide on the number of reminders needed.
  - Determine time frame for completing steps.

- *How can I put expectations and progress in a visual format?*

  - Develop documentation (chart, checklist).

- *What would make it worth his while?*

  - Decide on reinforcer for successful completion of routine within specified time.
  - Review steps of routine, tools (checklists, timers), and rewards with child.

certain tools, and, thus, building independence. They are mechanisms to remind a child or adolescent of what is expected *so you don't have to*. They convey a guideline, a time limit, a system of organization, a sequence, or a behavioral expectation—*so you don't have to*. Visual cues can take the form of a checklist, as was used with Theodore. They can also include calendars or timers.

CALENDARS

Another useful trick for establishing children's routines is to use calendars. They provide visual documentation of daily activities and can be used to resolve conflicts between child and adult expectations. Almost every household has a calendar; many even have a family calendar. But it's rarely used by anyone other than the parent.

Calendars can supplement daily checklists. Once the child masters the list, your expectations can increase to cover day-to-day changes (the band instrument on Tuesdays, for instance). Use supplemental visual cues. One way is to color code items according to the day your child needs them. With masking tape and Magic Markers, tag each item with a small square of tape colored with a marker. Use the same marker and highlight the appropriate day on a calendar—blue for Monday, red for Tuesday, and so on. The child checks the calendar (posted close to the door) and takes the items coded for that day. (To make this system work—at least initially— keep all coded items by the door with the calendar close by.) This system not only increases a child's ability to act independently, it also acquaints him with a meaningful use for a calendar.

Once your child has developed proficiency with a daily checklist, you can combine the calendar and list in one format. The calendar can include a list of things needed daily as well as color-coded items. This reminds the child of what he's responsible for on a daily basis—homework, assignment notebook, lunch or lunch money—without relying on parental support. Parents need to update the calendar list and, at least initially, double-check and reinforce compliance. But once he gets it right, you don't have to keep reminding him.

Also use calendars to schedule all family members' commitments in one place. When a child comes home and asks, "Will you take me to get poster board for my project?" (which, by the way, was assigned three weeks ago and is due tomorrow) and you have to take his brother to a piano lesson, the calendar can convey the bad news—so you don't have to. Your reply is "I don't know. Check the calendar to see if I have to be someplace else." So, too, when Maria comes home and asks if Anna can spend the night tonight (something you are the last to know since she and Anna have made all the plans), let the calendar convey the decision. If your household policy is, "*Ask two days in advance; if the answer is yes, it goes on the calendar. If it's not on the calendar it doesn't happen,*" the calendar communicates the response. One last example: Your younger child asks to go to the park on Saturday. You say, "We'll see," which by Saturday morning becomes interpreted as "*You promised!*" If the family policy is, "*If agreed to, it goes on the calendar. If it's not on the calendar . . .*" To make this system work you need to wean yourself from that parental cop-out "We'll see," which usually means "probably not" to you and "yes" to your child. If it's "no," say so; if you're not sure, set a definite time by which you will tell your child one way or the other.

Quick Tip

Use calendars to document family activities and privileges. If it's not on the calendar, it doesn't happen.

Calendars are also great for recording interim objectives and deadlines for long-term projects. Many children, especially those with ADHD and some learning disabilities, have difficulty breaking down large tasks into their component parts. Calendars provide a visual format for taking those parts, once established, and, working back from the final due date, determining short-term objectives and deadlines for each step. Children need this skill as they get older and the assignments' complexity increases. By middle school, teachers assume children have the ability to organize, work, and complete tasks independently. Therefore, introduce these tools as early as possible.

TIMERS

Timers provide visual and auditory cues to document time. Time has no meaning for young children and most kids with ADHD. To them, it is something controlled by adults. "It's time for bed." "Who says?" Or, "Let's get going, we're in a hurry." "Who's in a hurry? I'm not in a hurry." To them there is always more than enough time to do things they don't like to do and not enough time to do things they enjoy. When you stop a fun activity, they want to shoot the messenger.

The timer says "time is up" so you don't have to say it. Before your child turns on the television, sits down at the computer, or starts talking on the telephone, set a timer to determine when time for that activity has expired. Have the child set the timer, or at least get him to acknowledge what happens when the timer rings. When it rings, and he appeals or complains, your response can be: "I'd like you to have more time, but the timer rang." You can be on his side and still make clear that time is not something you control.

Quick Tip

Use a kitchen timer to determine when "time's up" for your child's activity. The timer enforces the rule—not Mom or Dad.

It is essential that you reinforce the timer's decision (even if your child strenuously objects). As long as you adhere to the policy that something happens *every time the timer rings* (and "that something" does *not* include resetting it) the timer will become the enforcer.

Pointer for Effective Parenting

Something happens every time the timer rings but
that does not include you or your child resetting it.

Timers are even more effective when paired with incentives.
Reinforce compliance with the timer and/or completing the task
before the timer rings. An incentive gives the timer special sig-
nificance, giving him a reason to respond. Simply keeping a tally
of times when your child complies with or beats the timer gives
it greater importance. Each success can earn a timer credit that
your child can accumulate and cash in for privileges. Set a minimum for each day. A half hour of television requires six timer
credits; ten credits keeps the light on twenty minutes later at
bedtime.

Quick Tip

Provide an incentive for your child to respond to the
timer. He can earn it by ending an activity when the
timer goes off or by completing a task *before* it rings.

Theodore: What has really worked for me is the sports watch I got for
Christmas. It has a stopwatch, timer, and alarm as well as a clock. Not only
does the watch tell me what time it is, I can use it to time myself on a lot of
things, like "screen time" I can earn to watch TV or play on the computer or
Game Boy. I also use it to time my Saturday morning cleanup.

I use my watch timer to remind me when it's time to take my medication
at school. Because my parents want me to be responsible for taking my
medication at home, when I remember, I set my alarm to remind me to take
my late afternoon medication.

For a while, to encourage me to wear the watch, I could earn ten cents
a day if I wore it and checked it off on my evening list. This was an easy ten
cents a day. My parents no longer have to use an incentive like money to

get me to wear it. I've learned how useful my watch is and I never forget to wear it.

Quick Tip

A watch with one or more alarms enables a child to take on more responsibility for managing his own time and obligations.

Sharon: The timer can also be a tool that protects the child's interests in his struggle against you, the timekeeper. In the past, when he wanted your attention, often his request was met with that maddening response: "In a minute." But how long was that minute? No wonder your child reacts so negatively to hearing that now. As far as he knows, it's that dreaded adult minute and you'll never show up. A timer can hold us to the same standard we impose on our children. When you respond to their request for time and attention with the suggestion to "get the timer and I'll set it for fifteen minutes. When the bell rings, I'll stop what I'm doing and come into your room," a child can accept this answer. If you adhere to the timer whenever it is used, your child can trust it to get you to stop, as promised.

ADDITIONAL VISUAL CUES

In many households, "trespassing" is the basis for a lot of arguments. Siblings invade each other's space and take things without first asking permission. What belongs to you, the parents, belongs to everyone. These infractions don't include the times when children get into things that are potentially dangerous. This is another opportunity to use visual cues. Colored dots (available at office supply stores) are perfect for color coding items to show ownership. Use red and green dots to mark areas or rooms that are either okay to enter (green) or are off limits (red). Put red dots on cabinets that hold "you need permission" or "these aren't yours" items. Label free-access cabinets and closets with green dots.

Quick Tip

Use red and green colored dots (available at office supply stores) to mark areas or rooms that are either okay to enter (green) or are off limits (red). This is especially useful for young children.

Labeled or color-coded milk crates can be the basis for organizing and marking ownership of possessions. A milk crate or carton in the front closet is the perfect place for shoes. Use a set of crates to hold different items—shoes in red, hats in blue, gloves in green. Their presence reminds everyone of the proper place to drop their things. (If all shoes are left there when family members come home, the box limits the scope of that last-minute, mad search for missing shoes.) Alternatively, colored crates can distinguish who owns what —Tommy's things in blue, Joe's in green.

Quick Tip

Use different colored milk crates in the front closet to organize or mark ownership of personal possessions.

Quick Tip

Using a milk crate, carton, or box in the front closet or by the front door to store all shoes eliminates that last-minute, frantic search for missing shoes.

Letter boxes on the homework desk labeled "finished" and "questions for later" act as visual cues that improve both organization and materials management. Completed work goes directly in the "finished" box rather than being shuffled (and lost forever) among other papers for later placement in a homework file or a student's notebook. The "questions" box allows a student to move on to something else rather than get up to seek help or sit and do nothing until assistance is offered. A child who needs a great deal of adult support will rarely get back on task once he's up and wandering the house.

Quick Tip

Use letter boxes labeled "finished" and "questions for later" for your child's homework. Completed work can be transferred later into the child's notebook or file folder for transport to school.

Of course, these visual prompts are only as successful as your support for their use. If you don't reinforce your child's use of the tools, it probably won't happen.

Evening Routines

Jan: Fourth grade triggered our next big effort to set up a routine. We had spent much of the summer traveling and Theodore had been away at camp. As a result, we had not gotten around to devising a new structure for getting him to bed. For one thing, he simply wasn't sleepy when bedtime rolled around at 9:30 P.M. Getting him to stop playing and focus on going to bed became a major battle once school began. He wasn't ready and dragged it out unmercifully until we had to scream, yell, holler, shout, and shriek to hound him off to bed. Worse yet, he wouldn't stay there. Up, down, drink of water, bathroom stop, and always "just one more question" he had to ask, or something that had to be done, answered, solved, or fixed. One of his most common ploys was "I'm hungry." I was frantic by this point because I needed quiet time in the evenings. I counted on the kids being in bed—maybe not asleep, but at least in bed behind closed doors and not bothering me after 9:30. No such luck.

Sharon: Parents expect their children to learn something in one context and then repeat that same behavior in a different setting. This process, called generalization, is very difficult for many challenging children, especially those with ADHD. Most parents don't use what has proved successful in one instance in a different situation. When Billy still won't go to bed without a struggle even though his mornings now go pretty smoothly, do his parents use the same techniques that led to that improvement? No, their response is to punish him. They expect him to put himself to bed as well as he gets himself up.

The solution is to create another routine following the same steps you did to get Billy out of the house in the morning. By paring down expectations to what is truly essential, putting them into a routine, documenting what you expect with a visual cue, and reinforcing adherence to the routine, your evenings will go more smoothly.

Remember, talk up success. Always pair social feedback (praise, verbal support, hugs) with primary feedback (privileges, etc.). The challenging child in particular has heard enough complaints about his behavior. The more challenged you are by your child, the less likely it is that you're able to be positive. And all children benefit from praise.

Reminding Jan and Jamie of the steps they took to establish a morning routine was all it took to do the same for bedtime. There were some extra difficulties because Theodore didn't fall asleep easily, but the process remained the same.

Jan: We got the picture. First, we had to more clearly define the problem. What was *really* bugging us? The yelling and screaming necessary to get Theodore into bed especially irked Jamie. For me, it was that Theodore wouldn't stay in bed. It also irritated me that it took so long to pick up the clutter around the house. Developing an evening list for Theodore to follow solved Jamie's problem. We solved my problem by turning our current "Five-Minute Pickup" into a broader concept called "Sweep," which is described in chapter 7. After much tinkering, we developed an evening list. If Theodore ate his dinner without fuss, he got the first half of his dessert. He could earn the second half by completing the following list:

THEODORE'S EVENING LIST

1. Sweep (solution to the clutter problem; see chapter 7)

2. Backpack/coat/shoes ready by front door

3. Get in pajamas

4. Make lunch for next day

If shower night:

- Pick up bathroom
- Comb hair
- Hang up towel

5. Dirty clothes in hamper

6. Socks in sock bag

Reward: second half of dessert if list turned in by 9:10 P.M.

Jan: The list solved many of our problems. It got everything done in time for a 9:30 bedtime. We subsequently added a set time for brushing his teeth and allowed him to take a snack box (generally a few pretzels or crackers with peanut butter) into his bedroom to eliminate "I'm hungry" delay tactics. Recognizing that Theodore needs less sleep than most children, we moved his "lights off" time to later, with the snack box removed and teeth brushed fifteen minutes before "lights off." However, he does need quiet time—

just as we do—so we kept 9:30 as the deadline for being in his room, door closed, and reading—not playing with toys.

Sharon: Jan and Jamie questioned whether it was right to use food—particularly sweets, like dessert—as an incentive. I think it's fine to do so since children learn that they can only have them when they have done the desired behavior. Most parents find that when the sweet is made contingent, it reduces the begging and arguing about if and when the child can have it.

Building Structure and Predictability through Routines

All children need structure in their lives. Some can develop it for themselves, but most—especially challenging ones—need adults to provide that structure for them. Similarly, most kids prefer predictability. They like to know roughly how the day will go, what will happen if they misbehave, and that there will be no school on holidays. For some children, however, predictability isn't merely desirable or preferable—it's essential.

Theodore: I like to know what's going to happen because then I can prepare myself. I need to know ahead of time exactly what's going to happen and for how long. Otherwise, I get upset if things don't go the way I expect them to. For example, when we're down at the beach, we used to have a lot of arguments because I got fidgety not knowing how we were going to spend the day. I'd think to myself that I'd be able to play Game Boy for much of the day, but I'd get mad when my parents would make me go for a walk on the beach. I'd get upset because I hadn't expected to do that. I had too much free time down there. Sometimes, partway through the week, I'd want to go home. Once we began drawing up a daily schedule for me, I did much better because I knew what to expect. If I knew I was going to take a walk on the beach because it was on my schedule, that was OK.

Sharon: Kids like Theodore, and that includes almost all challenging children, whether they have ADHD or not, need to know what to expect ahead of time. This information helps make their life predictable, giving them a sense that they can navigate their world successfully. Otherwise, they feel out of control or overwhelmed by the moment. When they feel out of control, they may act that way. They need structure and predictability. Without this, it is difficult for them to make lasting changes in their behavior.

Providing structure and establishing routines is easier than you think. Although children have difficulty doing so on their own, you can help them if you remember to ask the following:

- *What do I want him to do instead of what he's doing?*

- *What are the behaviors and/or steps that are most necessary to the situation?*

- *How can I put that in a visual format so he doesn't have to rely on me telling him what to do?*

- *What would make it worth his while?*

5

"That's It! I've Had It!!!"

How to Get Your Child to Do
What You Want Him to Do

Theodore: I really tried to do what I should be doing, but I could just never manage to get it all right. It seemed like I was always doing things wrong. My parents were always punishing me. I never knew what the rules were—what I could or couldn't do—because we hadn't written them down. It seemed like I was supposed to learn from experience. It was like a dog that jumps up on the couch and you yell at it to get down. Eventually it learns not to get up on the couch. That's how it felt to me. I figured out I'd broken a rule whenever my parents were yelling at me about what I just did.

Jan: It was now obvious that the things we had done for years weren't going to work for Theodore. We'd alleviated a lot of problems by structuring new routines for getting out of the house in the morning and for going to bed, but that was only the beginning. Establishing routines had drastically reduced the decibel level in our house, but we had a long way to go before our chaotic household could be termed a calm one.

Next we had to tackle those things we lumped under the term "bad behavior," such as watching TV without permission or throwing a temper tantrum when an errand had to be done after we picked him up at school, and get Theodore to do what we required. I felt like a broken record. We constantly reviewed what was wrong and extracted promises from Theodore (usually unfulfilled) that it would never happen again. The process was unproductive and incredibly frustrating.

As our frustration increased, I instinctively felt something else was going on. Theodore was not a bad child. He was not even a badly behaved child. He never hit anyone or threw things, nor was he aggressive toward other children. A gentle and endearing child, teachers always loved him, even as they despaired of his interruptions and constant talking. He wanted our approval—and that of teachers and other adults—and he wanted to do what he was supposed to do. Increasingly I began to feel that the problem wasn't disobedience. I realized it wasn't that he *refused* or that he was *unwilling* to do what he was told, but that for some reason, he *couldn't*. If that were the case, all the punishment in the world wasn't going to change his behavior. On some days it seemed as if punishment was his whole world. That made me sad.

Sharon: The vast majority of children, whatever the challenge they present, would rather be right than wrong. They would rather get it right, or do it right, and please the parent (when they're younger) or skip the hassle (when they're older). Therefore, if they knew the right thing to do and it came easily to them, they'd do it. They're not doing the wrong thing to get back at us and they're not doing it to drive us nuts. Since whatever we're asking of them is hard and takes effort, too often something else happens instead.

Don't take your child's behavior personally. Don't attribute negative motives to your child's actions. When you do, you react (or rather overreact) rather than respond to his behavior.

Pointer for Effective Parenting

Don't take behavior personally. Don't attribute negative motives to your child's behavior.

Think Ahead: Clarifying Expectations in Advance

My goal is that parents learn *planned* parenting and engage in *responsive* rather than reactive parenting. Planned parenting entails discussion of priorities, specific behaviors, approaches, and responses in advance of situations. Unfortunately, such discussions most often occur after the child has misbehaved. Parents argue, blame, agonize, and commiserate in reaction to a difficult situation. That process rarely, however, results in clear thinking, meaningful change in parenting, or advance planning for the next time.

To begin with, let your child know exactly what your expectations are for his behavior before there is a problem. More often, it's likely, you tell your child what the rules are right after he breaks them. This leads to a lot of frustration for both parent and child. To help you understand how unfair this feels to a child, consider the concept of a "mystery speed limit" day.

Imagine that every Thursday is mystery speed limit day. You get in your car and, although you are in a hurry and the usual speed limit is fifty-five, just to be safe, you drive at forty-five miles per hour. Within two miles a policeman pulls you over, explains that today's speed limit is thirty-five, and writes you a ticket. How do you feel? Welcome to your child's world. He often thinks that he knows the rules, but they seem to keep changing. Every time he turns around, there's some new thing he's done wrong. There's some new rule he's violated. And, furthermore, you tell him that he "should have known better."

Theodore: This is the one thing that I hate the most. My parents change the rules all the time. Well, they don't change them, they make new rules, then and there on the spot. For example, if I'm staying up late doing homework, my dad might say, "You've got ten minutes to finish your homework, make your lunch, brush your teeth, and get in bed, or you lose fifty cents." My usual reaction to this kind of rule making is "What? That isn't a rule! Since when is that a rule?" And they answer, "Since just now." Even though I've had multiple discussions asking them to stop doing this, they stop for a month or two, and then they go right back to doing it. Usually, they do it when they're really frustrated with something I'm doing—like homework.

Rules, Praise, Ignore: A Philosophy for Effective Parenting

Sharon: You can be a more effective parent if you:

- Establish guidelines and expectations in advance of the situation.

- Praise your child when he is following the rules rather than just punishing him when he doesn't.

- Ignore (disengage from) negative behavior that is often just venting or moaning.

RULES: CLEAR GUIDELINES ARE CRITICAL

One of the most fundamental keys to success in getting kids to stop and do what you want is to set clear guidelines that establish easy-to-understand, easy-to-follow procedures. Clear guidelines, like TV is allowed only after all homework is completed, eliminate arguments and allow children to understand your expectations.

Do's Are Better than Don'ts

Children need rules. They need guidelines and expectations established in advance of the situation, not in reaction to problems. Most households have rules, some of which are stated (over and over again), some of which are implied. Usually these guidelines spell out an almost endless list of don'ts. And this list gets longer as disagreements and meltdowns occur. Invariably, parents stress what they *don't* want a child to do. When asked what the rules are, most kids recite an incredibly long list of don'ts.

Usually, the rules a child starts with are those most recently introduced or reintroduced. One preteen told me the rules in his home were: "Don't run in the house, don't leave your clothes on the floor, and don't use the lamps for bowling." This was a first for me. I've interviewed a lot of kids and gotten many different responses to this question, but I'd never heard this one before (or since). It was obvious that someone had set up makeshift bowling in the last twenty-four hours. And the parents had reacted with a new household rule. If this was now one of the top three rules, what previous guideline had it replaced? As important as the lamp-bowling rule may have seemed at the moment, I'm sure the parents did not consider it one of *the* life lessons they want uppermost in their children's minds.

This underscores two important parenting points. First, whatever is most recently discussed at high volume will, temporarily, rise to the top of the list of rules, undoubtedly displacing something else. Second, your child's repertoire of behaviors is one item longer than your list of don'ts. He will, inevitably, come up with the one thing you did not think to prohibit.

Guidelines (a term I prefer to the word *rules,* because it goes over better with adolescents) need to be stated in positive terms. They need to specify what you *want* a child to do instead of what you don't want him to do. The guideline to "keep hands and feet to yourself" also covers hitting, pushing, shoving, grabbing, pinching, or throwing things. I know some families who have expanded this to include "hands and feet and teeth" and a few that use "hands and feet and spit."

Quick Tip

Frame household rules in positive terms. Doing so conveys what your expectations are—not just what your child isn't supposed to do.

Parents should include children in the process of developing and discussing guidelines because they will more likely remember a rule they helped develop. Moreover, a discussion with your children is a great way to find out what, after all these years, they really think are the important rules to remember.

Pointer for Effective Parenting

When you make the child part of the solution, he feels less like the cause of the problem.

Prioritize What's Important

Household guidelines should be so limited in number that, when asked to list them, *both* parents can accurately do so. Most of the time, I find that parents can't remember their own list of rules without giving it serious thought. You don't want to be like the family I worked with where Mom said she didn't think there were any household guidelines and Dad had a typed list of forty-two rules. Such a disparity in expectations inevitably leads to a huge gap in enforcement. Furthermore, no one can remember forty-two rules—not even that father. If you can't recall every rule, how is your child supposed to remember, much less abide by all of them? Keep in mind, these rules are far less important to your child than they are to you.

Parents must agree on household guidelines. You need to discuss what is important to focus on right now and what can wait. There are always things that need improving. But you can't work on everything at once. If you prioritize, making safety supreme, and limit guidelines to what is essential to family functioning, you can pare your expectations down to an achievable number.

In Jan and Jamie's case I did not need to convince them of the necessity for guidelines. Theirs was a problem of number and timing. They had lots of rules, many of which were developed in response to a situation that assumed equal importance to every other rule they had. Moreover, their rules kept changing. It was impossible for Theodore and Caroline to determine what was most important to their parents.

Having Too Many Guidelines Is a Problem

Jan: Coming up with rules was never a problem for us. Both Jamie and I believe in rules and we had plenty of them. We were so skilled at developing rules that, despite Sharon's previous experience, ours did not always start with "don't." We had a rule for everything, starting with simple manners, such as requiring "please" and "thank you" and progressing to such things as "no TV before homework is done" and "no dessert without finishing your dinner." Some rules were explicit; others were implicit. Our family had rules galore. Here are just a few:

1. Wet towels must be hung up.

2. Bagel crumbs must be wiped up in the microwave.

3. Dishwasher must be emptied before leaving for school.

4. Retainers must be stored in case.

5. Teeth must be brushed morning and night.

6. Toilet must be flushed every time.

7. Cap must be replaced on toothpaste.

8. Caroline has a half hour only to get ready for choir performance and must eat something (healthy) before she goes.

9. Turn off light if you leave the room for more than a few minutes.

10. No borrowing money from Mom or Dad.

11. No bad language or you have to put ten cents fine in the jar.

12. No leaving dishes in the sink or on counter.

13. No snacks except what is in designated snack box on kitchen counter filled by Mom or Dad.

14. No bugging Mom or Dad when they're on the phone.

15. No TV unless all homework is completed.

You get the picture. These were only a few of our many rules. We were constantly creating new ones to handle things that came up. That was both good and bad. We were trying to lay out our expectations in order to prevent explosions, conflict, and tantrums. But we also had trouble remembering all the rules and enforcing them consistently.

Caroline: I think we have way too many rules in our house. It's aggravating.

One Standard for All
Sharon: One pared-down set of guidelines, consistently reinforced, makes parenting easier on everyone. The existence of family policies or rules eliminates the need for different standards for each child. If the guideline is important, you want all of your children to abide by it. Having only one set reduces the chance that a more challenging child feels that all the rules are a reactive attempt to fix *him,* the broken child. By the same token, one set of household guidelines holds all children equally accountable for their behavior. Having one standard means all children know what is expected. That provides the structure and predictability that all kids—challenging ones, in particular—need.

PRINCIPLES FOR EFFECTIVE GUIDELINES

- All children need (and want) boundaries and limits.

- Guidelines exist in all families, though they may not be spoken or written.

- Try whenever possible to state rules in positive terms.

- Keep rules short and to the point.

- Have the fewest number of rules possible.

- Be consistent in using and enforcing the rules.

- Call attention to rules when the child is following them. Don't wait until he has violated them.

PRAISE: A POWERFUL TOOL FOR CHANGE

Praise is critically important in helping your child alter his behavior. Just as we need others to notice when we do something well, kids need that same feedback, especially when building new patterns of behavior. Be descriptive when giving a child praise. "I'm so pleased that you didn't interrupt when I was on the telephone." "You came the first time I called." "I think it's wonderful that you put your bike in the garage without a reminder."

Praise keeps a child on track and, when specific, clarifies what behaviors you want to see again. You can often see your child's face light up when you praise him for a job well done. Watch the light bulb go off in his head when you describe how much you appreciate his holding his temper in check.

Praise for good behavior goes a long way toward improving the whole family dynamic and helps build your child's self-esteem. This is particularly important for challenging children who are all-too-accustomed to hearing about what they are always doing wrong.

Finally, never forget that your attention is something your child needs. Be sure to use it in the right way and at the right time. Stay away from backhand compliments such as "I knew you could do it. It's a wonder that you never did it before." When you notice that Jack has brushed his teeth without your reminding him, don't miss the opportunity to tell him how you feel about it as soon as he comes out of the bathroom. Praise is most effective when you give it immediately.

Pointer for Effective Parenting

If you want to see the behavior again, pay attention to it.

Theodore: I felt good when my dad said he was proud I was getting myself up every morning and taking a shower with nobody telling me to do it. He said he was glad he could trust me to get up, that he didn't have to go back to my room every five minutes, worrying about whether I was doing what I was supposed to be doing. It made me feel good that he noticed I'd been doing something right.

PRINCIPLES OF EFFECTIVE PRAISE

- Praise keeps a child on track and on task.

- Praise helps to build positive self-concept.

- Provide extra praise for those behaviors that you want to build or increase.

- Your attention is something that a child needs. Use it in the right way at the right time.

- Be descriptive when giving a child praise. Say exactly what behavior you are praising.

- CATCH YOUR CHILD BEING GOOD!

IGNORE—OR DISENGAGE FROM—BAD BEHAVIOR

Sharon: It is harder than it sounds to ignore bad behavior. Many parents tell their children to "just ignore" annoying behaviors from other kids, but if your child even mutters under his breath, you overreact. It's easier if you think of it as "disengaging" from rather than ignoring the whining, moaning, foot stomping, or slammed doors. "Disengaging" sounds so much more clinical than ignoring. "Disengaging" will make you feel as if you are doing something. "Ignoring" probably feels like you're failing to do something. Effective disengagement, however, means no feedback. Don't talk, don't touch, and don't look—if necessary, walk away. If your child erupts or starts to argue, don't take the bait. Disengage.

Jan: When Sharon first explained what she meant by "ignore," I mentally redefined it as simply prioritizing which behavior to focus on. Since we were overloaded on rules, we had a lot to choose from. Gradually, it became clear to me that she wasn't just talking about setting priorities, she also meant that if we were going to ignore bad behavior, then we really had to *ignore it*. That was not easy for me to do. Ignoring meant I was supposed to give no physical, eye, or verbal contact. With difficulty, I can do that if the behavior's taking place in front of me but I find it hard to ignore (as in not notice) other admittedly inconsequential behaviors that really irritate me. Though I keep my mouth shut and turn off the light or flush the toilet, they still bother me.

Sharon: You can't ignore dangerous behavior. But pick your battles. Don't sweat the small stuff. As Jan points out, you may have more difficulty keeping the behaviors from bothering you—just don't let your kids know it.

GUIDELINES FOR EFFECTIVE IGNORING

Truly ignoring means:

- **No verbal contact**
- **No physical contact**
- **No eye contact**

- If you cannot ignore/disengage—leave the room.

- When you ignore, be consistent. Ignore the behavior every time it occurs.

- Heavily praise the opposite, positive behavior. Let your child know when he gets it right.

- When you first ignore a behavior, be prepared for it to happen more often (in an attempt to get your attention).

Jan: My ability to disengage depends almost entirely on my mood. If I am stressed out or frustrated, I'm unlikely to ignore anything. In fact, that is when I'm most likely to find fault with my kids' behavior. If I'm in a good mood, I'm far better able to just shrug off the little stuff. I have learned to disengage much of the time when Theodore mutters under his breath. As much as it irks me, as long as he's on the trail to following through on a request, I can let it go.

Theodore: I don't really know if my parents ignore stuff. Whenever they're in a bad mood, then everything I do is wrong. For instance, usually they won't notice if I have my shoes on in the house but if they're in a bad mood, they'll scream, "Take those shoes off!" Even worse, too often the bad mood of one of them will rub off on the other and then they notice *everything*.

Sharon: Be prepared for your child's behavior to get worse when you first start to ignore it. After all, she's learned from previous experience that if she cries or he stomps around the house or mutters under his breath, you will react. Now all of a sudden you don't. Your child concludes: "Maybe Mom didn't hear me. Maybe Dad just didn't see how upset I am. I'll have to do it louder to make sure they hear." So, be prepared. Instead, "catch your child being good" and praise him accordingly. This goes a long way to reinforce the behavior you want to encourage. Finally, when you ignore a specific behavior, do so consistently.

Behavior Change in Your Child
Starts with You

Jan: These principles made sense. They sounded logical, reasonable, and not too difficult to implement. We were already great on rules—in fact, we had a zillion of them. Clearly, this was one of our problems. We praised our kids for their successes, though we had a tendency to take their routine good behavior for granted. In fact, we were lousy at "catching our child being good," spending far more time yelling at them for what they did wrong. We were also bad at ignoring things. Since I have eyes in the back of my head, I seldom missed any of my kids' misdeeds. Since I have a mouth in the front of my head, I was constantly yelling.

All signs pointed to a need to change *our* behavior. That was not going to be easy. I was too addicted to yelling. I never had to control *my* behavior. I could just fly off the handle and feel justified in doing so. After all, Theodore had broken some rule. I was entitled to yell. Now I realized, change in Theodore started with change in me.

Incentives

WHAT MAKES IT WORTHWHILE TO CHANGE?

Sharon: Behavior change is a process of teaching skills that a child does not have. It is designed to increase the frequency with which a child uses one behavior instead of another. By reinforcing or rewarding a specific behavior in a way that is meaningful to your child, you enhance the likelihood that he will do it again.

Many things, including praise, stars on a chart, or privileges, can be meaningful rewards (see Sample Reinforcers for Use at Home, p. 106). An incentive needs to be powerful enough that your child will persist in trying a behavior that is otherwise very difficult for him to do on a consistent basis. What would make it worth his while to remember and do what is expected? What reward, praise, or privilege can you make contingent on whether your child does a specific behavior?

Pointer for Effective Parenting

Always ask yourself: "What do I want him to do and what will make it worth his while to do it?"

You can't require that he be good (that's too general) or that he does the desired behavior every time all day (that's expecting too much). Instead, you have to find a reinforcer that he can earn for doing one specific behavior more often than he does it now.

This is not bribery. Your goal is to induce your child to get it right. Remember, the vast majority of challenging children don't want to misbehave. They would love to be like others who seemingly breeze through life, effortlessly meeting adult standards of conduct. They are handling their world the best way they know how, or at least the best way they know how at the moment. What you're asking of them either does not occur to them or does not come easily to them. If it did, they'd be doing it.

By clearly defining the behavior you want and providing your child with an incentive to do it, you substantially increase the likelihood that the behavior will occur and reoccur. A reward makes your child want to practice a desired behavior, hopefully until he becomes somewhat proficient at it. Sometimes proficiency comes when he can make it part of a daily routine. For more occasional behaviors, practice—aided by an incentive—still remains the key.

Theodore: I hate cleaning up my room on Saturday mornings, but if I know I can earn chips for "screen time" to play my Game Boy, watch TV, or play games on the computer, I really try to do it faster and more efficiently. I get less distracted because I know I only have a certain amount of time to finish cleaning my room if I'm going to earn screen time. I'm less likely to pick up a book or read it for as long if I've got something to work for.

Sharon: Finding effective rewards isn't easy. Here are some you might try.

SAMPLE REINFORCERS FOR USE AT HOME

YOUNGER CHILDREN

Television (specified period)	Playing at special park
Computer games (specified period)	Video arcade
Video games (specified period)	Pizza (ordered in)
Video/video game rental	Chore pass (excused from a chore)
Playing outside	Allowance — or money

SAMPLE REINFORCERS FOR USE AT HOME

YOUNGER CHILDREN (CONT.)

7-Eleven (Slurpee)	Fast food
Watching TV in parents' room	Small toy/privilege grab bag
Special dessert	Extension on lights out (15–30 minutes)
Spending night at friend's house	Having a friend over for dinner
Dressing up in adult's clothes	Camping out in the backyard
Going somewhere alone with a parent	Planting a garden
Having a friend overnight	Control of car radio

ADOLESCENTS—ANY OF THE ABOVE, PLUS:

Phone jack in room	Curfew extension
Phone in room (1 hour per night)	Learner's permit/driver's license
Time to talk on phone	Use of car (specified purpose/time)
Screen time (privilege to use any screen —TV, video, video game, computer)	Use of Internet (e-mail and instant messaging)
Control of car radio	New CD or tape

You may have to change the reinforcer; you may have to find creative ways to measure and document progress. And, for more challenging children, you will certainly have to stay with the process, clarifying expectations, switching reinforcers, and giving lots of positive feedback.

You have undoubtedly noticed that children are very good at accomplishing things of high interest. But when asked to do something that doesn't interest them or is difficult, they can't or won't. You need to connect a high-interest activity—something he likes to do (or tries to get away with every time you turn your back)—to a low-interest activity. Make something he *likes* doing contingent on completing something you want him to do. Not only is the one behavior likely to improve, there will be fewer arguments over when and for how long your child can engage in the high-interest activity (playing a computer game, watching TV, or talking on the telephone). Access to the activity is not up for negotiation. He has to earn it.

Earning the activity gives him a sense of accomplishment—that he *can do it*. His prior experience is that no matter how hard he tries to get it right, he just cannot meet your expectations. He's always doing *something* wrong. Either he's done the wrong thing, or if he has, for once, done the right thing, he hasn't done it well enough.

To change your child's behavior you first have to alter your approach. It takes three steps:

- Clarify *in advance* in specific terms what you expect.

- Make a vow that you will notice when your child performs the behavior you desire.

- Provide an incentive to make it worth your child's while to perform that behavior correctly.

Don't be afraid of the term "behavior program." It's no more than a commitment to notice, as often as possible, when your child does a specific behavior correctly. Your child has a long history of people noticing when he does something incorrectly and being punished accordingly. Offering him an incentive, then being positive and noticing when he's done something right, takes a lot less energy than being punitive. And it feels a lot better—for both you and your child.

This positive approach to parenting puts responsibility back in your child's hands. To date, his experience is that you are in charge of whether he gets to do things. What time he goes to bed, how late he can keep the light on at night, and whether he gets a toy, is all up to you. Making such matters part of a behavior agreement puts your child back in control of whether he has access to them. If he performs the behavior (whether it is flushing the toilet, not hitting his sister for the next thirty minutes, or walking the dog), the privilege is his. If he doesn't, he doesn't earn the privilege. It's up to him. This approach gives him positive feedback and empowers him in a constructive way at the same time.

Theodore: We have a lot less arguments about when and how long I can be on the computer or play my Game Boy now that I have to earn screen time.

If I cheat, I lose screen time. If I watch TV an extra three minutes and they catch me, then I lose thirty minutes for just a measly three. So it usually isn't worth it to me to cheat. Sometimes, when I have plenty of chips, like three hours' worth, I'm more likely to take the risk of cheating. Screen time means I know exactly how long I can play or watch TV and we just don't argue about it anymore.

INCENTIVES FOR ALL SIBLINGS

Sharon: One of the best things about using a positive approach is that it is equally appropriate for all children in the family. Everyone has some behavior that needs improvement. Using praise and incentives increases the likelihood that a child or adolescent will work at whatever behavior is difficult for him and stay with it until it improves. You can use the same reward for different behaviors and offer different reinforcers for the same behavior. By offering incentives to all siblings to work on a specific behavior, you eliminate the inequity and resentment that could arise if you only did so for your challenging child.

One family I worked with decided that a later Friday night bedtime would be an effective reinforcer for both of their children. Jonathan earned his daily credits for keeping his hands to himself and not getting into fights in school. His sister, Susan, earned hers for a half-hour of violin practice daily. Each had a different behavior to work on to earn the same reward. Both Susan's and Jonathan's goal behaviors improved markedly in response to a program that rewarded their efforts with a later Friday night bedtime.

INCENTIVES IN ACTION: FIGURING OUT WHAT WORKS

Jan: With practice, we became adept at delineating behaviors we wanted to encourage and figuring out incentives to get Theodore to perform. For example, I am compulsive about turning off lights. Nearly every night, I delay dinner by running around turning off lights everyone else has left on. Theodore was the worst offender. It took several tries before we found a solution that worked—or, more accurately, found an incentive that made it worth his while to remember.

First we tried a visual reminder. Since he usually left the lights on in his bedroom, we hung a sign at eye level in his doorway that said: "LIGHTS OFF?" We figured he couldn't get out of the room without seeing it. Wrong. After a couple of days of remembering, the sign became part of the landscape. He no longer saw it, and started leaving the lights on again. Next, we offered ten cents each day he remembered to turn off the lights. That night, we'd record if he had turned off the lights. This was a total flop because ten cents was insufficient incentive for him to remember.

When I realized he needed a more powerful incentive, I told him I'd pay him fifty cents a day if he turned off all the lights. That made it worth his while. (At this steep a price, it's a good thing we didn't need to use the same incentive for Caroline too since she was much better than her brother or father at remembering to turn off lights.) After a few weeks of his consistently remembering because he had built it into his routine (leave room, turn off lights), we switched our focus to unflushed toilets. If his behavior lapses we reinstate the system. A short course of incentives (not always money—sometimes it's earning extra screen time) usually does the trick.

Pointer for Effective Parenting

It takes creative thinking—and consultation with your child—to find an incentive that will make it worth his while to do what you want. Since an incentive can lose value, offer a choice of a few and change them as needed.

Sharon: Incentives for changing a behavior don't need to stay in place permanently. Once your child is doing a desired behavior fairly consistently, you can reduce them by offering a larger incentive for doing the behavior over a longer period of time, such as one dollar for turning off the lights three days in a row. Keep in mind, however, that low-interest and more difficult behaviors that are not part of a standard routine, such as not hitting a sibling, are likely to require incentives in some fashion for a longer period of time, especially for kids with ADHD. Moreover, if the target behavior is part of a routine, the whole routine itself should be reinforced. If parents feel they're held hostage to constantly monitoring the child's behavior and rewards, the solution is to prioritize what's important to work on and set the other things aside for the moment. Remember, don't sweat the small stuff. And don't overwhelm your child by asking him to change too many behaviors at once.

Jan: This approach worked with all sorts of "Theodore" behaviors. Incentives proved to be a more lasting way to get him to change his behavior than any punishment would have been. For example, it drove me nuts when Theodore would forget materials needed for homework. Too many times I had to traipse back to school for a frantic search. Finally, I trained myself to check Theodore's homework assignment book and backpack every day before leaving school to ensure he had what he needed. Why couldn't he remember to do this himself? Because as a child with ADHD, he was distracted, didn't think to check, and had no incentive to make it worth his while. My solution put the responsibility on me instead of on him where it belonged.

Sharon: Jan and Jamie needed to specify what they wanted Theodore to do before he left school. They had to find something he wanted to reward him for bringing home everything necessary. First, Theodore helped Jan and Jamie develop a list to remind him what to check for in his backpack. Then, they decided where to keep the list so it would be readily available. (Attaching it to a Velcro dot just under the backpack's flap keeps it handy.) Finally, they had to determine what would make it worth his while to check the list before departing. (If you don't know, ask your child.) I suggested that Jan and Jamie carry a jar of quarters in their cars and give Theodore a quarter—on the spot—if he had everything he needed in his backpack without reminders from them.

Theodore: Knowing I'd get money each day if I remembered to bring every-thing home from school made me more likely to stop and think about what was in my backpack. The incentive didn't work all the time. Sometimes I just plain forgot about it or assumed I had everything but didn't. Still, I remem-bered more often than not. How often depended on how much I wanted the money.

Jan: When money ceased to be a sufficient motivator, we switched to earning a chip for screen time that he could use to watch TV, play Game Boy, or play computer games.

When we saw how well this worked, we applied it to his writ-ing down all his homework assignments—with due dates. For doing so he could earn a chip toward screen time every day. Not only was Theodore able to rack up much-desired screen-time chips, he was inadvertently learning a skill he critically needed as a distractible child—to think ahead and organize himself and his belongings. Double victory. Now we rarely have to make trips back to school.

THE BACKPACK CHECKLIST

1. Work with your child to develop a backpack checklist that includes everything he needs to bring home, such as homework assignments and materials, school forms, and flyers.

2. Determine where to keep the list.

3. Decide on a reinforcer such as money, special snacks, extra playtime, or any other reward that motivates your child.

4. Check the backpack for materials as compared to the assignment notebook and pay up *immediately*.

OBSTACLES TO EFFECTIVE USE OF INCENTIVES

Sharon: Delivery of an incentive is as important as its selection. One real difficulty is in follow-through by parents. Here are examples of some of the most common obstacles to incentives' effectiveness:

- Insufficient or delayed follow-through by parents
  - Parent forgets to pay allowance.
  - Parent waits too long to rent the earned movie.
  - Parent can't find time to get to the park.

- Promised incentive is too inconvenient
  - The fast-food restaurant the child likes best is too far away.

- Promised incentive is too expensive
  - Disney World is *really* expensive.

- Earned incentive is not delivered because a different negative behavior occurs
  - All week, child is in bed on time. But, because he talks back, parent takes away reward for going to bed on time.

- Parent promises to do something as reward that parent absolutely hates and therefore spoils activity or doesn't follow through
  - Parent cuts short afternoon at video arcade.

- Incentive is available someplace else, not just as reward for specified behavior
  - Dad shares his Klondike Bar with Susie—but she's supposed to *earn* it.

If the incentive is too inconvenient, you won't be consistent in providing the reward when your child earns it. If you delay, your child may do something that causes you to take away the privilege he's already earned—which you should not do. You have to find an incentive that you can—and will—deliver immediately.

Another problem arises when a parent agrees to a reinforcer that will be like nails across a blackboard to deliver. There are, for example, places I dread so much that I'm not going to agree to go there, no matter how well a child behaves. I like pizza and enjoy games but I am not going to sit and eat pizza with bells and whistles going off and a large rodent walking around.

If there are things parents hate to do they will often delay fulfilling their end of the deal or make the experience so unpleasant for the child that it's not a real reward. The choice is simple. If you absolutely loathe the racket of a video arcade, don't promise to take your child there (or find someone else who will).

It is also critically important that *the selected incentive is not available at any other time, for any other reason, no matter what.* You can't give it out as a treat because you're in a good mood. If allowance is the reinforcer, you have to talk to Grandma and ask her to refrain from slipping Sally five dollars on weekend visits. If you use a video rental as a reward, your child must do what's required before you rent one. He can win the Nobel Peace Prize, but no video rental unless he does that one behavior.

Making effective use of reinforcers is not easy. If there are only two things that motivate your child and six behaviors you want him to change, it's a challenge. Prioritize the behaviors, focusing on only one or two at a time. If the behaviors are serious enough, you will have to initially let some of the less disruptive behaviors slide. Chores take a backseat to physical aggression. Verbal abuse takes precedence over homework. As each improves, you can increase your expectations so that he must do more to earn more of that one reinforcer. If he goes for a day without aggression or threats, he earns his allowance, plus a bonus.

Provide separate opportunities to earn a reinforcer. For example, if money is the motivator, set up two accounts—one for discretionary spending and an activity budget for favorite pastimes. He may use his discretionary money to buy things, but activities such as movies, video rentals, and arcade trips depend on what's in the activity account. Keep the monies separate. Link a separate behavior to each (e.g., one behavior earns money for movies; another for video rentals; and a third for arcade trips).

Here are guidelines for using reinforcers (or rewards) to encourage your child's good behavior.

RULES FOR REINFORCEMENT

1. Select an appropriate reinforcer for the child.

2. Give the reinforcer only when the desired behavior happens. To be effective, the reinforcer cannot be available at any other time for any other reason.

3. Reinforce immediately after the desired behavior happens.

4. When building new behavior or strengthening behaviors that occur infrequently, reinforce every time.

5. Reinforce improvement. Do not expect perfect performance on the first try.

6. To keep new behavior going, reinforce it every so often.

7. When using food, objects, or activities as reinforcers, always present them with a social reinforcer. Example: "I like the way you put the toys on the shelf" (social reinforcer); "Now you may go out to play" (activity reinforcer).

8. Reinforcer needs to be feasible to adult in terms of interest, time, and money.

Tip: Use an activity he likes to do and does all the time to reinforce a behavior or activity that is less desirable to him.

Pairing praise with rewards helps build the relationship between you and your child and break the negative cycle of punishment and recrimination. Equally important, positive feedback gives you the opportunity to clarify exactly how your child earned the reinforcer. Your praise should always include a specific description of the behavior you saw that you want to see again.

Jan: Periodically we had to change Theodore's incentives. Money often worked. When his money box was full, however, cash diminished in value as a reward. Sometimes we increased what we paid and sometimes we changed the reinforcer altogether. When *Pokémon* was the rage, Theodore badly wanted to watch the half-hour TV show. We began to videotape *Pokémon* and doled it out in thirty-minute increments that he could watch by cashing in his screen-time chips. When he lost interest in the show, we had to find something else. When we bought the computer game Age of Empires, it proved to be a powerful incentive for earning screen time. New and different computer games had a similar result.

Sharon: It is the use of structure and incentives that result in behavior change and teach new skills. But both positive and negative consequences are necessary to really make a difference. There will be times when your child's behavior warrants a punishment. It is a necessary tool when children violate clearly established, reasonable guidelines and policies or behave in a way that is dangerous or destructive. To determine if the punishment is effective, watch the behavior. If you find yourself punishing the same behavior over and over, the punishment is not working. If your child is saying "I don't care. It doesn't matter to me," but the behavior occurs less often, stick with it, you're on the right track.

Punishment

Jan: In looking back, I can see now that our parenting style, which was fine for our daughter, was completely inadequate for Theodore. Somewhere along the line, punishment had become a way of life. *"That's it! I've had it!!!"* was the theme. He did something we didn't want him to do; we got angry and reacted emotionally. It didn't change his behavior. Whatever he had done wrong invariably happened again, and we again overreacted.

We made all the usual parenting mistakes, but when we didn't see progress, we made even more. We nagged Theodore unmercifully. We punished excessively. We constantly sentenced him to "time-out." Because we were perpetually taking things away, he always seemed to live "without." Often, out of impatience and anger, we punished Theodore when he didn't even know what he'd done wrong.

PUNISHMENT 101: IT WON'T CHANGE YOUR CHILD'S BEHAVIOR

Sharon: Jan and Jamie are intelligent, rational adults who take seriously their child-rearing responsibility. In this respect, they are representative of the vast majority of parents I see. And like the vast majority of both parents and educators, they often reacted to child misbehavior with punishment. The behavior reoccurs; they punish again. The child continues to repeat the behavior and they ratchet up the level of punishment, thinking that if the penalty is strong enough, they will finally get through to him.

Though I do not believe in speaking in absolute terms, here is an exception. I have *never* had to introduce punishment as a novel concept to *any* adult. It seems to be the one approach that comes naturally to parents (and educators, for that matter). But *punishment does not change behavior,* especially when it is the only approach used.

Pointer for Effective Parenting

Punishment rarely changes behavior because it doesn't teach a better way to handle a situation.

Punishment tells a child what not to do, but it doesn't tell him what to do instead. Let's be honest. You've tried every form of punishment you can think of to get things to change and, so far, how well has it worked? Punishment doesn't teach a better, more appropriate alternative. It must be paired with information and feedback about what *to do*, not just what not to do. Don't get me wrong. Some kids seem to get the message with just one or two redirections (my euphemism for punishment). But you're not reading this book because you're raising that child. You're raising the child who makes you wonder if you'll ever get through to him.

PUNISHMENT 201: YES, IT'S STILL PART OF THE PICTURE

Bad behavior does happen and it's important to know how to respond when it does. Don't delude yourself that punishment will be well received. Expect a negative reaction. It amazes me that parents are surprised and incensed when punishment results in more negative behavior. Their expectation is that "he did something wrong and he should accept the consequences of his actions." That's wishful thinking. There may be some question in your child's mind as to whether he did anything wrong or not. Even if he knows he did, it wasn't his fault. It was somebody else's fault, often yours (or the closest available living being, including the dog).

Often, the more challenging the child, the more difficulty he has making the connection between cause and effect, especially in behavioral or social situations. And most children, challenging or not, try to avoid the negative consequences of their behavior.

FIRST WARN, THEN PUNISH

Children need to know ahead of time exactly what the consequences will be if they misbehave. Otherwise, any punishment seems unfair. Don't make the mistake of parenting on the basis of implied "risk aversion" ("If you do as I ask, I won't scream and yell at you"). Such threats aren't effective because you haven't let your child know exactly what the negative outcome will be if he doesn't do what you want. When you hear him say, "That's not fair," what he really means is "I didn't know that was coming." If your child knows what will happen before the behavior occurs, he can make an informed decision about how he wants to behave. One boy told me he would have finished the chore "if I had known my dad was not going to let me go to Sam's party."

If you're like most parents, right now you're probably thinking, "I've told him a hundred times . . ." The problem is that your child could not be sure whether you'd snap on 85 or on 102. Which time would be a warning and which would result in enforcement? If you find yourself even thinking *"That's it, I've had it!"* you're about to deliver punishment without warning—and your child undoubtedly will believe you are being unfair. When you hear that phrase, *"That's it, I've had it!"* in your head, your next words ought to be "The very next time you do or say that, it will cost you fifteen minutes off your bedtime," or some such penalty, and follow through.

Theodore: My parents used to make things up left and right. They do it a lot less now that we have rules we all know about. Now they only do it once or twice a week. When they do, it's usually when they want me to get something done and it's taking me a while to do it. If it's taking me a long time to get my homework done, they'll tell me if I don't get things done by 9:45 P.M., then I'll lose two chips for screen time. That's unfair because that isn't one of our rules.

AN INFRACTION EARNS THE SAME PENALTY EACH TIME

Sharon: Although you can't anticipate your child's every misdeed, you probably know how he is likely to misbehave. So, you must lay out your expectations for good behavior and define what will happen if bad behavior occurs. For example, say you've been having a problem with Sam punching his brother Robbie. Though you offer an incentive for the boys to keep their hands and feet to themselves, you still need to tell them what will happen if anyone hits. Then if Sam hits Robbie (or vice versa, since the rule applies equally to both), he knows, because you've already told him, that he will have to go to his room and it will cost him a half hour of TV.

Now, what happens if Sam hits Robbie a second time? You fly off the handle and take away the TV privileges for a week? Guess again. For punishment to be effective, it has to be imposed at maximum intensity each time the behavior occurs. If he hits Robbie again, Sam loses another thirty minutes of TV. It's the same punishment each time—no escalator clause. If the procedure is ineffective, make sure your punishment costs him more than the behavior gives him. Sometimes it may be worth the loss of TV to get his brother upset. Maybe losing TV is not the right deterrent. Better still, check the incentive for keeping hands to self. A more powerful incentive may be needed.

AN INFRACTION EARNS THE SAME PENALTY *EVERY* TIME

Effective punishment doesn't increase in intensity or duration for additional infractions, but the penalty has to be imposed every time the misbehavior occurs. Just because Sam hit Robbie twice today, and was punished both times, it doesn't mean you ignore the third time he hits Robbie because you're sick and tired of dealing with it. He has to know there will be a consequence—and exactly what the punishment will be—each and every time he behaves badly.

If your teenager violates curfew, each ten minutes he is late costs him ten minutes off curfew time the next night. Twenty minutes late means he must return twenty minutes early the next night. Likewise, a child who gets up ten minutes late in the morning goes to bed ten minutes early that night. Twenty minutes late getting up costs him twenty minutes at bedtime. When established in advance, the exact consequence can be based on the severity of the infraction.

MAKE PENALTIES ENFORCEABLE ACROSS SETTINGS

Effective punishment must also be enforceable across people and settings. That means Grandma can levy the penalty the same as Mom or Dad and that it is imposed whether Sarah's in the grocery store, the car, or surrounded by ten friends at her own birthday party. If time or circumstance makes it impossible to implement the punishment at the moment of infraction, hand over an I.O.U. that signals that the punishment will still be required. Your child must understand that a specific behavior earns the punishment whenever it occurs, regardless of where you are.

IMPOSE PENALTIES WITH *NO* EMOTION

The most difficult guideline for effective punishment is that you have to deliver it in a matter-of-fact tone. If you're jumping up and down like an animated cartoon, your child can't even focus on what you're saying because of the way you are saying it. Besides, given the way you look at the time, it's hard for your child to associate his own behavior with the punishment. He thinks that it's a direct result of the fact that *you* lost it and so now he's being punished. "Mom got mad so I have to go to my room." "Dad's furious, so I'm grounded."

The hardest thing for parents to do is to hold their own frustration or anger in check and curb their tongue. The less said the better. With as little emotion as possible, you say: "You must be home fifteen minutes early tomorrow because you came in fifteen minutes past your curfew tonight." No discussion, no accusations, no ranting and raving. Believe me, your child isn't listening to your lecture anyway.

Right after your child gets nailed for doing something wrong, his only thought is to get out of the situation and away from you. So limit communication to a brief message that identifies the rule that was broken, the transgression and the associated consequence, all stated in a matter-of-fact tone. "The rule is 'Be home by five.' It's five forty-five; you're late. That will cost you forty-five minutes the next time you go to a friend's house—then you will have to be home at four fifteen." This increases the likelihood that your child can separate what you say from how you say it.

Jan: I'm not as good at this as I should be. I really have to work hard to contain my own frustration or irritation when my kids do something wrong. Having a list of rules with set consequences acts as a check on my natural inclination to harangue. It helps me say: "That's one dollar in the fine jar for lying," and not lecture Caroline or Theodore on why they shouldn't lie about having walked the dog.

LYING: TELLING THE TRUTH DOESN'T CANCEL PENALTY FOR ORIGINAL INFRACTION

Sharon: In their zeal for truthfulness, most parents err by letting their child off the hook "if you just tell the truth." In their relief that their child has told the truth, all too often, parents don't impose any punishment for the original misbehavior. This is a big mistake. Telling the truth then becomes a way to escape punishment for the original infraction. The only punishment is a long-winded sermon on the virtues of telling the truth and the evils of lying.

All kids lie. They lie because they got caught. They lie to escape punishment. They lie because it's the first thing that comes into their head. The solution is a separate penalty for lying that is *always* imposed in addition to the penalty for the infraction. If you want them not to lie, they have to know they will be punished for the lie *and* for whatever they did wrong. The choice is theirs: one punishment for the original infraction or two punishments, one for lying and one for the misbehavior. Give them time alone to weigh their options. Be consistent in imposing the punishments, one or both.

One more comment before leaving this topic: Don't set your child up to lie. If the rule is no cookies before dinner and your child approaches you with crumbs on his mouth, crumbs on his hands, and the top is off of the cookie jar, don't ask him if he's been eating cookies. The only question should be "What's the rule about cookies before dinner?" Similarly, if the rule is no TV on Saturday morning until he walks the dog, and you find your child lounging in front of the television, the dog whining at the door, tail between his legs, don't ask him if the dog has been walked. Just say: "What's the rule about TV on Saturday morning?"

In changing your approach to punishment, your guideline

should be that punishment is something your child *earns*—not something you impose because you're in a bad mood. You want him to understand that a certain behavior *earns* a specific punishment and that another behavior *costs* him a predetermined privilege. Your language and demeanor help your child associate the punishment with his behavior. For this to happen, you have to be consistent, even-tempered, and use language that helps your child make the connection.

MAKE CLEAR WHAT POSITIVE BEHAVIOR YOU EXPECT

Finally, since punishment used as the only behavior change mechanism is not likely to work, the real key is to pair a positive approach with it. If you are like most parents, punishing the negative behavior over and over hasn't made a dent. The more diffi-

---

RULES FOR EFFECTIVE PUNISHMENT

Effective punishment:

- Is preceded by a warning.

- Has a set beginning and end.

- Happens immediately.

- Occurs at maximum intensity (does not increase in intensity or duration for additional infractions).

- Is enforceable wherever your child is when the misbehavior occurs.

- Is delivered in a matter-of-fact tone.

- Is imposed every time that behavior occurs.

- Is always accompanied by acknowledgment of the appropriate behaviors he should be demonstrating.

cult the child, the more likely it is that he lives in a highly punitive world. He has endured every form of negative feedback—and still hasn't changed his behavior. This is the opportunity to interrupt that negative, unproductive cycle. You're more effective when you convey to your child: "If you do this behavior, it will earn you this privilege and if you don't, it will earn you this punishment." Specify what behavior you want to see and reward it when he does it. Positive acknowledgment, paired with punishment, judiciously applied, is the most effective way to change behavior.

Evaluate any set of procedures by its results. If your child's behavior changes for the better, then the reinforcements and punishments you've selected are effective, regardless of what he says.

Pointer for Effective Parenting

Don't kid yourself that punishment will be well received. If, however, your child's behavior changes for the better, the punishment is effective—regardless of what he says.

On the other hand, if the behavior doesn't change in two weeks, you have to reevaluate your approach. Remember to make your child part of the solution. When you decide what infractions to focus on, ask him to help design a meaningful penalty.

Pointer for Effective Parenting

Get input from your child on what penalty would be meaningful. Input, however, does not mean decision-making.

Finally, posting a list of infractions with consequences on the refrigerator, bulletin board, or wall is a way to ensure consistency for both parents and child. Clarifying household rules with similar lists can help tone down the decibel level.

Pointer for Effective Parenting

Posting lists of infractions with consequences in places where kids can't miss them—refrigerator, bulletin board, or their bedroom door—helps reduce arguments over consequences. Since all you do is refer to the list, the rule—not mean Mom or Dad—decrees the punishment.

Jan: This system was as beneficial for our teenager as it was for Theodore. It substantially reduced arguments because we could just say, "What's the rule? What's the penalty for violating that rule?" Pointing to a piece of paper eliminated a lot of the nagging and arguing. The list reminded her of what the rules were and limited us to saying no more than, "Caroline, you have a half hour to get ready for your chorus performance and you must eat before you go." No nagging allowed. She knew the penalty if she dawdled in the bathroom getting ready.

Caroline: It was useful to post rules because it meant there were set guidelines everybody agreed on. It reduced my parents' tendency to increase punishment on the spur of the moment because of their anger. It also meant they had to stay off my back. Plus, there was no longer anything to argue about—at least for those things on the list.

Sharon: If something works, figure out where else you can apply it. Analyze behaviors by using the questions discussed in chapter 4: *What do I want him to do instead of what he's doing? How can I put it in a visual format so he understands what is expected of him and doesn't have to rely on me to remind him?" What will make it worth his while?* Doing so makes it easier to be positive in your approach to behavior change.

When a problem occurs, reflect on what's worked in the past. Maybe all you have to do is adjust the routine. Move a chore or responsibility to another time of day when not as much is going on. Establish a procedure that allows for a change in chores every two weeks. Ask questions that are specific to that situation and make the necessary modifications.

Don't overlook the benefit of added structure to help produce the desired change. An additional list or using a schedule, calendar, or timer can go a long way toward addressing the issue. Once any improvement occurs, jump on it. Notice it in a way that matters to your child.

Ensure that reinforcers don't compete with each other. Make sure that your child can't get a reinforcer some other way. Ensure everyone understands the procedures. Find a way to document both expectations and results. Use lists to clarify expectations and formally check them off as they are completed. This documents success. Provide larger, more powerful rewards for longer periods of success. Offer a bonus if the desired behavior occurs three days in a row or four out of five days. Allow your child to earn a different reward for exceeding expectations.

Don't expect perfection but be prepared to reward it. Stay with the program for at least two weeks. It takes two weeks, minimum, to change a behavior pattern. Expect ups and downs. Children who are more oppositional need to experience both up- and downsides of behavioral contingencies. So don't be discouraged if there are rocky periods. Expect to have to apply the negative consequences (which may only be that he does not earn the privilege or other reinforcer). Stick with the structure.

It is unrealistic to expect your child to get it right for the rest of his life. The purpose isn't to ensure that whatever behavior you're focusing on never happens again. Rather, your goal should be that the negative behavior doesn't happen as often, doesn't last as long, and isn't as intense.

Pointer for Effective Parenting

There are no permanent cures or solutions. Aim for reducing instances of negative behavior, decreasing their duration, and reducing the intensity of your child's negative reactions.

Finally, don't raise the bar too quickly. Once you have achieved some success, stay with the program as it is. Don't increase your expectations just yet. Allow both yourself and your child the opportunity to enjoy the moment. He's not yet proficient at whatever has been achieved. It's still a work in progress.

How to Handle Unforeseen Behavior Problems

Jan: No matter how many lists, charts, and rules we have plastered all over the refrigerator, bathroom mirrors, and bulletin boards, our children can come up with something we haven't thought of. Often something happens and we don't have a rule, much less an incentive to change the behavior or a penalty to punish it.

By having procedures we can fall back on, we have learned reasonably well how to respond in ways that work. We rely on the three principles: "Rules, Praise, Ignore." We decide if we need to adopt a new rule or policy, ignore the behavior if it isn't that important, or find an incentive to help change it. If the behavior warrants punishment, we are learning to give a warning first. We have to clarify our expectations so that the kids know that a specific behavior will result in a penalty instead of imposing punishment out of the blue the first time it happens. We've had to alter *our* behavior to change that of our children's.

Effective parenting, particularly changing the behavior of a child we find challenging, takes constant vigilance. It is difficult and can be taxing and very time-consuming. But the effort has paid enormous dividends in a much calmer household. Moreover,

STEPS FOR CHANGING BEHAVIOR

1. What she/he should do *instead* of what she/he's doing:

_____

2. What she/he shouldn't do (in this situation):

_____

3. How often and when does it happen?

_____

4. What reward will get her/his attention and make it worth her/his while to change the behavior?

_____

5. How will you document performance?

_____

6. How often will you check on her/his behavior?

_____

7. How will you measure progress/improvements? (charts/chips/points):

_____

If you answered all of the above, you're ready to help your child make changes.

If she/he does this positive behavior . . .	then she/he earns this following reward . . .
_____	_____
_____	_____
_____	_____

If this negative behavior occurs or this desired behavior does not occur . . .	. . . then she/he earns this punishment . . .
_____	_____
_____	_____

now that we know how, we have the confidence that we can design a solution for almost any behavior problem that arises.

What to Do When Things Fall Apart

Sharon: When a program or approach that was successful for a while stops being so, the reinforcement is the culprit. In some way, this aspect has broken down. Either delivery is off (delays have rendered the reward meaningless) or the reinforcer has lost its potency. In both cases, swift action is necessary. Either improve your performance in delivering the reward or find a new one that will be meaningful as an incentive to spur your child's performance. If, however, the program or approach never was successful, either your expectation was unrealistically high or you didn't explain it well enough so that your child fully understood what was expected.

STEP 1—FIGURE OUT WHY THINGS AREN'T WORKING: IS IT YOU OR YOUR CHILD?

Jan: There have been many times when things have suddenly gone downhill. Although medication is sometimes a factor, more often it is because we have become inconsistent in enforcement or Theodore (or Caroline) loses interest in the incentive for good behavior. The usual sign that the system needs fine-tuning is that the decibel level goes up. If I find myself doing a lot more yelling, then I know I have to figure out where we've gotten off track. Sometimes, the fix is as simple as making myself stop and give Theodore a written list of short tasks. Too often, I lapse into telling him to "do this, do that, and then do this." If either of us is already grumpy, that can result in raised voices, but sometimes he'll stop me and say, "Can you please write it down on a list?" Then I know it's me—not him—who has to change.

STEP 2—REINSTATE PROCEDURES FOR PREVIOUSLY SOLVED BEHAVIORS

Sometimes behaviors that we thought we had "fixed" reappear. When Theodore arrived home from camp one summer, we had to reinstate incentives for flushing the toilet and turning off the lights. The latter was hardly surprising since he'd been gone for five weeks without electricity in his cabin—no lights to turn out there.

STEP 3—ALTER THE REINFORCEMENT

At other times, the reward stops being effective. When the pig-gybank is bursting, money isn't much of an incentive for Theodore to do his morning list. If, however, we shift to letting him earn screen time, he goes back to getting everything done.

STEP 4—ALTER THE PENALTY

Similarly, fines are not much of a penalty if his money box is full—but taking away screen time is if he is enthralled by a new computer game. In Caroline's case, having to wash the dishes several extra nights for a week was a more effective penalty than fining her.

STEP 5—WHEN NEW BAD BEHAVIOR EMERGES: GO BACK TO THE BEGINNING

Sharon: Now you have the tools. Remember the general principle: Rules, Praise, Ignore. Now answer the following questions:

- What do I want him to do instead of what he's doing?
- How can I document the expectation and progress in a visual format?
- What would make it worth his while to demonstrate this new behavior on a consistent basis?

Theodore: Even though it may seem they do, incentives don't make jobs any easier for me. I have to do as much work to get the incentive as I would if there wasn't one. But incentives make me more willing to do a job without complaining and do a better job. They make me stop and think: "Oh, I have a chance to earn some money or some screen time if I do what they want." That makes me more willing to do it.

It's obvious that incentives are better than punishment because all that punishment says is "OK, if you do this again, then something bad will happen." Incentives say, "If you feel like you're about to do this, but you don't, then you'll get the reward." I like incentives. They motivate me. I hate punishments.

6

"Where Did I Go Wrong?"

Shedding Bad Habits

Theodore: When we started making rules and using incentives our house got a lot quieter. There was a lot less screaming ourselves hoarse. Things still weren't perfect. I still would get distracted and they'd forget to count me out (give three warnings before time-out)—and they'd get so mad, they would forget to use the new way of doing things. They'd just punish me and forget to give me a reason to change my behavior.

Jan: Things were better. For the most part, everyone knew what was expected, and Jamie and I were better about making short lists of tasks for Theodore. We were more likely to think of incentives to get him to do what we wanted. But some days new things came up or nothing on the lists got done and the decibel level rose accordingly.

It was so frustrating. For every two steps forward we took at least one step back. I knew we were making progress but it didn't seem like enough. Why weren't there long stretches of calm?

Defining What Constitutes Success

Sharon: Jan and Jamie's lament is typical. They had made great progress with new routines and had adopted new ways to get Theodore to do what they wanted. He had made many changes in his behavior. But even after all this hard work, they still were looking for a way to "fix" everything. Jan still clung to her wish for a magic wand.

It is hard to give up unrealistic expectations. No matter what they do, Theodore will remain a challenging child. Jan and Jamie now had better skills, but their inflated expectations jeopardized that progress.

Unrealistic expectations are one of the biggest obstacles to change. They can infect your definition of progress, the kinds of changes you will see, how long they will last, or how quickly you expect them to take place. If you don't notice the small changes, you won't see success. Progress is success.

Pointer for Effective Parenting

Be aware of—and praise—the small improvements in your child's behavior. If you don't notice progress, you won't achieve success. Progress *is* success.

If your child is disrespectful, it is unrealistic to expect that anything will result in him holding his tongue from this day forth. If the frequency of negative comments decreases from three to two a day, that's progress. The goal is not that your child will *never* talk back. Nor that your child will *always* respond respectfully. The terms *never* and *always* do not apply to behavior. Any parent who waits for perfection is missing many opportunities to savor and praise progress.

Pointer for Effective Parenting

Banish the words *never* and *always* from your vocabulary in connection with your child's behavior. Behavior does not occur in absolutes. Don't expect anything to work all of the time.

Progress is measured in steps. It doesn't happen all at once and it doesn't happen overnight. You need to recognize it when you see it—in whatever forms it takes. If you want a negative behavior to decrease, then progress is that behavior occurring less often, for a shorter duration, or at a lower intensity.

Melinda and Joe's eight-year-old daughter had at least one tantrum a day. Although she didn't blow up at every frustration, when she did it was a loo-loo. Erica's tantrums could go on for hours. As long as Melinda and Joe measured progress only in terms of how often the tantrums occurred, they continued to over-look success. By shifting the focus to duration, they realized that Erica's outbursts now lasted only half as long. The steps they had taken had, indeed, produced change. If frequency had been their only measure, they might have given up on an effective approach.

Measure progress by trends. Everyone has bad days and mo-ments. Is the positive behavior occurring, on average, more fre-quently? Improvement doesn't occur at a steady pace. The more challenging the situation, the more you must measure progress in small increments. Be prepared for frequent setbacks. When posi-tive change occurs—and it will—rest assured that whatever is going right will not last. The best of behavioral changes, like the worst, invariably passes. That's inherent in raising any child. If you anticipate the lapses, you'll be less frustrated when they happen.

When improvement occurs, some parents fail to recognize it; others start thinking, "cure." When the inevitable regression hap-pens, they are twice as disappointed than if there'd been no change at all. Their inflated expectations result in increased frus-tration despite the improvement. Therefore, it is essential to nar-row your focus, define changes in terms of improvement (not perfection), anticipate the ups and downs, and reinforce any and all success.

Jan: We slowly began to change *our* behavior, so we could help Theodore change *his*. The key was clarifying what constituted truly "bad" behavior. Distinguishing between behavior that frus-trated us (such as "dawdling") that could be improved by struc-turing routines and true disobedience (watching TV without permission or playing on the computer instead of doing home-work) was essential. That also made us realize how much of what we had previously seen as defiance or not following instructions on purpose was a function of Theodore's ADHD and needed to be dealt with differently. Prioritizing our rules helped us determine what we could encourage through incentives, what warranted punishment, and what we should ignore.

We made all sorts of mistakes and often plunged into what Sharon calls the "Seven Key Parenting Pitfalls." I'd like to say we didn't after we learned better ways to deal with Theodore—but at least we did it less often.

Seven Key Parenting Pitfalls: Traps to Avoid

1. Having unrealistic expectations

2. Relying on punishment alone

3. Sermonizing and dramatizing

4. Punishing without warning

5. Extending punishment too long

6. Failing to give clear directions

7. Establishing too many rules

PITFALL 1: HAVING UNREALISTIC EXPECTATIONS

Sharon: Not only must you have reasonable expectations for the rate of change, you need to have realistic expectations for what your child can achieve. You must see your child as he is—not as who you thought he was or who he ought to be. If he has a devel-opmental disorder, it's unreasonable to expect him "to act his age" without training. Similarly, most children with ADHD are easily distracted by anything that crosses their radar screen at the mo-ment. Therefore, when you send him upstairs to put his shoes on, he may never come back. The fact that his younger sister returns promptly should not be your measure of whether your child with ADHD can realistically be expected to do so. Nagging, yelling, and lecturing won't increase his ability to successfully complete the task. You are increasing his stress level and raising your own blood pressure.

Unrealistic expectations frustrate parents and defeat their children. Knowing what your child is reasonably capable of achieving makes it easier to recognize incremental progress. Based on past performance, what would constitute improvement? Using this measure assures that your expectations are reasonable. Stepping back and focusing on what your child is actually doing (not what you wish he'd be doing) will help you recognize progress when it occurs.

Pointer for Effective Parenting

Knowing your child for who he is, not who he ought to be or who you thought he was, enables you to better recognize progress when it occurs.

How to Drive Yourself and Your Kids Nuts

Jan: We were (and remain) guilty of having too high expectations. We have such "nice" kids (even if one of them is challenging), that I expect perfect behavior all the time. I know he's easily distracted, but if I can do it, why can't Theodore remember to hang up his towel every time after he takes a shower? The dog *has* to be walked every night. It's Theodore's job, so he shouldn't gripe about it. Right?

Not only do we expect Caroline and Theodore to do all their (considerable) chores, we expect them to complete them on time and do them thoroughly and cheerfully—or at least without complaint.

Each child has to clean his or her room on Saturday morning. Now, when I say clean, I mean *everything* picked up, clothes neatly folded or hung up on hangers (buttons buttoned, zippers zipped so they don't fall off), all toys put away (properly), desks cleaned off (and wiped), books straightened (all spines facing out, books lined up in same direction), room dusted, and floors vacuumed. Now, is that too much to expect? To our kids, cleaning their rooms means shoving stuff into the closet and swishing a dust cloth around for a second or two. Suffice it to say that we've battled over what's "clean enough."

Caroline: I don't see why I have to clean my room in the first place. I keep it relatively neat anyway. It's not like anyone's stumbling over clothes and books thrown everywhere. And I live in the place. They're not the ones living in it. It's aggravating that it has to be perfectly clean. It's clean enough for me.

Jan: The problem is that the gap between my expectations and those of my children needs to be closed. That requires taking steps either to pare down my expectations or more clearly delineate exactly what my definition of "clean" is and how they can achieve it instead of just saying: "That's not clean enough. Go finish your job."

PITFALL 2: RELYING ON PUNISHMENT ALONE TO CHANGE BEHAVIOR

Sharon: The children who most challenge us are usually those who have been punished the most. Although this approach comes naturally to parents, it does not result in effective behavioral change. Punishment doesn't change behavior because it does not teach your child a better way to behave.

Despite the fact that it hasn't worked, parents keep right on punishing their kids "to make them behave." They punish and punish until "there is nothing left to take away." These children descend into a cycle of misbehavior that results in their digging a hole from which they cannot emerge. To break this cycle, you need to help your child climb out of that hole by looking for positive behavior and rewarding it as soon as you see it.

Pointer for Effective Parenting

Punishment alone doesn't change behavior because it does not teach your child a better way to behave.

Punishment with No Reward

Jan: I did everything I could to ensure my children became readers. Well, I succeeded. Theodore, in particular, reads voraciously. For him, that comes with liabilities. Reading—books, any of the numerous kids' magazines we subscribe to, and comic books—became one of Theodore's two most common distracters, with LEGOs a close second. While I was never tempted to take away any of Theodore's books as punishment, comic books were another matter. He read *Calvin and Hobbes* comics obsessively, dawdling over them at breakfast, in the bathroom, and when he was supposed to be getting dressed or ready for bed. Periodically, we would sweep them up and hide them. Eventually we'd give them back.

Needless to say, punishing Theodore by taking them away didn't teach him not to dawdle, or get him to do what he was supposed to do. Taking away Theodore's comic books did nothing to change his behavior. We denied him access to them in a fit of pique, but rarely gave him an opportunity to "earn" them back.

Since the real problem was the "dawdling" and not the actual reading of comic books, using incentives to get Theodore through routines where he was distracted by them proved far more effective than just taking them away.

PITFALL 3: SERMONIZING AND DRAMATIZING AT THE POINT OF INFRACTION

Sharon: Punishment can interrupt the behavior for the moment. Your child may (if you're lucky) make the connection between the penalty and his own behavior—but not if he attributes it to your outburst. The more talking you do when a child misbehaves, the less likely your message will get through. Emotion diminishes the capacity to think, let alone speak. And since this isn't one of those Hallmark moments, when your child is interested in hearing what you have to say, why say anything? As Will Durant said, "Nothing is often a good thing to do and always a good thing to say."

Pointer for Effective Parenting

When misbehavior occurs, the less said, the better.

Jan: Resisting my natural inclination to lecture and simply say, "You used 'bad' language. That's ten cents in the fine jar," took discipline, but resulted in a lot less yelling and a calmer household.

PITFALL 4: PUNISHING WITHOUT WARNING

Sharon: Imposing punishment without previously having told your child exactly what the consequences of his behavior would be invites meltdown. Your child can only make the connection between his behavior and the punishment if he knows what the punishment will be in advance. Otherwise, he believes you're being unfair.

Prevent meltdowns by posting lists of infractions with specific penalties that will be imposed every time. This eliminates arguments and helps your child make the connection between punishment and his own behavior.

Pointer for Effective Parenting

Punishment without warning is unfair and perpetuates your child's notion that the punishment is a function of parental whim rather than a consequence of his own behavior.

The Perils of Punishment without Warning

Jan: We were frequently guilty of punishment without warning. Getting Theodore to bed was difficult enough; getting him to stay there was even tougher. One night after he had wandered out repeatedly, finally announcing, "I'm just not tired," I snapped in exasperation: *"I don't care! Just go to bed!"* Shortly thereafter, I glimpsed light under his door, pushed it open, and discovered him reading with a jacket blocking the light under the door. I thundered in, yanked the book out of his hands, unscrewed his lightbulb, and stormed out of the room.

In retrospect, I think he'd been pretty clever. His solution had fixed *my* problem (that I was weary of him coming out and bothering me) and it had solved *his* problem (that he wasn't tired). My response, however, was dreadful. I had doled out punishment without warning. Since I'd made no threats ahead of time, he had no idea this was what I'd do. Worse, I'd unsolved both his and my problems. I'm not sure who was punished more that night.

PITFALL 5: EXTENDING PUNISHMENT TOO LONG

Sharon: Taking away a toy or privilege for an extended time only teaches your child to do without it. This may not be bad, but it probably isn't what you'd intended. Moreover, the longer he goes without, the more likely he will focus his resentment on you rather than connecting its loss to his own behavior. Punishments that last too long usually end up punishing the parent and the whole family as much or more than the child.

Moreover, extended loss of a toy or privilege doesn't make sense. There's no logical relationship between leaving a bicycle outside and not being allowed to ride it, because the penalty doesn't teach the child to put it away. Short-term loss of bike-riding privileges paired with the following procedure will more likely teach him to put it away. If your child leaves his bike out he 1) loses the privilege to ride for the next twenty-four hours and 2) can't ride again until he has practiced ten times walking the bike between the point where he left it and where it belongs, parking it with the kickstand down each time. He can't ride any bike (not just his own) until he fulfills both requirements.

When you take something away for a long time, you deny your child the opportunity to handle that item or privilege appropriately. Grounding a teen for being late precludes the possibility of practicing checking his watch and coming in on time. Taking away toys for a month when your child fails to put them away doesn't give him practice at tidying up. Eventually, he'll be adept at putting his toy away because that's all he will have—one toy. You will have taken the rest away.

Pointer for Effective Parenting

Extended punishment doesn't allow your child the chance to practice doing something right. Such punishment only teaches him to do without the toy or privilege.

PITFALL 6: FAILING TO GIVE CLEAR DIRECTIONS

Only give directions when you are prepared to enforce them.

Unless you are willing to get up and ensure immediate compliance, avoid using the term *now.* You're inadvertently teaching your child to ignore you when you delay or don't follow up your direction to, for example, "turn off the television now." What child in his right mind would promptly respond when experience tells him that no one will check for at least ten minutes? If you tell your child he must pick up his room before he gets to play outside, don't convey that it's all right to ignore your direction by not checking that he has done what you have asked.

Pointer for Effective Parenting

Only give directions when you are prepared to follow up. Otherwise, you teach your child to ignore what you say.

When you give directions, state them clearly. Don't phrase directions as suggestions or questions. Your child's obvious response to the pseudodirection "Are you ready to go to bed yet?" is "No, I thought I'd watch Jay Leno but thanks for asking." There's no room for ambiguity or negotiation if you say, "It's time for you to go to bed."

Offer choices of acceptable options. "You can take a bath and then have a story or story first, then bath. It's your choice." The sequence is optional; the bath is not.

It's okay to make requests if you don't care if your child says no. "Do you want to take a bath tonight?" makes it clear a bath isn't mandatory. Be careful not to cloak directions as pseudosuggestions. Otherwise, you'll find yourself furious with your child after he fails to go along with something you phrased as if it were mere suggestion. "It would be nice if you took a bath tonight" sends your child the wrong message. You want him to learn that you mean what you say and be able to differentiate suggestions from directions.

The number of instructions you give at one time is as important as how you give them. Too often parents confuse their child's inability to remember multiple directions with willful noncompliance. If you give more than one instruction, *write them down*. Many challenging children need the visual reminder of what to do.

Quick Tip

Write down multiple directions. A visual reminder helps your child remember what to do.

If it's inconvenient to write it down, at least be sure you have your child's full attention before you give directions. If he's working on the computer, your talking is merely background noise. There's little chance he realizes you're talking and less chance he cares. To avoid screaming at your child, first get his full attention, then tell him what you want and, whenever possible, seek acknowledgment. Get some sign that he has processed what you said and seek some commitment that he plans to follow through.

PITFALL 7: ESTABLISHING TOO MANY RULES

Too many rules frustrate everyone. Your child has no chance of remembering (much less abiding by) all of them if you can't even keep track of them. An excessive number of rules makes consistency between parents impossible and enforcement a function of whoever is present, their mood, and what they remember. Too many guidelines lead to arbitrary parenting, which can make a child angry. Then, when he can't meet your expectations, you'll fall into the trap of pointing out each of his errors. When he continually fails to get your approval, your child feels like a failure.

Trying for All the Pitfalls at Once

Jan: "I'm sick of you cheating on TV. Every time I turn around, I find you cheating on TV. You go downstairs to collect the garbage and you turn on the TV. 'Just to see what's on,' you say. Well, *that's it! I've had it!* No TV for *six* months!"

You can imagine how effective that punishment was. Lashing out in anger and frustration, I had taken away Theodore's television privileges many times. He knew he wasn't allowed to watch without permission. Yet he did. Repeatedly. And just as often, we took it away—for a few days, a week, a month—and now six, long (futile) months.

I'm sad and embarrassed as I think back on this incident. Taking away television for six months failed as punishment and certainly didn't "teach" Theodore not to cheat. He still did. Much later we understood that impulse rather than disobedience drove Theodore's cheating. Sometimes he simply couldn't resist "just checking to see what was on."

By taking away television for six months, we had fallen into almost all the most common pitfalls in just one incident. We had:

1. *Sermonized.* And with all the emotion I could muster. The only message Theodore could have gotten was that I was really angry.

2. *Punished in isolation.* We certainly didn't cure him of cheating on TV. Worse, we gave him no incentive to earn back the privilege.

3. *Extended the punishment for too long.* What was the point of six months? Did he learn any lesson except that we were arbitrary and capricious? Or worse, that he was warranted in thinking we were mean, unreasonable parents?

4. *Punished without warning.* "That's it! I've had it!" Theodore didn't know what hit him when we took TV away for six months. Why six months *this* time?

5. Expectations that were too high. The perfect child never turns on the television without permission? Get real.

6. Too many rules. Not turning on the TV without permission was just one of a gazillion rules we had—many of which were unspoken.

I still cringe when I remember this episode. We didn't think of ourselves as arbitrary. But at times, we were. Looking back, I can see how deeply we fell into parenting pitfalls from lack of understanding and zeal to get Theodore to "obey."

Sharon: Reviewing their household policies allowed Jan and Jamie to understand where certain strategies went wrong and why they didn't work. They recognized that capricious punishment resulting from too many rules didn't work. It certainly hadn't changed Theodore's behavior. Understanding and applying the rules for effective punishment helped them craft penalties that worked.

Sliding Back into Old, Bad Habits

Jan: Although we knew consistency was crucial, it was also exhausting. It was a struggle to make the effort to do things a new way, day after day. Partly that was our own fault since we had so many rules, so many possible infractions, and so many specified penalties. Remembering to enforce the rules each and every time took so much effort. We're whizzes at devising rules; we're not as good at consistent enforcement. At times we found ourselves sliding back into bad habits of yelling, imposing punishments out of the blue, and forgetting to use much of what we'd learned. The decibel level in the house was our barometer for recognizing when we'd gotten off track.

That raises the issue of yelling. We yelled at Theodore constantly. Worse, we didn't just yell, we berated. We yelled to get him to do something since he usually ignored—or, in reality, didn't hear—simple requests. We yelled to get him to stop doing something (ditto). We yelled in frustration; we yelled in anger. In short, we yelled in reaction to everything. And, I'm ashamed to say, we yelled to make him feel bad. We yelled because we didn't understand. And even when we did understand, we fell back on yelling because it was what came naturally.

Pointer for Effective Parenting

- -

If you start to hear yourself yelling more than usual, it can be a warning that you've fallen into old, ineffective patterns that will not change your child's behavior.

ON YELLING

Yelling seems to be many parents' punishment of choice. It comes naturally and requires no special training. It fits almost any parenting style and can be utilized in response to any behavior. One father earnestly asked me: "Why does he make me yell at him? I try asking him nicely; I'll even repeat myself. But he just ignores me or refuses to do what I say and winds up making me yell at him." I'm sure he's not the only parent who feels this way.

First, it's important to understand that kids do not set out to *make* their parents do something like yell at them. No child consciously says to herself, "Hmm, what can I do to get my mom to start screeching at me? Shall I lie through my teeth about breaking the lamp?" "Should I break my curfew just so Dad can rage at me in front of my boyfriend?" I don't think so. So, let's agree that children do not *make* parents do these things. In fact, they'd consider their life a whole lot less stressful if their parents didn't yell at them.

Second, they are not ignoring you or refusing to follow your directions. They're doing something that, to them, is far more important and certainly much more interesting than listening to you. Their full attention is on that something else and can barely process that you're speaking to them. In fact, much of the time, especially if you yell a lot, you're background noise.

Third, in most homes children have learned that they don't have to pay attention the first time. From another room, parents raise their voices, calling out inquiries without waiting for responses and giving directions without any clue as to whether that child is paying attention. After a while, a child learns to grunt or say "OK" in response. Don't delude yourself that he heard or paid any attention—much less understood—what you said. He didn't. The only reason he says anything is because experience has taught him that if he doesn't say something, you'll keep bugging him. This pattern has led to most children's unconscious realization that if the direction is important, a parent will repeat it. And if the direction is really important, the parent will repeat it at high volume. Therefore, when parental noise hits a certain decibel level, they've learned it's time to sit up and pay attention. So, go find him and then give your direction. Don't waste your time yelling from another room.

Quick Tip

It is more effective—and less taxing on everyone's nerves—to expend the effort to walk to wherever your child is, touch him on the shoulder or otherwise ensure you have his attention, and then give your direction.

Yelling may be an indicator of household stress. It may be a function of job-related pressures, financial problems, marital difficulties, or your own mental health problems. It may even be a by-product of coping with a challenging child. Whatever its cause, yelling is not going to improve the situation. It certainly won't change your child's behavior and it can increase the stress level. If you find yourself yelling, determine which of your child's behaviors you're trying to change and decide how to reinforce the behavior you want to see.

Yelling may also signal the emergence of some new, annoying behavior in your child. These are normal limit-testing, impulsive, immature, too-little-sleep-last-night (child or parent), Mom's-just-about-had-it behaviors. For these, we have a different approach.

Reducing Negative Behaviors

"COUNTING OUT": AN EASY TECHNIQUE TO REDUCE BAD BEHAVIOR

Sharon: Parents love to count. "I'm telling you, you have to the count of three to get up those steps and into your room." Or, "I'll give you until the count of ten to pick that up and put it back where it belongs." Then there's the countdown to explosion. "You have until the count of five to stop that. And I mean stop it completely. That's one. This is not a game. You're really trying my patience. That's two. Did you hear me? I'm not going to put up with this. That's three. I'm telling you, don't do that again. That's four.

You don't want me to reach five. Okay, that's five. You really pushed me too far this time . . . !"

In wrestling, the referee counts to ten, but in a family, children have no idea what today's count is. They don't know whether to expect a lecture at the end of each number or the consequence for failing to comply with the mystery count. Moreover, parents use counting differently every time. And with all that talking between numbers, who can keep track of the count? To be effective, counting needs to be done the same way every time.

A counting procedure gives your child a limited time to change his behavior before he incurs the consequences. With a structured—and unvarying—counting procedure, your children know how long they have to shape up . . . or else . . . and it's critical that they know what that "or else" will be. For example, give Junior until the count of three to stop teasing the dog or he has to go to his room for five minutes. Give your children until the count of four to stop bickering or you'll pull the car over and sit for ten minutes (making them late to the movie).

GUIDELINES FOR COUNTING

- Each time a negative behavior occurs, the parent counts one number. That behavior "earns" a number. (Emphasize that the behavior "earns" the number to help your child make the connection between his own behavior and the outcome.) You can count different negative behaviors to reach "time-out."

- When you announce each number, hold up one, two, three, or four fingers, as appropriate, and identify the behavior that earned the number. For example, "That's one, for yelling. That's two, for calling names. That's three, for arguing. That's four, for arguing. You've earned a time-out." The most serious behaviors, such as hitting, earn an instant time-out.

- If you reach the final number (often three or four—but make clear ahead of time what it is), the child "earns" a quiet time or time-out.

- Set a timer for one minute. If he gets to the designated place for serving time-out before the timer rings, he owes a short time-out (e.g., five minutes). If he's not in the time-out place when the one-minute bell rings, he owes a long one (e.g., ten minutes).

- If he refuses to go to time-out, he will have no family privileges until he serves the time-out. That means no screen time (anything that uses a screen—TV, videos, computer, video games, Internet, etc.), no snacks or sweets, no outside play, no friends in the house— none of the big stuff you can readily control.

- Once in time-out, set the timer for the predetermined time, e.g., one minute per year of age. When it rings, calmly tell him time's up. No lectures, nagging, or sermonizing is allowed.

- If your child doesn't reach the final count within a fixed interval (such as twenty or thirty minutes), you start over. Any new misbehavior earns a new starting count of "one." You can't count him out for three behaviors that occur twelve hours apart.

- *Important:* Reinforce your child for intervals when he doesn't hit the final number. Offer an incentive to stop before he reaches time-out, rather than just the disincentive for going too far. Tell him he can earn the incentive if he doesn't earn time out during a specific interval such as an hour, a half day, or a whole day.

- If you're heading for a difficult situation where there is likely to be trouble, up the ante. Offer a double bonus if your child doesn't reach the final number.

Dr. Thomas W. Phelan, clinical psychologist and nationally known expert on ADHD, wrote an excellent book, *1-2-3 Magic,* which lays out a complete program that relies on counting to interrupt negative behavior. Whatever name you choose for it, once you establish a counting procedure, you should use it in all situations and the same way every time. Jan and Jamie named it "Three Strikes and You're Out." Another couple titled it "Four Balls and You Walk."

Briefly explain the counting procedure to your children, then check back with them later to see if they have any questions. Role play or practice the procedure so they understand what behaviors you will count and what the result will be.

For counting to work, the time between one and the final number must be relatively short (around a half hour, less if the child is younger, a little more if the child is a preteen). If he doesn't hit the final number until forty-five minutes after you first said "That's one," you start counting him out all over again. Make sure you allow time for him to understand what he has to do, pull himself together, and decide he'd rather knock it off than end up being counted out. Designate a specific time-out location in a quiet place where your child will have no access to TV, video games, or computer. Time-out isn't a reward; it's a brief exile away from anything that might keep the behavior going.

It is important to reward your child for not reaching the final number. That balances out the counting, especially on rough days when it feels like all you do is count. If your final number is three, by rewarding your child for going a period of time without reaching it, getting that reward eventually becomes the motivator for stopping at two (or one).

Counting has numerous benefits as a technique for interrupting negative behavior. Because it is so simple, anyone can do it. With only a brief explanation, your child easily understands it. Moreover, any approach that makes your response predictable will seem more reasonable to your child. When used properly, it meets all the criteria for effective punishment. (See Rules for Effective Punishment on page 123.) Counting provides a warning as well as a set beginning and end to a predictable punishment. Since punishment is most effective with a minimum of discussion, counting encourages your use of that all-important matter-of-fact tone.

Jan: This technique made sense and seemed easy to use. Even though we'd already made many changes in how we dealt with Theodore, we still needed a systematic method for halting the highly annoying, but not earth-shattering, stuff like Caroline and Theodore's bickering. Sharon suggested that we start with an adaptation of Phelan's *1-2-3 Magic.* Our version was: "That's strike one; that's strike two; that's strike three—you're out. Off you go to time-out." Then we'd set the timer for one minute for each year of Theodore's (or Caroline's) age. Initially, that meant Theodore went off for eight minutes; Caroline for eleven. When the timer rang, we'd go tell them they could come out of their rooms. Occasionally we'd add five minutes to the time if there'd been egregious mouthing off.

We usually forgot to specify what behavior we were counting, although the kids always seemed to know. We also didn't give them one minute to get to time-out because often they were as eager to get away from us as we were to get them there.

One of our goals was disengagement—time for all of us to cool off. The time apart almost always defused the situation. Using Theodore or Caroline's age for the length of time-out made sense as did having the timer, not us, determine when time was up. Since it was hard to curb our tendency to lecture, counting and time-out reduced our sermonizing by giving us the opportunity to cool down.

We had a real problem with Theodore's constant talking and questions when we watched a movie together. Although the incessant questions and comments stemmed from curiosity, his behavior was disruptive and drove us nuts. Answering all his questions meant we couldn't follow the movie ourselves. We would keep telling him to be quiet, "or else" (usually unspecified), but that didn't work and we invariably ended up yelling. So we decided to try this new counting procedure—but we didn't have much hope it was going to work.

We knew, however, that the purpose of counting was to establish a procedure and count when it was violated. In this case, that meant telling Theodore that if he talked during the movie, we were going to count. If he reached three, he would have to go to his room for eight minutes.

We settled ourselves in front of *Men in Black*, with Theodore fiddling with LEGOs. After no more than two minutes, he piped up with a question. "That's one," we said. No response. Shortly thereafter, he glanced at the TV and asked another question. "That's two," we declared. He looked up, startled that we were actually serious about this. He remained quiet another few minutes,

GUIDELINES FOR TIME-OUT

- The time-out procedure puts space between parent and child and between the child and anything that might perpetuate the behavior.

- Time-out should be in a quiet area, away from family "traffic," with no access to TV or computer. It can be on a mat, in a chair, or in a separate room.

- In a matter-of-fact tone, parents state the behavior, remind the child of the rule that was broken, then say "Time-out." No discussion until after the time-out, if then.

- Set timer for one minute to allow time for the child to go to the time-out spot. If he's there before the bell, he owes a short time-out. If not, he owes a longer one.

- The rule of thumb is that the length of time-out is based on age. A short time-out for a five-year-old is five minutes. A long time-out is ten minutes. Once he is in the time-out area, set the timer.

- Time-out is over when the bell rings, not before.

then piped up again. "That's three," Jamie said. "Off you go for eight minutes to your room." After a brief protest, he trudged upstairs. Eight minutes later, we told him he could come back downstairs, where he watched the rest of the movie without reaching three again. Surprised that this technique had worked, we began using it to halt those annoying, but not earth-shattering behaviors.

Counting was effective because it kept us from engaging in arguments with Theodore, which we never won anyway, and eliminated our delusion that we could persuade him through reason that behaving better was the right thing to do. We chose to use Theodore's room for time-out. There he could read books, play with LEGOs, or listen to music, but he could not use his Game Boy (which we removed) and he had no access to TV or the computer.

Theodore: The first time my parents used "Three Strikes and You're Out" I didn't really think they'd enforce the punishment, that it would just be a threat to stop what I was doing—"or else." Once I got used to it, it gave me a chance to calm down alone, which I really needed. It also worked for my parents because it allowed them to get away from the problem and cool off.

Sometimes, when I was really peeved at my parents, I would get myself counted out on purpose. I knew that my parents wouldn't let me just walk out on them—either I'd have to get counted out and be happy to be away from the yelling or put up with it for another half an hour. Nowadays, I've learned to better control my impulses and curiosity—all the things that would usually make them angry—and I don't get counted out much anymore.

7

"I Can't Take It Anymore!"

Devising Solutions for Specific Problems

Sharon: Children don't stop negative behavior because they suddenly realize it is better to engage in saintly, or merely appropriate, behavior. If they stop it's because there is some powerful incentive to do so, generally paired with a good reason not to go back to old ways. But stopping the behavior certainly isn't a result of suddenly seeing the light, much less being convinced by your lengthy sermons.

If you are the parent of a challenging child, or are challenged by a less-easy child, you're going to spend years figuring out ways to deal with your child's behavior. For the more serious behavior—such as substance abuse and violations of the law—you should seek professional help. For the less serious, but highly irritating behaviors, let me reassure you, you can make a difference. Some behaviors are easy to change; others are more difficult. Sometimes the structure you have in place to change behavior suddenly stops working. Sometimes new behaviors crop up. The solution is the same. Just keep going back to the basic process for changing behavior.

Follow the Steps for Changing Behavior at the end of chapter 5 (page 128). That process can get you back on track and help you cope with new negative behaviors. Sometimes incentives aren't enough. If the negative behavior continues to occur, you may have to add penalties. If so, refer back to the punishment guidelines we laid out in chapter 5. Remember that you have to make your expectations clear, lay out what the rule is, provide an incentive for following it, and stipulate what consequences will occur for violations. Be sure you have a way to document the process. Be careful not to put too many new things in place at the same time.

While the process may seem daunting at first (and time-consuming), and you find it takes effort to stay on top of it, it will come more easily with practice. The more you use this method for changing behavior, the better you will get at it. The more change you see, the more confidence you will have that you *can* deal with your child's difficult behavior in a positive fashion. Once you have these skills you can get back on track if things start to slide. Shedding old habits isn't easy but the results are worth it. You'll have a calmer household, happier child, and less stressed-out parents.

What follows are specific examples of behaviors that Jan and Jamie tackled. Keep in mind they targeted these behaviors one or two at a time and made changes over a long period of time. You might find some of their solutions useful for your family.

HOUSEHOLD CLEANUP—THE "SWEEP" CONCEPT

Jan: Nightly cleanup drove me nuts. I would nag a little, the kids would clean a little, I would yell a little, they would clean a little, I would scream a lot, and the house might finally get picked up. Sharon recognized regression to an old pattern and had a better idea. We should clarify our expectations, define a procedure that would include a negative consequence if expectations were not met, and introduce it on a daily basis. The result was our adoption of "Sweep."

"Sweep" is a procedure for household cleanup whereby kids scurry around picking up and putting away and the parent then checks, confiscating anything left behind, returning these items only after a child earns it with a subsequent clean "Sweep."

Sharon: Getting children to put things away is often a catalyst for family strife. Their definition of a clean room differs from yours and they rarely agree that your time frame or consequences are reasonable. "Sweep" does three things. It establishes a consistent definition of "cleanup," reinforces adherence to it, and provides a means to earn the return of confiscated items as soon as possible.

SWEEP
A PROGRAM FOR HOUSEHOLD CLEANUP

- *Define the area to be cleaned* (bedroom, family room, community property area).

- *Provide definition of "clean."* For example:
  - Books and magazines on the shelf.
  - Trash in the trashcan.
  - Dirty clothes in the hamper.

- *Determine time of sweep.* Sit down with all your children to explain the procedures at a time not connected with cleanup. (Use a timer to limit length of discussion.)

- Sweep occurs the same time every day.

- Give reminders ten minutes and five minutes before sweep.

- At time of sweep, adult enters with bag. Any items left out go into bag and are not available for use until they're earned back.

- A subsequent clean sweep earns child one item returned.

- A second consecutive clean sweep (next night) earns two items from bag, etc.

- If trash is left on floor, adult chooses one item properly put away and adds it to sweep bag for each piece of trash left out.

Taking away items permanently or for long periods of time only teaches children to do without them. Returning them when they have earned them gives children experience putting all toys away, rather than just learning to clean up a reduced inventory. Children do not necessarily like "Sweep" at first, but when used consistently, they adjust and cleanup becomes routine. Be aware that the value of the confiscated item can influence how hard a child works to get it back.

Theodore: Sweep was difficult to get used to because I would put things on my desk and my parents would sometimes sweep them. They hadn't completely explained what they meant by "clean." I would often forget to check places like the powder room and the sun porch and so I'd get things swept from there. I didn't like that.

Some things would get swept that I didn't much care about. Whether there was something in the sweep bag that I really cared about would often affect how hard I worked at sweep the next night. But now my sweeps are cleaner and I have to worry less and less about losing things. I'm also more careful about making sure that the things I care about are put where they belong.

INTERRUPTIONS WHILE ON THE TELEPHONE

Jan: Being a magnet for my kids (Theodore especially) when I was on the phone really irritated me. As soon as the receiver was in my hand, they'd come and pester me with questions that had to be answered that very instant. These often took the form of "permission" queries such as "Can I have a snack?" "Can I watch TV?" "Can I play on the computer?"

It's hardly surprising that the best time to ask parents for anything is when they're on the phone. Kids know that when you're focused on something else (like a telephone call), you're more likely to say yes just to get rid of them. Sometimes the converse is true—you're more likely to say no just because you're annoyed they're bugging you. However, I tended to say yes to get Theodore (or Caroline) to go away. Sharon devised a plan that clarified procedures for when I was on the telephone.

Over time, I altered how I handled telephone interruptions. I taught Theodore to distinguish between answers he *had* to have immediately and those he could postpone. Generally, of course, he concluded he *had* to have an answer immediately. My solution was to have him write down his question and put "YES. . . NO" after it. I could quickly scan it and circle my answer. This has worked reasonably well, though it took some instruction that

---

POSITIVE PRACTICE FOR TELEPHONE INTERRUPTERS

Experience has taught your child that by interrupting (usually insistently), you will give in and say yes to the cookie, TV, or going to the mall to get him or her to go away.

To teach your child not to interrupt, practice as follows:

1. Set a timer for a short period (1–3 minutes).

2. Announce that your child must play or wait quietly while you're on the phone, and promise that when the timer goes off, you will answer his questions.

3. Then practice by making a call. Call the weather, an understanding friend, the Sports Score Line, whatever.

4. When the timer goes off, hang up, praise him for being quiet, and answer questions.

5. Gradually increase the time he must not interrupt.

6. Practice the same procedures for incoming calls by having an understanding friend call at a specific time.

Note: This only works if you do not respond to or converse with your child before the timer rings.

when I circled NO, I was not going to explain *why* then. He had to accept my answer and wait for the explanation until I was off the telephone.

Sharon: This is an excellent example of teaching a preferable behavior *before* the situation arises rather than when it's already happening. When you're on the phone trying to get through a conversation, it's already too late. For a very young child, adapt the procedure by handing the child a card or picture depicting what she will earn if she waits to talk until the timer rings. When the bell sounds, you trade the picture for the earned treat. For an adolescent, Jan's adaptation of writing the question or comment is a great one. In both examples, the procedures are outlined and the positive outcome is the treat or an answer to Theodore's question. The negative consequence in the telephone training is a loss of the treat and, in Jan's adaptation, no answer to the question. The key to success is explaining your expectations in advance and clarifying what the outcome will be for both positive and negative behaviors.

GETTING THE DOG WALKED

Jan: Theodore wasn't the only one whose behavior needed to change. When we developed a morning routine for Theodore, we did a similar one for Caroline. One of the tasks on her morning list was to feed and walk the dog. However, since she caught the school bus before anyone else was up, we weren't always certain she'd done it. We began to suspect she was neglecting, at least occasionally, this unsupervised chore. One morning after she'd left, the dog seemed hungry, so I put some food in her bowl. When she wolfed it down and barked to go out, where she promptly did her business, I felt certain that Caroline had neither fed nor walked her—even though Caroline claimed she had when questioned later. After this happened a few more times, with a highly unusual "accident" indoors, we had to do something. We knew we had at least one option—Jamie or I could get up to ensure that Caroline did her job. That was unpalatable, but worse, it smacked of policing our generally responsible then twelve-year-old daughter, which we didn't want to do.

Sharon: Jan and Jamie wanted to be able to trust Caroline to walk the dog, but they needed a system to ensure she did. Caroline had to know that her parents had a way to check up on her, without overt policing. I recommended that they use a technique that Jan called the "Dog Walker's Check-In."

We agreed the procedure should be self-enforcing so it wouldn't entail the policing Jan and Jamie wisely wanted to avoid. I suggested that the night before, they place a colored marker (ribbon, piece of colored string) on a fence or post halfway through the

DOG WALKER'S CHECK-IN

1. To ensure that your child has walked the dog (in the morning), the night before, tie a brightly colored ribbon or highly visible piece of cloth or string to a fence, signpost, etc. at least halfway along the route.

2. Require the child to retrieve the ribbon to get credit for having done the walk. If it's not returned, count the job as not having been done. The ribbon can be left on counter as evidence of walk completed.

3. Vary where you put the ribbon so the child has to look for it.

4. Put it up after your child has gone to bed.

5. The ribbon can be used for evening walks as well. Just position the ribbon or cloth ahead of time.

6. Phase out the procedure by using the ribbon on an occasional basis.

usual route for the walk. Caroline would have to retrieve the marker to demonstrate she had indeed walked the dog.

The obvious benefit is that placing the marker takes far less time than accompanying the child while he completes the task. When parents insist on supervising, they eventually find themselves resentful at having to do so, which is not good for the relationship. Moreover, constant supervision takes time, which most parents can't afford. The result is that, in no time, parents quit and things go back to the way they were before.

USING A PRIVILEGE WITHOUT PERMISSION

Jan: We needed Sharon's assistance to solve another problem about which we often overreacted and punished Theodore excessively. He tended to sneak forbidden time on the television or computer and punishment alone hadn't stopped him.

Sharon: I devised a procedure that required Theodore to earn time to watch television. Earning chips for not cheating on TV proved to be such a powerful incentive that Jan and Jamie have adapted the basic concept extensively.

EARNING TV TIME

Instead of taking away TV for a month the night you catch your kid cheating and watching it when he isn't supposed to be, make your child earn TV time.

For each day the child doesn't cheat on TV, reward him with two paper clips (poker chips, etc.) entitling him to a half hour (or whatever agreed amount) of TV time. Record it daily on a chart on the refrigerator and put the chips in a jar. Make television time available every day. If he has enough chips in the jar, he can redeem them.

EARNING TV TIME (CONTINUED)

The penalty for cheating is removal of one chip for cheating plus the number of chips equivalent to the time the child watched TV—even if it was "just to check what was on." Or simply subtract ten minutes, or whatever amount was watched without permission, from the start of the next day's earned television time.

Note: You can also use this method for your child to earn "line time"—telephone, Internet, instant messaging, etc.

Sharon: This establishes a policy that includes a predictable response when he cheats on the privilege of watching TV. Theodore knows what will happen when he abides by the policy and what will happen when he doesn't—a good example of structure and predictability.

Jan: Earning TV time has worked remarkably well. The only problem is that occasionally we forget to put the chips in the jar when we're supposed to.

Theodore: This system has helped me stop cheating (though I still do sometimes). What I hate is when they catch me cheating when I'm just checking to see what's on and they take out two chips, even though I've only been watching for two minutes instead of a lot more.

PROVIDING PARENTS WITH INFORMATION ON SOCIAL ACTIVITIES

Jan: Once we had become somewhat adept at designing solutions for behaviors we wanted our kids to change, we started to look at setting up procedures that could *prevent* problems. One Saturday morning, we had to track down Caroline at the house of a friend where she had spent the night. She had neglected to tell us whether she would be at the house of the girl's father or mother—and phone calls to each place went unanswered. Suddenly, a little stolen TV time didn't seem so bad.

When we related this incident to Sharon, she recommended that we develop a "Party Permission Contract" and start to use it before Caroline's social life heated up.

Sharon: When your child goes to a party, as parents, you want to know where he will be, that the party will be adequately supervised by responsible adults, and that he'll return—safe and sound—when he's supposed to. Your child's goal, however, is not necessarily the same. Teenagers may not want you to know those details. They may not know them themselves.

How do you prevent fights over this? Establish a clear and simple guideline (preferably in preadolescence, before the party scene begins): no signed form, no party. This entails a standard form for your child to complete that provides you with the following: date; time; location of party; supervising adult(s) in attendance; telephone number at which the adult(s) can be reached; transportation to and from the party, with specified, designated nondrinking driver; and required time of return. The benefit of consistently using such a form is that it eliminates arguments. Moreover, it puts the child on notice that all of the points covered on the contract are important to you (and verifiable). There are several factors to making this system work.

1. Your child must fill out the form and hand it in before you grant permission to attend the party.

2. Requiring that your child fill out the time of return—regardless of whether he or she already has a standard curfew—serves as a visual reminder (without arguments) of what that curfew is.

3. Having both parent and teen sign reminds both sides that they have agreed to a contract. You've agreed that the child can attend; the child agrees that he is able to do so only if he observes the stipulated conditions.

4. Penalties for contract violations should be laid out in advance, preferably in written form. You can set specific penalties for violations of the contract in toto or, more reasonably, for violation of

any given provision. For example, if your child does not return by the stated time, he should know exactly what the consequences would be. For example, if he's fifteen minutes late, he must return fifteen minutes early from the next social outing; twenty minutes late means twenty minutes early next time, etc. Or he must do the dishes every night for the next week or he won't be permitted to attend the next social gathering; etc. If your child leaves the party for another location without first seeking your permission, the penalty could be requiring him to complete the form for post-school, weekday activities for one week.

5. Tell your child that if there is ever any question of drinking and driving, he or she must call you. In return, you will immediately drop what you're doing and pick your child up with no recriminations and no lecturing. This fosters trust between you and your child, acknowledges that some teens unfortunately do drink and drive, and encourages your child to feel safe in calling on you for assistance without incurring any penalty. This is particularly important for challenging children who are already more likely to take risks than their nonchallenging counterparts.

6. You should not penalize your child for using transportation home from a party other than that stipulated on the form if the designated driver has been drinking. Preferably, your child should seek your permission first. If you aren't reachable either to give permission or to pick your child up, it is better to trust him to get transportation with a nondrinking driver without your permission than to risk driving with someone who has been.

Jan: We first called it a "Party Permission Contract" but rapidly recognized that its utility covered far more than parties. So we renamed it "Social Activity Contract." We use it for everything: spending the night at a friend's house, school dances, going to the mall with a friend, private parties, and dates. Caroline responded with resistance, complaints along the lines of "I don't see why I have to go through all this rigmarole," and eventual sulky compliance. That doesn't deter us. We just remind her of that time when we couldn't find her.

SOCIAL ACTIVITY CONTRACT

I, _____ (child's name), request permission to attend a party, sleepover, or other social activity _____ (specify type) on _____ at the house of _____, located at _____ (address) or at the following site _____ located at _____ (address), from _____ A.M./P.M. to _____ A.M./P.M. The supervising adult(s) (must be over 25) are _____. Their phone number(s) are _____ and _____ and _____ and _____. I will be transported to the activity by _____ and from the activity by _____. If by car, the designated nondrinking driver is _____. I will be transported to activity #2 by _____ and from activity #2 by _____. If plans change, I will call you and leave a message regarding the activity, time, and change of location. If transportation is by car, the designated nondrinking driver is _____. I will return home by _____ A.M./P.M. I agree not to go anywhere other than the activities at the listed locations without seeking your permission first. If I cannot reach you, I will not go anywhere else. I agree to call you for a ride (without incurring any penalties) if the designated driver has been drinking. Note: there will be penalties for infractions of contract.

Signature _____ (your child)   Date _____

I agree that you may attend the social activity(ies) under the above conditions.

Signature _____ (parent)   Date _____

ARGUMENTS OVER SNACKING

To put it mildly, Theodore is a picky eater. He'd far rather eat snacks (particularly sweets) than well-balanced meals. Though he is very thin, we didn't want that to be an excuse for him to always snack on sugar-laden, fatty foods. We wanted him to have healthy long-term eating habits.

First we tried to ban snacks altogether to try to get him to eat meals. (Rule #1: No snacks between meals.) That was a flop. He either didn't eat snacks or he would sneak food out of the pantry, but he didn't eat his meals either.

Then we tried to link snacks to eating good meals. (Rule #2: No snack tomorrow unless you eat a good dinner tonight.) Another failure. Next we tried to control snacks. (Rule #3: The only snacks permitted are those in the prepared snack box.) That was a partial success, but he still sneaked food occasionally. It also led to arguments: "But I don't like what you put in the box." So we added consultation on snack contents. Then came: "But it's old and stale and I don't want to eat it." That led to refinement of Rule #3, or rather the creation of Rule #4: (Finish what's in the snack box, even if it is old, before getting new snacks.) While this now works fairly well, it's one (or rather, two) of those rules we have trouble remembering to enforce consistently.

SNACK GUIDELINES

- Make a list of acceptable snack foods. Include the quantity that constitutes a serving. For example, one apple, one package of cheese crackers, two packages of string cheese, two cookies.

- Use a lunch box or large pencil case.

- Decide on times when snacking is permitted. For example, between 3:00 and 4:30 P.M.; after dinner until 8:30.

- Write down time and quantity limits and post on the lid of the snack box.

- Reward snacking according to policy with increased say as to what goes into the box.

- Alternatively, each morning, pack your child's snack box with the designated amounts of allowable foods. You might offer your child several choices (graham crackers or pretzels; peanut butter and crackers or cauliflower and bean dip) as a reward for adhering to snack guidelines. The guideline is: When your box is empty, you're out of snacks for the day.

Sharon: Jan and Jamie originally implemented the snack box policy to reduce the small, daily skirmishes over what Theodore could eat and when he could eat it.

Theodore: The snack box works well sometimes and not as well other times. It doesn't work when I don't finish everything and let it sit for several days. The "eat what's in the box before you get new stuff" leads me to throw stuff away and hope I don't get caught so I can get new, fresh food. I get really mad if they catch me and won't let me replace what's in the box.

> ### Quick Tip
> ---
> A snack box can control access to and timing of between-meals food. Your child can earn a say in its contents by abiding by the rules governing its use.

Jan: The snack box has been especially useful at bedtime. It allows Theodore to have something to eat when he's reading in bed and it has eliminated (when we remember to use it) the "I'm hungry" excuse for not staying there. We remove the snack box before lights-out so he can brush his teeth.

THE FINE JAR: JOBS NOT DONE, CRUMMY JOBS, AND BAD LANGUAGE

Sometimes we've had a compliance problem—weekly chores don't get done or they are done poorly. Or the adults violate an unwritten rule and use bad language. We began to handle these compliance issues with one solution—the fine jar.

We posted on the refrigerator a written list of infractions we were focusing on, with the penalties written next to them. Monetary penalties were paid not to Jamie and me, but to the fine jar. When there was enough money in the fine jar, we ordered pizza. For example, when we concluded the kids were not doing some of their chores, up on the list went:

| *Job not done* | 1 dollar |
| *Towels left on floor* | 50 cents |

As circumstances changed, some things would be taken off the list; others would be added; and some would be refined. For instance, the kids complained that only their misdeeds were subject to fines, so they added:

| *Using bad language* | 10 cents |

That was aimed at Mom and Dad. When Theodore complained that "some people were doing a crummy job" on their chores (he meant Caroline), he added to the list:

| *Crummy job* | 50 cents |

Then, for the fifth day in a row, I had to wipe up bagel crumbs because Caroline hadn't put her bagel on a plate. Up on the list, I scrawled:

| *Bagel crumbs in microwave* | 50 cents |

Everyone got to identify problem areas and add things, which made each of us more willing to abide by the rules. All of us were subject to these rules, including Jamie and me. They were entirely separate from allowance and incentives earned for current target behaviors. (Theodore could earn fifty cents for turning off the lights, but still be fined for doing a crummy job vacuuming the breakfast room.) Penalties were exacted on the spot and enforced by Jamie or me—including if the kids caught us using bad language or forgetting to do one of our chores. Because the money in the fine jar was used for a family treat, that made it somewhat less onerous to pay fines.

Sharon: Some people aren't going to get bent out of shape by bagel crumbs left in the microwave like Jan. Others won't have to worry about walking a dog. But every family—even those without challenging children—has issues that are irritating and negative behaviors that can be tackled by behavior change principles, incentives, and creative thinking.

Techniques for Getting Back on Track

Jan: The truth is we get off track a lot. Progress is invariably followed by increasing expectations on our part that Theodore "ought" to be able to get it right every day since he got it right the last five days. Or because he's cleaned his room so well for five straight Saturdays, we expect him to do it well on the sixth. Then we blow up at him because he's not focused that day. No matter how many changes we make in his routines, how many structures we set up to help him get things done, or how many incentives we use to encourage good behavior, he still remains a challenging child. None of these things "cure" ADHD.

Worse, we get tired. Or overwhelmed. Or frustrated that it isn't all "fixed." We've got fine jars and mayonnaise jars filled (or not filled) with paper clips littering the kitchen. We have to make a special trip to tie a ribbon on the fence to ensure the dog gets walked. Yellow Post-it reminder notes compete with grocery lists and doctor appointment cards to litter the kitchen counter. We have to reprint morning lists and evening lists, fill snack boxes . . . it goes on and on. It is time-consuming and exhausting to have to be consistent. Theodore needs structure and predictability. Sometimes we get tired of the effort necessary to provide it. We get lazy more often than I care to admit.

When we do, we have to work at getting back on track. Here are some things we do.

GETTING BACK ON TRACK #1: WRITE IT DOWN

One of the best ways to get Theodore to do something is to *write it down*. Like many challenging children, he has difficulty following a series of directions. I started to keep Post-it Notes around the house so I could quickly pick one up and make a short list for him to follow. Lists serve several purposes. While they principally provide Theodore with a visual reminder, they also make us prioritize what he needs to do and force us to break down into achievable steps what we mean by such directions as "Pick up your room." So, instead of just verbally telling him, "Pick up your room," we write down:

Put dirty clothes in laundry basket
Put magazines on shelf
Put LEGOs back in box and put box on closet shelf

Theodore has become so attuned to this that when we forget and tell him, for example, "Set the table, then put your soccer shoes away, and take that box downstairs," he sometimes asks us to put it on a list. If we tell him, "Go pick up the stuff you left in the sun porch" and he embarks on that task, but we then remember we want him to set the table and tell him to do that, he'll sometimes complain, "I can't do two things at once. If you want me to do several things, write it down."

Whereas Caroline usually remembers the two or three things we ask her to do, Theodore's distractibility requires us to be more careful about issuing multiple directions and give him a visual reminder to keep him on track. We've reconsidered our thoughtless manner of issuing directions. While we are far from perfect, we have become more careful about how we ask our kids to do things.

Pointer for Effective Parenting

Write down your directions. Use bullet form. Then post it so your child has a visual reminder. Doing so has the added benefit of getting you to stop yelling.

GETTING BACK ON TRACK #2: START WITH INCENTIVES, NOT PENALTIES

We know we're in trouble if we catch ourselves meting out penalties to "solve" problems, instead of searching for an incentive that will make it worth Theodore's while to do what he's supposed to do.

Theodore: It really bugs me when we get off schedule, like for my evening routine, and it's my parents' fault. Then they get mad at me for not having my stuff done even though it was their fault. Because they're mad, they'll give me a time limit that's too short to get it all done and penalize me if I don't make it. It's not fair and it doesn't give me a reason to get things done faster. It works much better when they realize that it's their fault and let me earn chips for TV or computer if I get it all done. They don't do this often enough.

Jan: When we see we're running late, we start harrying Theodore and set a time limit to get things done. Too often we use a penalty, such as "If you don't get your lunch made and into bed in five minutes, we're going to take away a chip," instead of an incentive to make it worth his while not to dawdle.

Sharon: This is a classic illustration of why structure and predictability are so important. The family needs to adhere to the agreed-upon time, a half hour before bedtime, when homework stops—whether it's done or not. Theodore needs to know that every night all activity halts at 9:00 P.M. and he gets to eat dessert, then head for bed and read until time for lights-out. This example also illustrates why imposing penalties out of the blue doesn't work. It just ends up with your child convinced you are unfair and the punishment is unwarranted.

Theodore is absolutely correct that incentives are more likely to work. If your routine is disrupted, pick an incentive, not a penalty to spur compliance. As Theodore says, an incentive is far more effective.

Maintaining Good Behavior

REVIEW, REASSESS, AND RESTRUCTURE REINFORCEMENTS AND PENALTIES AS NECESSARY

If you want your child to continue to do what's required, you have to periodically review and reassess his behavior and the structures you've put in place—especially the incentives you're using. Today's problem may vanish tomorrow. But there is sure to be something that takes its place. Although parents must be vigilant about all their children's behavior, it is doubly important that they review and update approaches with their challenging child. Constant adjustments in the process are essential to ensure that the child maintains success.

Jan: To illustrate the importance of this reassessment, let's go back to "Earning TV Time" (page 161) and examine how we altered it as Theodore's interests (and behavior) changed.

EARNING SCREEN TIME

1. Award two chips at the end of each day during which your child does not sneak time at the computer, TV, or Game Boy.

2. Place chips in jar. They are then available for cashing in for playing time on the computer or Game Boy or for watching TV. Require your child to hand you the number of chips he intends to use. Then set a timer to ensure compliance.

3. No chips, no screen time.

4. It is your responsibility to ensure that your child has ample opportunity to use chips. It is your child's responsibility to ensure you put the chips in the jar each night they are owed to him.

For his tenth birthday, Theodore received two new computer games. These rapidly became of far greater importance to him than TV—at least for a while. Cheating on TV promptly ceased to be a problem; stealing a few moments (or considerably longer) with Sim City 2000 took over. So, we revamped "Earning TV Time" to include what Sharon called "screen time."

Initially, Theodore earned chips he could cash in for screen time if he went an entire day without sneaking time at the computer, TV, or Game Boy. Because this became such a potent incentive for him, we allowed him at different times to earn screen-time chips for everything ranging from completing his morning list to turning in homework to bringing home all homework materials. When money ceased to be an incentive, earning chips for screen time generally was.

The number Theodore could cash in was limited only by time available (including bedtime). Homework, chores, and scheduled sports or other activities came first. Sometimes we would allow him to use a limited number of chips as a break from long periods of weekend homework.

Earning screen time has consistently been the most powerful incentive we have had for Theodore for the last two years. While it has worked for a long time, I know the time will come when it will stop motivating him. Much though I hate the thought, no incentive lasts forever. We know that money is an inconsistent incentive, dependent on how full Theodore's money box is. Increasingly, giving him a mini menu of possible incentives helps us figure out what will work best.

Quick Tip

Provide your child a mini menu of incentives to choose from when adjusting procedures and structures to get back on track.

Similarly, we're constantly modifying systems we set up to help Theodore. Sometimes a structure works for a while and then stops.

So we have to adjust. Too often, it isn't the system's fault; things get off track because Jamie and I slack off. Maintaining consistency is hard work. I keep telling myself that putting forth that effort is what it takes to provide the predictability and structure that Theodore badly needs. The payoff has been a happier child and a far calmer household. That's worth it.

8

"How Is My Kid (How Am I) Ever Going to Make It through School?"

Parents and Educators Working Together

Theodore: I really like going to school a whole lot even though sometimes it can be a pain! What makes school hard for me to handle and keep my cool about is that I always try to push myself to do my very best and sometimes it doesn't pay off—like when I make careless mistakes on math (I knew what to do but copied something wrong). Or when I do something that takes a long time and I forget to turn it in on time. I get really frustrated because it feels like I wasted all that time and hard work.

Sharon: Challenging children and schools can be an explosive mix. Sometimes, just the demands of the setting—sitting quietly for extended periods, following multistep directions, and sharing the teacher's attention—are too much for the child. Difficulty in school is not a signal that your child is destined to struggle and fail later in life. School does not represent any experience or situation that will need to be repeated as an adult, unless your child becomes a professional student. Where else will he be asked to sit for six hours every day, exposed to information half of which he will not use again or has little or no interest in, without being paid to do so? His classroom difficulties therefore may have nothing to do with his intellectual functioning or his potential for mastering the academic material, but may stem from the school's having behavioral or processing requirements that are not a good match for your child.

The challenging child often encounters a rocky educational road. Those years are likely to be equally tumultuous for you as the parent sharing the experience. Sometimes a teacher first calls attention to your child's struggles. Often, however, an educator merely confirms what you already knew on some level. In either case, the conference that initiates this difficult and unsettling relationship with the educational community is one a parent never forgets.

SIGNS OF A CHILD'S STRUGGLE TO GET BY

On the preschool level, teachers notice the child who can't sit still, doesn't stay with the group, has trouble following directions, is too aggressive with peers, or can't share. Teachers' concerns increase when they see behavioral outbursts. This may include refusing to follow directions, running out of the room, destroying peer materials and more purposeful aggression, even toward adults. Signs that things are not as they should be include a child's wanting to avoid school and saying that nobody, including teachers, likes him. A preschool child should not feel this way except occasionally.

In elementary school, attention and academic issues add to the mix. Teachers become concerned if a child is easily distracted, doesn't finish work, can't keep up with the others, and isn't picking up concepts. Sometimes they notice a child isn't making friends. A teacher's report of social difficulties can confirm parents' worst fears as they see birthday party invitations drop off, play dates become scarce, and their child's peers calling less and less often.

At this stage, school should be a positive experience. It's a valid concern if your child says he doesn't want to go to school—and he's only in second grade. There are so many years ahead of him. How will he (and you) get through them?

By middle school, a challenging child may know administrators and counselors as well as he knows classroom teachers. Worse, they probably know him equally well. Six educators—instead of just one or two—may echo reports of your child not getting work in on time. A floundering child may vacillate between the role of class clown and class tough guy, or he may become withdrawn, unusually reactive, or moody—that is, if he hasn't given up entirely. Peers notice these behaviors and the teacher's response. Most children who come home with nothing to say about school can name every child who got in trouble that day. Your child may acquire a reputation that is hard to live down. A struggling child may be the victim of teasing or he may be the troublemaker on the bus (if he makes the bus at all). And, to make matters worse, the preadolescent attitude that was just starting to appear in fifth grade has emerged.

By high school, that adolescent attitude is full-blown. Some parents can't even talk to their child—challenging or not. If they can get him up and to school, his peer group—not his classes—is the lure. Monitoring his schoolwork is next to impossible because he refuses to show his parents his assignment notebook—and resents their asking to see it.

Unless they communicate directly with teachers, interim grades or progress reports (if the school system has them) are the first parents may know of impending failure. By then, it is almost too late to complete all missing assignments, get the projects done, and study enough to offset poor test and quiz grades.

Every challenging child faces some of these issues at one time or another. Your challenge is figuring out when the situation is serious enough to warrant taking action. Look for trends instead of reacting to incidents. One or two rejections are part of growing up; chronic rejection should not be. Chalk up an occasional missed assignment to forgetfulness; constant missed assignments may indicate a larger problem. Get more information from teachers *before* you draw conclusions. Talk with your child, not at him, and listen more than you talk. Listen when he's in the backseat talking to friends. You may learn a lot. Then talk over your concerns with someone else—your spouse, another parent, or the guidance counselor—to get some perspective.

Jan and Jamie struggled with many of these problems. They also faced a host of other difficulties, including the daily nightmare of trying to get homework done, other children teasing Theodore, and teachers who did not understand his needs, much less know how to accommodate them. They had to learn strategies for working with and educating teachers and school administrators.

PICKING UP ON SCHOOL PROBLEMS

Jan: Theodore started day care at three months, and though he wasn't as easy as Caroline, we didn't receive complaints about his behavior until kindergarten. At the age of four he attended a Montessori preschool where we thought he would thrive in the intellectually stimulating environment. To our surprise, he didn't. Much later we understood that because of his ADHD, he lacked the self-direction needed for an unstructured Montessori environment.

Kindergarten was not a success either. His teacher was inflexible and considered his classroom behavior disruptive. He interrupted and talked constantly. While we knew that his rapid speech could make it hard for others to understand him, we attributed his interruptions to his vast intellectual curiosity. He always had "just one more question" that had to be answered, whether it related to the teacher's lesson or some tangential thinking on his part. The teacher tried to modify his behavior, but we thought her approach was too punitive. She imposed penalties for interrupting but no rewards for not doing so. (We didn't recognize until his ADHD diagnosis that we approached behavior problems the same way.) Theodore got plenty of penalties, but his behavior didn't change. I couldn't decide whether she didn't like the behavior—or Theodore.

We also sensed that he didn't fit in well with his classmates—a problem that would later become more pronounced. Theodore had fewer friends than in preschool and more trouble getting along with his peers. We weren't sure what to make of this.

First grade was better. He had a respected teacher and his class was also unusually small. However, the teacher's strict behavioral expectations weren't a good match for Theodore. Although no one said he was hyperactive, his restlessness (bothering his neighbors, fiddling with stuff in his desk, and difficulty sitting for long periods) created some problems with the teacher and his classmates.

We got accustomed to complaints about his interruptions. At home, we encouraged him to say: "Excuse me, I have something to say." That worked reasonably well, though not always. We had to acknowledge his desire to talk and assure him that we would listen, if not immediately, then shortly. It taxed everyone and wasn't a strategy likely to work at school.

The first academic problem surfaced with spelling. He hated it, couldn't remember how to spell many easy words, and dreaded the weekly tests. We grew to hate it too since we had to drill him. Those sessions often ended with us yelling and him in tears.

Theodore's marvelous second-grade teacher was more flexible in her expectations for behavior. Complaints diminished, but didn't cease. By then, we'd started warning teachers about his retreating into books when overstimulated or upset. As the homework load picked up, getting it done became a daily struggle. Spelling continued to be a nightmare. Moreover, his teacher reported Theodore's increasingly strained relations with his classmates, which neither she nor we understood.

In third grade, the intensification of his problems resulted in testing that led to a diagnosis of attention deficit disorder. At last, with a label, we were able to begin to understand what was creating the difficulties for him and his teachers.

SHARING TEST RESULTS

While we had always worked with teachers, Theodore's diagnosis meant that working in concert with them became essential—not merely desirable. Since his teachers had suggested the testing, we shared the results with them and the principal with the caveat that we did not want the system formally to label him as having ADHD. While not ashamed of it, neither were we comfortable having Theodore stigmatized as a "disabled" or "dysfunctional" kid.

Although we understood that ADHD was a diagnosis that entitled him to special assistance by the school, we also saw it as something that could be used by others to label him as "different." His ADHD didn't impair him to the extent that we felt he needed special accommodations by the school, such as extended time on tests. But we knew that Theodore already felt "different," and did not want attention drawn to that by a formal ADHD label. Moreover, we knew there were teachers who didn't believe ADHD was real—that the behavior manifestations were merely "bad" behavior. While we trusted his current teachers, we couldn't ensure that he always would have understanding and sympathetic ones. We preferred to work informally with his teachers and the school system—at least for the time being. We provided each of his teachers with the test results but retrieved the copies so they wouldn't inadvertently lodge them in his file. While we may have overreacted, it felt necessary at the time.

I don't necessarily recommend that all parents do as we did. Rather, they should think through carefully what the school's general attitude is toward students with disabilities and what the best approach may be to getting the help they need for their child. In most cases, having test results in the child's file will better serve his needs.

Sharon: If you receive a formal diagnosis for your child or consult with specialists, you may be uncertain about whether to share information with the school. In the case of a formal diagnosis, you may struggle with whether to seek formal, legally mandated accommodations.

With some reservations, I advocate sharing information. I have concerns about telling a teacher your child's diagnosis without providing supplemental reading material that explains the disorder. Specifically, if your child is enrolled in a private school that is known for its rigid stance regarding individualizing for students with special needs, discretion is advised (at least until you find an alternative program). However, there are teachers in such schools who will be attentive to problems once they become aware that testing has determined that there are specific issues that should be addressed.

Whether you share the results of testing formally, or informally as Jan and Jamie did, depends on your individual situation. Education is a partnership formed on your child's behalf. You can't have a real partnership if one side withholds information. Separate the decision to share information from your fear that doing so may result in some sort of label. Tailor what you say and some of the terms you use to what you already know the teacher's views to be. If you are unsure, meet first with the counselor or the school's special-education specialist to learn when and in what manner to present the information.

Parents of other children whose needs the school is meeting successfully are often good sources of information. They have already struggled with the same issues you face and have insights you may find helpful. Their information can spare you unnecessary work and angst. Many school systems have parent resource centers, ably staffed and run by those with information, experience, or access to both.

Be wary, however, of gathering all your information from disgruntled parents, as there often is more to the story than they can or are willing to say. They have their own axes to grind. Often, their situation is the result of having gone about their mission the wrong way. Or they may not have exhausted all avenues available to them. Unfortunately, some parents have unrealistic expectations of what the system legally is responsible for providing. Even if the information is correct, what you learn from someone who is disgruntled is what not to do.

IMPORTANT FEDERAL LAWS

Jan: We knew that we had legal leverage to ensure that Theodore's school would meet his needs. Sharon filled us in on our legal rights.

Sharon: The two relevant federal laws are the Vocational Rehabilitation Act Amendments of 1973 (Section 504) and the Individuals with Disabilities Education Act (IDEA) or Public Law 101-476 (1990), which is the new name for the Education for All Handicapped Children Act (Public Law 94-142) of 1975. Under IDEA, children with disabilities who are demonstrating significant difficulty in their school and/or academic performance are guaranteed a "free appropriate public education." "Appropriate" (not "ideal") means the school system is responsible for providing an education by teaching in a way that enables the child to learn. Therefore, the school must determine a child's level of cognitive and academic functioning, what he needs to learn, and how to meet his educational needs. If the school system cannot provide an appropriate education, it must explore other options, including paying to send the child to a private or residential school.

Once a child is found eligible for services and/or accommodations, based on evaluations, parents, educators, and often the child meet to develop a written Individualized Education Program (IEP). The IEP spells out exactly what accommodations the child needs to achieve academic success. These mandates apply to students with a full range of disabilities—including developmental delays; emotional, physical, and learning disabilities; hearing and visual impairments; and, in increasing numbers, ADHD. Accommodations are child-specific and depend on what is already available. They can range from Braille textbooks for a blind student or a full-time aide for a severely developmentally disabled child to extended time on tests for a child with ADHD.

Jan: At the time of his diagnosis, Theodore did not need special accommodations. Although we and his teachers believed he was not performing to his capability, none of us felt that the usual accommodations for children with ADHD were necessary. We recognized, however, that we might later conclude otherwise.

Working with Teachers

ESTABLISHING REGULAR COMMUNICATION

The most important step we took with Theodore's third-grade teachers after his diagnosis was to establish a system for regular communication. We agreed to talk at the end of each week. Both teachers gave us their home telephone numbers, which allowed us to reach them outside of regular school hours. We didn't have to rely on a formal conference or catching a few moments before or after school.

Quick Tip

Develop an effective method of communicating on a regular and frequent basis. Talk with the teacher and agree on the method for exchanging information. Use a form that asks one or two questions, a journal, e-mail, and conferences, or, when a teacher offers, home telephone numbers. On an as-needed basis, leave a note in a teacher's mailbox or a voice-mail message.

In subsequent elementary grades, we adopted different strategies. When we let regular communication lapse with his fourth-grade teacher and she had not recognized that deteriorating grades and behavior signaled that his medication was no longer working, we set up weekly before-school conferences with her and Theodore. That gave her an opportunity to review his behavior over the past week and alert us to any problems. Regular conferences also gave us an opportunity to educate her about attention deficit disorder and suggest ways to deal with problems. Having Theodore present told him we were all concerned that he do well and were working together to that end.

Quick Tip

If you have specific concerns, establish a regular time to meet with your child's teacher. Though useful on a weekly basis, meetings can become less frequent as needed. Including your child, if appropriate, makes him part of the process and conveys that you are all working together on his behalf.

Theodore: I think parents and teachers meeting on a regular basis is good because parents can find out how their child is doing and if there are any problems. I liked them because they helped me learn about things my teacher was noticing so I could work on changing them.

Communicating with Post–Elementary-School Teachers

Jan: It was much harder to coordinate with six middle-school teachers than it had been with a single elementary teacher, but the need for regular communication didn't diminish. Written notes that had been effective with elementary teachers didn't work as well with Theodore's middle-school teachers because I couldn't rely on him to pass them on. Voice-mail and e-mail messages worked better; so, too, did occasionally stopping in to see a teacher before or after school. With one who always had lots of kids for after-school assistance, I could count on talking with her after she finished with her students. I knew this was a special situation and was careful not to abuse it. Jamie and I also periodically scheduled conferences with Theodore's team of teachers.

The benefits of regular communication were obvious. We wanted to elicit teachers' cooperation—not hostility. Letting them know we cared about how Theodore performed in their classrooms made it more likely that they would deal with him in positive ways. Regular communication also allowed us to educate teachers (at least those who were willing) about how ADHD affected him. Theodore was able to perform better when he felt a teacher liked and supported him. It wasn't so much that we wanted teachers to cut him some slack (though I longed for that at times). Rather, we wanted them to understand him. If he read while the teacher was lecturing, it wasn't that he was being disrespectful—or even that he wasn't paying attention. Some teachers would try to "trap" him by calling on him when they thought he wasn't paying attention—only to find that he could repeat what they said verbatim.

Theodore: I generally like my teachers, but some I like even more, especially those who understand who I am and how my mind works. Teachers usually treat me like any other kid, which I'm glad for. I respond best to teachers who really push kids to learn, but not too much. It's the right amount when I'm pushed to do more than my usual standard, but not until

I'm doing more than I really can do comfortably.

Jan: Regular communication also gave us early warning of problems. We repeatedly discovered when we let communication lapse things cropped up that could have been nipped in the bud if we'd known about them.

Other Ways to Get Information on Your Child at School
Jan: Observing Theodore's elementary class was allowed, but I rarely did it since it made him self-conscious. Instead, I attended activities to which parents were invited, particularly those in his classroom, which would let me observe him discreetly. In-class performances, sometimes followed by lunches, and opportunities to talk to his class on "career day" or report on overseas travel for social studies helped me assess how he was doing. I also went on occasional field trips.

Theodore: I don't think that any kids like to have their parents watching them because they'll feel embarrassed. I know that I didn't want my parents there. Sometimes I wouldn't even let them come to a performance if I was afraid I might screw up. Whether I wanted them to come on a field trip depended on what the trip was. I wanted my parents to come on certain trips, but not on others. The zoo was OK, but Colonial Williamsburg or Outdoor Lab—uh-uh.

Jan: On one field trip, the long, noisy bus ride convinced me that Theodore should no longer ride the bus to and from school. No wonder he arrived at school too overstimulated to settle down when the teacher called the class to order. Driving him to school meant I delivered a far calmer child and could occasionally check in briefly with his teacher.

Quick Tip
- -
Consider taking your child off the bus. Some kids do better if they walk or go by car, carpool, or bicycle.

> School buses can be crowded, noisy, and poorly su-
> pervised. That environment is difficult for many kids,
> but for others it can be a disaster.

Theodore: I always hated riding the school bus because kids were so rowdy and the bus was too noisy. It would get me too pumped up and made it hard to settle down once I got to school. It was much better when I stopped riding the bus because I had more time to do my morning list and I didn't get pumped up. I was able to start class and be focused.

Sharon: Jan's idea to remove Theodore from the bus was the ideal solution for Theodore. Because the bus came so early, the new plan gave them fifteen extra minutes in the morning. But it just as easily could have exacerbated the morning stress. After all, now if he was late, so was Jan or Jamie. In many cases, family demands and schedules make it impossible for a parent to transport the child to school.

The bus driver's principal focus is safety and transportation, not behavior management. If the bus is a hotbed for behavior problems, it's unreasonable to expect the driver to address, much less solve them. Instead, parents should work with the school to establish a procedure for addressing bus issues. A process to reduce the frequency of certain problems should include:

- Guidelines for proper bus behavior

- Consequences for violations

- Enforcement mechanism, such as safety patrols

- Procedures for reporting and discussing problems, which should include getting the views of kids other than those involved in any incident.

- Ways to implement changes.

ESTABLISHING A POSITIVE PARTNERSHIP WITH TEACHERS

Jan: Regularly exchanging information helped us bolster what the teachers were doing and vice versa. By sharing what we did at home, the teacher could reinforce cues we used with Theodore by doing the same at school (such as a silent hand motion to "slow down your speech").

Sharon: Parents are an excellent resource for teachers. While some teachers are more receptive than others, how the message is delivered is critical for all. If your suggestions are made as demands, the teacher's response is likely to be defensive, if not hostile. Don't make your first communication confrontational and demanding. Likewise, if you toss off valuable techniques as passing comments when you pick up your child in the afternoon, the teacher will not give them the weight they deserve—or even remember them. While most teachers appreciate your interest and your sharing useful information, the written word, followed by the opportunity to discuss it, is more effective. Write a letter with your suggestions that the teacher can read at her convenience. Then meet at a mutually convenient time. This two-step process helps create an atmosphere of mutual respect and professionalism conducive to a productive partnership on your child's behalf.

Everyone has something to bring to the table. You know your child and may have insights on what works for him at home. The teacher knows the current classroom situation, the students, the curriculum, the problems, and the approaches tried to date. You both want to establish a partnership for successfully educating your child. Once you've learned which approaches work at home, you can suggest techniques that can be adapted for classroom use.

Most strategies effective with challenging children also help typical children. A teacher quietly giving a student a thumbs-up rewards the child for being on task. Holding up a blue legal pad as a prearranged signal that there is too much noise and "I'm taking names" is a useful, anonymous, visual cue. As a class-management technique, the blue pad gets everyone's attention. Most teachers appreciate approaches that benefit all children in a classroom.

Quick Tip

Approaches and tools that work with challenging children are equally useful for all students.

Only a very small percentage of educators receive any formal instruction in behavior management. Specific information on special needs is often limited to a survey course on special education. Teachers, therefore, may be ill equipped to address the challenges your child presents.

The best techniques, particularly visual cues, which are effective for virtually all kids, are fruitless unless a teacher explains them thoroughly—including what the positive and negative consequences will be for the student—and then uses them consistently.

Quick Tip

Visual cues are effective because they don't disturb the flow of teaching.

Informing a teacher of what has worked for past teachers is particularly profitable. Doing so spares teachers the job of reinventing some wheel that's already proved effective. All too often, the most successful approaches die at the end of the academic year. Rarely is there a formal system for passing on this information. If you ask a teacher to jot down aspects of classroom structure and techniques that were especially helpful to your child, you can provide this information to next year's staff. Be aware that some of the best teachers just know what to do intuitively and can't always identify what they do that works for your child.

Finally, ask your child's current teachers to meet with next year's staff to share information about your child. That way the new teachers know that whatever you suggest already passed muster in the classroom. Teachers are more likely to adopt a technique that you know works for your child if another teacher recommends it.

> ### Quick Tip
> --
> Ask your child's teacher to write down what techniques and classroom structure have worked for your child. Then you can pass it on to next year's teacher—or better yet, ask the current one to do so.

Whatever strategies teachers implement will be far more successful if parents support them. Support, however, can take many forms. Some teachers will seek your advice and assistance whereas others just dump the problem back in your lap. Those looking to you for ideas do so because they've exhausted their own bag of tricks. Offer your cooperation and input with a tactful reminder that if you knew how to solve your child's problem, they wouldn't be seeing it at school. Pass along what you have read and approaches used by past teachers that were successful. Make sure that your response conveys a spirit of partnership and collaboration. The goal is to reinforce one accomplishment that can often lead to others. Nothing breeds success like success.

Whatever their teaching style or classroom structure, teachers should consider the following in developing their behavioral interventions:

- Define and reinforce the behavior you want to see.

- Assign a role or responsibility to the student.

- Then make sure he gets noticed for getting the job done.

ACTING AS YOUR CHILD'S ADVOCATE

Jan: We've learned the hard way that there is a difference between trying to solve your child's problems for him and acting as his advocate when he's in over his head or unable to resolve something. By the time Theodore was diagnosed with ADHD, I had realized that he didn't have the emotional resources or the ability to solve all the problems he was encountering. I tried not to step in too quickly to give him time to work things out on his own. Sometimes holding back worked. Other times, I waited too long. The reality is that a challenging child has to have an adult on his side—someone who not only can but will intervene on his behalf. My goal is to reach the point where we never have to intercede on Theodore's behalf—that he can negotiate the system on his own, whether it is at school, with other kids, or in activities he participates in.

Although I have the same goal for Caroline, with Theodore, the need for help was more apparent and the obligation to back off was less evident. Accurately assessing where we are on that continuum is difficult. Until he can be his own advocate, Jamie and I have to do it for him. As he has gotten older and more adept at handling things, we have had to do it less often, particularly when he needs a teacher's help with schoolwork.

Differentiating between Advocacy and "Crutch" Behavior

Sharon: All parents, at some time, face decisions about whether to step in or let the chips fall. When your child is more challenging, this dilemma occurs more often. The hardest line to walk is between being an advocate for your child and becoming a crutch. When does championing his cause and helping others understand his needs become enabling his dependency and excusing his shortcomings?

Unfortunately, there is no definitive measure of where one ends and the other begins. There are no alarms to signal when you have moved from the necessary role of advocate to that of crutch. If you bear in mind that independence is one of the greatest gifts you can give your child, the distinction is easier to see. When you do the task for him, you effectively say that his limitations are so debilitating that he is unable to do it himself. You are telling him he is too handicapped to do this without you. When you go to the teacher and "explain" his behavioral or academic lapses, you are asking her to excuse him from learning how to handle that situation better.

Think of what message your child gets when a behavioral issue arises. Typically, a note comes home, you meet with the teacher, then interpret the problem and solution to your child. The message that conveys, however, is that you have to handle these matters,

---

TEACHING YOUR CHILD TO TAKE RESPONSIBILITY FOR SOLVING BEHAVIORAL PROBLEMS AT SCHOOL

1. When a behavior problem arises, meet with your child's teacher (or appropriate school administrator) to determine:

   • What the problem is
   • What needs to be done to address it

2. Arrange a follow-up meeting that will include your child.

3. Before you discuss what you learned from the school, ask him what he thinks the school's concerns are. Only after you solicit his views should you convey what you've learned. (This gives your child a feeling that this is an exchange of information, not just an attempt to "fix" him.)

4. Brainstorm solutions.

5. Prepare your child by practicing ways to respond to what the school will say.

6. Have your child attend the meeting with the school— without you if appropriate or with you if necessary.

7. Get feedback from the school on how the meeting went.

8. Ask your child how it went from his perspective.

not him. That may be fine when your child is six, but it's not OK when he's older. Moreover, it inadvertently teaches him not to talk directly to teachers. It shouldn't be surprising that he is unwilling to go to the teacher for extra help or to resolve concerns when he's in the higher grades.

There is a better way. Meet with your child's teacher to determine what the problem is and what needs to be done to address it. Arrange for a follow-up meeting to include your child. Then ask your child what he thinks the school's concerns are and brainstorm strategies for handling the situation the next time it occurs. Prepare him by discussing what he thinks are appropriate responses and have him practice what to say. It may not even be necessary for you to attend. Ask the teacher to let you know how it goes from her perspective. Compare that with your child's assessment.

Training your child to solve his own school problems is essential. After all, it's his life—not yours. Moreover, while it is important for you and the teachers to understand the problems of a child with special needs, it is equally if not more important that *he* understands them. It is the only way he will learn what works and how to advocate for himself. Teachers change every year and you won't (and shouldn't) always be there to interpret for him. The choice is simple. He can either come to the conclusion that he is less intelligent or lazy (an adjective often used by educators and parents to describe these children) or he can understand that he learns differently. This difference means that he may have to work harder or demonstrate mastery of academic material in a different way. It is not an excuse; it's an explanation.

The Role of the School Administrator

Sharon: Your child's teacher is a crucial factor in his educational success or failure. A bad match rather than poor teaching may be the cause of an unsuccessful year. A good principal is often the most reliable judge of a teacher's style and strengths. Whereas teacher selection and class placement are an important part of the elementary principal's responsibility, on the secondary level, the school counseling staff often participates in or oversees that process. In either case, you can look to the administration for determining a good fit between teacher and the more challenging child.

For children with special needs, you may have to deal with a range of school officials—primary classroom teachers, counselors, and special-needs instructors. Whether accommodations are made for your child or not, your goal is to have everyone working as a team on his behalf. Often it is the principal or other administrator who can best facilitate that. Successful cooperation requires tact, diplomacy, a polite demeanor, and persistence to ensure your child's needs are met.

Jan: In elementary school, we developed good working relationships with Theodore's principal and school counselor, not just his teachers. This mattered because we needed them to intervene at times when difficult problems arose, especially in the after-school program and on the playground. Tact, a deliberately nonconfrontational attitude, and careful cultivation of the relationship all contributed to building a good partnership. Most important, we prioritized and limited our requests. Administrators knew we already had tried to resolve problems directly. We worked hard not to antagonize and conveyed our desire to work together on Theodore's behalf.

Pointer for Effective Parenting

Tact, a nonconfrontational attitude, and careful cultivation of teachers and school administrators are essential for developing a cooperative team approach on your child's behalf.

However, we had to stay on top of his situation at school. It pained me that Theodore endured years of teasing and bullying and angered me that his elementary school did so little to stop it. The harassment didn't cease until his move to middle school, where he was no longer surrounded by that particular group of kids. For too long, we placed the burden of responsibility onto Theodore, believing that he needed to learn how to handle teasing. I regret that we didn't intervene more forcefully to find a way to halt it. No child should have to endure the hostile environment Theodore did.

PREPARING FOR TRANSITIONS

I started to prepare for Theodore's transition to middle school twelve months before. Because Caroline had attended the same middle school, we already had a good relationship with the principal. Preparing for Theodore's move, however, seemed more like launching a military campaign. Throughout the year before, I kept the principal apprised of Theodore's progress and then had a meeting that spring to discuss him in more detail. I got to know the head counselor, had Theodore's fifth-grade teacher meet with her, and asked Sharon to share her insights with both principal and counselor. Aware of his needs, the principal and head counselor weighed class placement and teacher assignments accordingly. Before school started, Jamie and I met with his new teachers to highlight Theodore's strengths and alert them to potential problem areas. All the effort paid off in a remarkably smooth changeover.

Theodore: I really liked moving to middle school. My new school was large with lots of kids. Because there were so many I didn't know, it was like starting all over in making friends. None of them knew I had ADHD, none of them knew I talked fast, or any of the things that had kept me from making friends in my elementary school. I began to make many new friends.

I liked my teachers a whole lot. They were all really nice—and very challenging. I also liked being in classes where the kids were really smart. I found the workload challenging to manage. Even though I had done a lot of work in fifth grade, I wasn't prepared for this much. The teachers all offered time for me to come in for extra help before, during, or after school. They did this for everyone—not just for me. It was a good chance for me to go in and ask them about things I didn't understand.

CHOOSING THE RIGHT TEACHERS

Jan: "Choosing" teachers is controversial for both schools and parents. Schools don't want pushy parents dictating class assignments, whereas parents want to ensure that their child has the "best" teachers. I switched from a laissez-faire approach to conveying our views about the next year's teachers after Caroline had a poor match one year.

In elementary school, I consulted with Theodore's current teacher about who would be a good fit for the next year. With the school's permission, I observed teachers in their classrooms to make my own assessment, which allowed me to make an informed decision. Some committed, excellent educators' teaching style or classroom structure weren't a good match for Theodore. I also paid attention to other parents' assessments of their children's experiences. Jamie and I then expressed our preference to Theodore's current teacher and the principal—and once even went to the next grade's teacher to let her know we hoped Theodore would be in her class. Our views represented what was a good fit, not an evaluation of teachers' competence. Providing useful information increased the likelihood that the school would consider our views when class assignments were made. There was, of course, no guarantee that the principal would honor our request.

Middle school was more complicated. We already knew some but not all of the teachers and since each grade was divided into teams of teachers, we needed to determine which group of teachers would best meet Theodore's needs. We focused on developing a good relationship with the head counselor and principal rather than on expressing a preference for a specific teacher or team. They did well by him.

"Expressing a preference" is a more accurate description than "choosing" teachers. I never felt it necessary to put our views in writing, though I knew a number of parents who did. A teacher at another school told me that school administrators looked more favorably on a parent's letter outlining the teacher characteristics that would serve their child's needs best than on a request for a specific teacher. Expressing our sense of what would be best for

Theodore gave us some voice (and, we hoped, influence) in the process, but we recognized it was the school's decision—not ours.

Specific School Problems: Homework and Projects

HOMEWORK

Theodore: Homework has always been hard for me. Usually it takes a long time to do because I have so much of it and it's difficult for me to pay 100 percent full attention to it. It's also not a lot of fun because it involves so much writing and I'm not good at writing with a pencil and paper. Because of that, I find it hard to organize my ideas and get them down on paper. I'm much better on the computer where I can go quicker and be much neater.

Usually homework is a war zone if I haven't taken my medication because then I get distracted so easily. That doesn't happen very often. But even when I've taken my medication, sometimes I don't understand the directions and think I've done something right. My parents know I haven't and we end up in a big fight and I storm off to my room and slam the door, which makes them even madder.

I really like to learn because I'm so curious about everything. What bugs me about school is that I really do work hard, but when it doesn't pay off, I get upset. I wish I had less homework.

Sharon: Parents are not educators. Even if you are, you should refrain from acting the part at home. Your role as parent is more important. Homework brings out the worst in everyone. It turns students into dolts and patient, understanding parents into inept, seething tutors. The process is rarely good for family relations, which is why it should not be a family endeavor. It should be an individual endeavor that needs structure and adult support.

The following is a four-step procedure with built-in incentives for structuring homework. With your child's input, it sets performance expectations based on his abilities and reinforces his behaviors with praise and rewards.

Discuss the process in advance, preferably several times over a few days to ensure everyone knows the drill. Do not spring a new structure in the midst of a homework battle, as if it were punishment for poor cooperation. After you've explained the new system, consider preliminary feedback like "You've really gotten a lot done on your own. If we were using the new system, this would have earned you five credits." You may even want to mark the points as earned for when the program actually starts.

Your child earns homework credits or points for each step. Award more points for the most difficult part of the process. If it is a huge battle just to get him to gathter his things and sit down, then step one should be worth more points. If the main obstacle is willingness to try anything without your talking him through it, then weight steps two and three more heavily.

Decide what privileges or rewards your child can earn. A certain

---

FOUR STEPS FOR STRUCTURING HOMEWORK

1. Sitting down without argument

2. Getting started independently

3. Working on and completing assignments

4. Reviewing work and making corrections

PROCEDURE

- Tell your child he can earn homework credits (chips, points, whatever) for each step.

- Agree on the number of credits he can earn for each step. Make the hardest steps for your child worth more points.

- Determine what privileges or rewards he can earn with homework credits.

- Decide how many credits he needs for each reward or privilege.

number of homework credits might buy screen time (television, computer, Internet, videos, video games), telephone time to talk to friends, a later lights-out or video-rental money. (See chapter 5 for more information on how to set up behavior change programs.)

STEP 1: SITTING DOWN WITHOUT ARGUMENT

List two or three acceptable places to do homework. Believe it or not, it doesn't have to be a place that is free of all noise and distraction. And it may not be necessary for your child to sit at a desk. Some children get more done lying on the floor, propped up on their elbows with a radio on, than seated at a desk in a quiet room. Provide a time sheet listing half hour increments. Determine an ending time for homework. This should be no later than a half hour before bedtime. You don't want your child using homework as an excuse to stay up later. Nor do you want such a potentially inflammatory activity to be the night's last task.

Ask your child to choose where he'll do his homework (from the

---

HOMEWORK TIME AND LOCATION SHEET

Location: _____

Start time: _____

Half-hour homework intervals (check times you plan to work):

3:00–3:30	_____	6:30–7:00	_____
3:30–4:00	_____	7:00–7:30	_____
4:00–4:30	_____	7:30–8:00	_____
4:30–5:00	_____	8:00–8:30	_____
5:00–5:30	_____	8:30–9:00	_____
5:30–6:00	_____	9:00–9:30	_____
6:00–6:30	_____	9:30–10:00	_____

A similar chart can be drawn up for weekends.

acceptable options) and to check on the time sheet when he will work (one half hour, two half hours, or whatever is an age- and grade-appropriate time to complete it).

Finally, ask him how many reminders he wants of the approaching start time. Generally, one or two reminders are necessary and sufficient. Your child earns credits if he is at the right place at the designated time, with only the one or two reminders.

Shortly before the agreed-upon time, announce, "Five minutes to homework." At the set time, announce, "Homework time, this is your second reminder." Walk to the designated place, even if you have to step over your child on the way, and if he beats you to the spot or, miraculously, is already there, he earns the first set of credits.

STEP 2: GETTING STARTED INDEPENDENTLY

After noting on the chart the first set of credits as "earned" or "not earned," set a timer for five minutes and *leave the room.* Your child earns the second set for taking out/assembling all needed materials including the assignment book, reading the directions, and actually putting pencil to paper or starting to read (whatever the first assignment calls for). At the five-minute signal, return to the work area and award points accordingly. Any evidence that he is prepared to start or has started earns the second set of points. Some children with specific learning disabilities need parents' help to read the directions and understand what needs to be done. You may need to be a scribe (for the child with writing difficulties) or reader (for the child with a reading disability). But they can demonstrate readiness by organizing their own materials. Remember, as long as you are in the room, you are an audience for questions or complaints. That sets you up for arguments. Answer any questions your child may have but *do not do the work with him.* However, make it clear you will return to give assistance or answer questions at the next interval. Initially, that interval may be two or three minutes. But it will gradually increase over time. Reset the timer and leave the room.

STEP 3: WORKING ON AND COMPLETING ASSIGNMENTS

This step is critical for building independent work skills. Often teachers report that students "won't get started" when the real issue is that they are so reliant on adult support to jump-start them and keep them going that they can't get started. This puts them at risk for poor performance or negative feedback at school, where they won't receive that kind of individual support.

Having reset the timer for fifteen, ten, or even five minutes, depending on how much help your child needs, return when the bell rings to give feedback, answer questions, or explain concepts. Your child can earn credits by having worked for the duration of the time or having completed a specific amount of the assignment (first five problems or questions, completed a paragraph or an outline). Before he begins, it might help if you break down a worksheet or task. Dividing an assignment into manageable parts can help your child get through it. Many times, a task that looks too long and overwhelming brings on homework-induced stupor or a tantrum. Awarding credits as each part is

HOMEWORK CHART

HOMEWORK BEHAVIORS	NO. OF POSSIBLE POINTS	POINTS EARNED
Step 1: Sitting Down without Argument:	_____	_____
Step 2: Getting Started Independently:	_____	_____
Step 3: Working on and Completing Assignments:	_____	_____
Step 4: Reviewing Work and Making Corrections:	_____	_____
Total Points Earned	_____	

completed reduces anxiety and facilitates your child's ability to work independently.

When you check in, do not stay more than one to three minutes—just long enough to comprehend the question and demonstrate how to do the problem or find the answer. The longer you stay, the more likely you will fall back into old habits of talking him through the process. That fuels his sense of dependency—that he can't do it without you. Demonstrating how to do something or find needed information gives him a visual reminder of the steps and instructions that he can refer to after you have left the room. Leaving the room gives him the opportunity to study the example and understand your explanation without the pressure to perform while you stand over him, asking, "Now do you understand?" While constantly going back and forth may seem hard, it's less wearing to reset the timer than to engage in pointless, unproductive fights.

When you help him, bear in mind that the deck is stacked against you. You are explaining something your child has little interest in understanding, at least not at the level you think he should. You won't be able to explain it the way the teacher did, a fact your child will point out repeatedly. ("That's not the way Mr. Williams said to do it.") Furthermore, after your first explanation, your child hears every subsequent clarification as "You were too stupid to get it the first time, so now I have to say it again." It doesn't matter that such a thought never entered your mind; that will be his interpretation. Often, you have slowed your speech down, overenunciating and there's a good chance your voice has a slight edge the second go-round. So give a concise explanation using written examples whenever possible.

STEP 4: REVIEWING WORK AND MAKING CORRECTIONS

This is the one aspect of homework for which you get clear support from the teacher. If you don't check it, the teacher will (or, at least, should). Most kids think homework is over when they're finished; going back and fixing mistakes isn't necessary. Counter this by awarding step-four credits during the last ten minutes for checking it with you and making corrections. For older students, award credits for showing you their work. First focus on what your child has done well. Emphasize the work he completed, the answers or parts that are correct, and the good work behaviors he demonstrated.

You may need to set specific standards for accuracy. If the homework before review is 90 percent accurate, he can leave it as is and still earn the credits. If he makes changes on the 10 percent that needs it, he earns bonus points. This encourages more careful work while reinforcing a willingness to make corrections.

Allow your child to exchange homework credits as he earns them, but don't give him advances. Modify your point system (how many points it takes to earn something) as needed, but keep it the same for a minimum of two weeks. It usually takes at least that long to establish new behaviors. Discuss with your child any changes in procedures before incorporating them. Sit down with him regularly (not while trying to get homework done) to evaluate how it is going and to express your appreciation for any positive changes you have noticed.

SOME FINAL THOUGHTS ON HOMEWORK

Homework is a large part of your child's education and is not going to go away. The earlier you establish homework guidelines and procedures to find positive ways to reward his efforts, the better the outcome will be for the whole family. If homework is already a battleground, you have nothing to lose. There are a number of excellent resources on study skills and homework strategies, including *Seven Steps to Homework Success: A Family Guide for Solving Common Homework Problems* by Sydney Zentall and Sam Goldstein and *Study Strategies Made Easy: A Practical Plan for School Success* by Leslie Davis et al., both listed in the Resources section.

If your children are still young, start a daily quiet time to establish the precedent. Having a daily homework interval of a set length makes excuses such as "I don't have any homework," "I finished it at school," or "I forgot my book" moot. If fun, more desirable activities are contingent on your child making good use of homework time, then excuses and rushing through assignments become pointless.

Talk to the teacher if, despite your and your child's best efforts, homework still drags on for much longer than it should. Ask how long the assignments should take. Most teachers want to know if a student is struggling. Since homework, especially in the elementary years, is principally for practicing concepts already covered in class or in the text, if a student is unable to grasp the material and perform in a traditional way, brainstorm other strategies with the teacher. Shortening assignments, such as ten math problems instead of twenty-five, or having a child dictate paragraphs instead of writing them out longhand, can help. Such adjustments may indicate your child needs special attention from the teacher or individual support from educators trained to address learning difficulties. If you continue to tackle these issues on your own and no one at school knows, your child's problems won't be addressed.

SCHOOL PROJECTS

Jan: I have a love-hate relationship with school projects that involve long-term deadlines and mixed media—the oral report accompanied by a poster or research project with a diorama. Although Theodore can allow his creativity to soar and impress teachers and classmates with such projects, they make our life a nightmare. They're so embedded in the curriculum of our school system that they even infect math—not just social studies and science. If Theodore could do them on his own, I'd think they were a great mechanism for in-depth learning. But he can't. Since we won't do them for him, that means we have to supervise, which more often feels like policing. School projects—and the accompanying tantrums and tears of frustration (Theodore's and mine)— have ruined innumerable weekends, holidays, and school vacations.

Theodore sees a project as this huge looming thing. Invariably we spend extensive time talking through what needs to be done, then helping him plan how to accomplish it. We have to help him divide the project into smaller tasks. Then we have to supervise. That includes helping to choose colors, outline maps, and oversee every step of the way to make sure he gets it all done. Jamie is usually designated as project coordinator.

Theodore: I'm not exactly enthusiastic about all the projects I have to do because there are so many. In sixth grade, I came home with a project to do almost every single week. Then I had to work like crazy over the weekend, which didn't leave any time for fun. Depending on what kind of project it is I may find it easy or hard.

I'm not crazy about projects I have to present to the class orally. I don't like standing up in front of people, especially my peers. I'm afraid I might speak too fast and they won't understand me. I'm also afraid they'll make fun of me if I'm told to slow down. The part I like is making a visual prop—like a poster or a diorama—because I like to do the artwork.

Sharon: Theodore isn't the only one who finds projects difficult. Most children—challenging or not— have difficulty with them. It is the rare parent who describes a child who accurately gauges the length of time it will take to complete everything, gathers the necessary materials, and has it ready before the due date. More often parents describe projects as nightmares.

Douglas's parents had a miserable two days when they discovered, quite by accident, that he had a major science project due on Friday—and it was Wednesday night, late. When Carol sat down with a resistant Douglas to help him determine what he still needed to do, she found out he hadn't even picked a topic. A screaming argument yielded a materials list that she had to find time to purchase the next day. Thursday afternoon and evening Douglas shut himself in his room, working feverishly. At 2:00 A.M. Friday morning, Carol found him putting the finishing touches on a volcano that belched smoke and spit some kind of lavalike goo. He had forgotten, however, to write the report that was to be 60 percent of the grade.

The problem with projects begins with your child's sense of time and urgency. If it isn't due today, it isn't urgent. Moreover, he believes that the date a project is due is another day to work on the project. While this sounds like an exaggeration, if your child's project is due Friday, he assumes he has all day Friday to work on it. He doesn't understand that the teacher will collect it at 9:00 A.M.

The second major problem some students have with doing a project is that they can't break it down into smaller tasks. That makes the assignment seem overwhelming. Sometimes they start off with gusto only to run out of steam before the project is finished. Or they only do the parts that interest them, which for some kids are the hands-on, creative parts. Others race through the written report, but hit a roadblock on the accompanying artwork, which feels to them like pointless coloring.

Whatever your child's pattern is, a few tools can help him complete projects with less parental supervision and reduced moaning and groaning on his part.

TOOLS FOR SMOOTHER-SAILING PROJECTS

- A checklist or form your child completes with your assistance to break projects into smaller tasks. The form should include space for interim due dates. (See sample on p. 206.)

- The form or an accompanying calendar to record interim due dates for each part of the project. It is important to update the form as deadlines are met or missed.

- A daily homework time during which he is required to work on school-related things—including projects—whether he has any other homework that night or not.

- A check-in and privilege system that encourages him to start, stay with, and complete long-term assignments on time. (See section on structuring homework, pp. 196–203.)

PROJECT CHECKLIST

Project title/type: _____

Date due: _____

Project completion date (1–2 days before due date): _____

Materials needed: _____

_____

_____

_____

Date materials purchased/assembled: _____

Steps for completing project: **Date:**

1. _____   _____

2. _____   _____

3. _____   _____

4. _____   _____

5. _____   _____

6. _____   _____

7. _____   _____

Examples of steps include:

Reading

Research—review books, articles, Internet research

Notes or note cards

Outline

Draft(s)

Charts/maps/costumes/products

Practice (oral presentations, memorization)

Coordinate with others (project team)

A Necessary Perspective

You must help others recognize your child's strengths as the avenue to address his deficits. Although schools have requirements for what must be taught, they can also have multiple ways to measure what a child has learned. When you have a conference with teachers, ask whether there is a creative way for your child to demonstrate mastery of the material. Possibilities include an oral report with a question-and-answer period, instead of a test. Or a debate to demonstrate a good understanding of the subject matter. Having the child teach a lesson can provide a measure of his understanding. Teachers' focus, especially on the secondary level, is to teach the material and determine level of mastery. When you suggest creativity, you are not asking them to lower their standards. You are only asking that they be flexible in determining criteria for mastery.

Above all, make sure your child gets the message that he is more to you than just a set of grades. Make it clear that you don't measure his worth on the basis of his academic performance. As important as school is, your relationship with your child is more important. Don't let school destroy it. When he is no longer in school, he will still be your child.

9

"What? I Have to Do It Myself?"

Fostering Independence and Responsibility

Theodore: My definition of independence is that I am allowed to do things like read when I want to and do things I have to in any order I want. I can also do those things without my parents standing over me and telling me what to do. Independence also means that I have some freedom to do what I want. I think that I have some independence. I wouldn't mind having more.

Being able to do things responsibly means I am able to do things without reminders (like my morning list, walking the dog, and other things). I think I'm better at responsibility than I am at independence.

Jan: Overall, Theodore is a responsible kid and he's learning to do things on his own. However, sometimes it takes a lot of reminders to get him to complete tasks.

Sharon: Independence should be among a parent's highest priorities. It is one of the greatest gifts you can give to your child. Some children seem to come by independence more easily than others do. They set out to do something and accomplish their goal with little or no adult help. They exercise good judgment about what to take on and how and when to work on it.

Others want independence but lack the skills to be self-reliant. These children repeatedly argue for the right to do something on their own or decide things for themselves. Experience has taught their parents that acceding to their demands will mean things will go unfinished or end in disaster. They know their kids' tendency not to consider certain important information when they make decisions. But these kids haven't seemed to notice that they aren't any good at systematic planning, organizing details, and time management.

Finally, there are the children who avoid autonomy. These kids expect assistance for everything and are angry when someone is not there to support them. Resistant to trying anything new, they want help with the most mundane matters and larger tasks easily overwhelm them. A child like this can be exhausting.

Most parents who are challenged by their children face one of two independence dilemmas. In either case, changing their behavior starts with parents. First, let's examine how children get this way. Consider the following scenario.

You wake your eleven-year-old and leave to get yourself ready for work. You return to find her still asleep. After you make many forays into her room, she is finally up and dressed. Then she disappears into the bathroom. Multiple reminders later, she wanders into the kitchen, glances at the clock, and rushes around yelling that she's "going to be late." What irks you is the distinct impression that she considers it *your* fault. Everything in her attitude and tone makes it clear that you are the culprit—especially her comment: "So why didn't you get me up earlier?"

Unfortunately, she's right. You have established a morning pattern of waking her, then talking, cajoling, pleading, nagging, and verily even yelling to get this girl up, dressed, and out the door on time for school. Therefore, if she is running late, it is obvious that you did not talk, cajole, plead, nag, or yell loud or long enough to get the job done. So it *must* be your fault.

ENABLING "LEARNED HELPLESSNESS"

Learned helplessness, a term coined by psychologist Martin Seligman, results when it is easier for you to do things yourself than get your child to do them. This applies to any task. While performing the job yourself gets it done faster, and sometimes (but not always) reduces nagging, it teaches dependence and communicates to the child that he can't do it himself. This pattern of helplessness is one he learns over time. And he couldn't learn it without a lot of help from someone.

Jan: Jamie and I believe our job is to raise Caroline and Theodore to be independent, responsible adults. If anything, we have tended to impose independence and burden them with responsibility (they sure seem to do a lot more chores than their peers do). However, we have also inadvertently fostered elements of "learned helplessness" in Theodore.

From the time he was born, we were aware, as my clinical psychologist mother-in-law noted, that Theodore scored low on "the self-help scale." That meant he would rather have somebody else do something for him than do it himself. He wasn't particularly late to talk, but he got by on "uh-uh" grunts and pointing for a longer time than Caroline did. When he got older, he'd ask one of us to get down a cereal bowl rather than get it himself. It wasn't especially annoying, but we were aware that he preferred to let others do things for him.

As his other behavior problems commanded more of our attention, we became less stringent in enforcing his getting chores done because they would so often trigger tantrums or huge fights. By the time Theodore was diagnosed with ADHD, he had more than a few elements of learned helplessness.

There were times when both Jamie and I sounded like broken records. "Why couldn't he organize his school binder himself?" "Why couldn't he put his own dishes in the dishwasher?" Although Theodore now follows a morning list, we still tend to nag: "It's seven thirty-five. You only have five minutes to get your teeth brushed or you won't get your fifty cents for completing your list." (We do this instead of letting him experience the consequences of our system—no completed list, no fifty cents.) Unfortunately, it is ingrained in my nature that if a dish is left on the counter, I'll stick it in the dishwasher—but I'll mutter under my breath at the same time, "I'm not your maid!"

Sharon: I hear the same concern from parents over and over. "I just want my child to take responsibility for his own behavior."

Well, he doesn't have to if *you* keep taking responsibility for it. If you get him up and out, take his work to school whenever he forgets it, or rationalize his behavior to his teachers, then he has no reason to take responsibility for these things. If you pick up after him and organize him, he has no need to develop these skills for himself. If you are more than a resource while he does his homework, you are enabling his helplessness. If you act as a tutor, mentor, scribe, cheerleader, or drill sergeant, then he will not be able to function at school without similar support. Teachers are likely to interpret his overreliance on adult support as noncompliance.

Some children do need support. Without some reminder or visual cue, they will not be able to complete daily tasks. What they need is something to replace *you* as the reminder. Without a list, a reminder note, a calendar, or timer there is nothing to tell your child what to do or how much time he has to do it. The list (or timer or calendar) alone isn't enough. You need to find a way to make him pay attention to it.

Tools for Developing Independence

Start by using the following tools yourself as an example of how and when to use them. Then make them a meaningful part of your child's life.

CALENDARS

The household calendar should not only be your personal reference for the family's activities, it should contain information that is important to both you and your child. Not just the dentist appointments, but also the play dates, birthday parties, and sleepovers that are special to him.

Include a "calendar check" in the family's daily routine. Once a day, you and your child (or preferably everyone in the family) should review the information on the calendar. Cross off things done the day before, add new dates and activities, and plan the day accordingly. Making it part of the daily routine gives your child practice using the calendar as an organizing tool. Taking the time to do it daily reinforces its importance.

Quick Tip

Include your child's favorite activities on the house-hold calendar. Check it together daily. This reinforces the calendar's importance as he organizes and plans for the next day and upcoming events.

LISTS

Lists help organize thoughts, sequence tasks, and prompt memory. They are even more important for your child because they shift responsibility onto him. Show your child the importance of lists by using them yourself. Include him when developing a grocery list. Discuss items from a "to do" list with him. Prepare short lists he can check off as he completes household chores. Use a task list or homework notebook so he can check off each assignment as he completes it. Make lists to break down large projects into smaller tasks with interim due dates. Then provide an incentive for each part he completes on schedule. After you both have been using lists for a while, ask him when he thinks using a list would help him. Implement at least one of his suggestions and give reinforcement each time he uses the list.

Jan: I am an inveterate list maker, but no one else in the family is. Theodore recognizes it helps if we make a list when we give him multiple directions, but he doesn't make lists for himself. I wish he would check things off, but he doesn't seem to feel the sense of satisfaction I get every time I scratch something off one of my many lists.

Theodore: I usually don't make lists because I find it too difficult to sort out what I need to do, when I need to do it, and in what order. Writing stuff by hand isn't easy for me. When someone makes a list for me, I follow it, but I don't bother checking things off because I can remember what I've already done.

Quick Tip

Lists can facilitate independence. They communicate what needs to be done so you don't have to.

Sharon: The time and energy you take to demonstrate the utility of these tools is an investment in your child's independence. If your child is able to successfully complete a process—any process—without you, then you know he's becoming independent.

ALLOWANCE

I'm a big believer in children's allowances. An allowance has enormous potential as a teaching device. If a child has easy access to money, he develops little understanding of its value. His only experience is that when he needs it, money magically appears. He has no need to budget and save or prioritize his spending if money is always available.

Moreover, allowance is a useful tool for rewarding your child's new skills and behavior changes. Use it to reinforce successful completion of specific tasks and independent performance of routines.

I divide allowance into three parts. Of the total, a child should receive one part without fail just for being part of the family. How much he receives of the other two parts should depend on what he earns.

- 20 percent should be provided unconditionally so that he will have funds to learn the value of money.

- 30–40 percent should be earned for your child's contribution to the household, i.e., chores.

- 40–50 percent should be earned as reinforcement for behavioral changes.

The total amount depends on age, the child's present concept of money, and what expenses you will require him to shoulder. A five-year-old has very few expenses, but his allowance will be more meaningful if he is exposed to the idea that he can only buy those things that are within his budget, i.e., what he already has. If not, he has to wait and save more. As a child gets older, the range of things he would like increases so make him responsible for some small budget items as well as some big ticket ones. Here the message is best delivered by making him cover some of his own small expenses (candy, snacks, the second video he wants to rent) and make a contribution (matched by the parent) for a more costly item (a video game, a new computer software program, etc.).

Hold adolescents accountable for their discretionary spending money. For that to work, they may need a higher allowance. Their expenses are larger and they are more often in situations that require money. If you are not going to subsidize them, they need to earn allowance to cover their expenses. It is not unreasonable for a fifteen-year-old to earn an allowance of fifteen dollars. It is not, however, reasonable for a five-year-old to earn five dollars. At five, he won't have the expenses that he'll have at fifteen. However, five is a great time to begin learning the value of budgeting and saving.

VALUE OF MONEY FUNDS

Even if your child earns no other allowance that week, he can spend or save the money he gets just for being a member of the family. Having some funds gives him the opportunity to decide between spending or saving. Pay this part of the allowance at the start of each week. That will make him consider what he wants to do with it and may be a catalyst for him to earn more throughout the week.

HOUSEHOLD CONTRIBUTION FUNDS

Although every family handles chores differently, most want their child to do something to contribute to the household's general functioning. Some make their child only take care of his own space or room. Others require small daily chores such as setting and clearing the table. Some include more substantial jobs such as lawn care, laundry, housecleaning, and cooking.

Whatever your expectations, you may have already realized that your child's interest in and expertise at completing chores is substantially different from yours. Despite this, if you are like most parents, you probably badger your kids with repeated reminders, recriminations—even threats—and still end up doing at least some of their chores yourself. It is fatiguing and infuriating. You keep up this self-defeating process because you rightfully refuse to abandon the notion that your child should be a contributing member of the household. Some of you even insist, despite past failure, that your child should do his chores without pay. After all, no one pays you to do the grocery shopping or pick up the dry cleaning.

Even for those parents who use allowance as an incentive for completing chores, past experience probably has taught you it doesn't work—or at least it doesn't work very well. More to the point, your kids don't work.

Before you start muttering that your child should want to contribute to the running of the household, let me assure you that it's a moot point. He really doesn't see why many of the chores need to be done at all. He doesn't notice when the trash piles up or his clothes are on the floor. It's just not on his list of priorities.

Timing may be an additional problem. Parents tend to pay allowances at the end of the week, even though chores are spread throughout. Having done the work on Monday and Tuesday without meaningful reward, there is less incentive for your child to do more as the week wears on. Hence, his performance deteriorates.

Moreover, when payment is delayed, allowance is less likely to be linked to performance. If you refuse to pay on Saturday because your child didn't complete chores on Thursday and Friday, his successful efforts on Monday through Wednesday go unrewarded.

And if you religiously pay allowance no matter what, why would he do any work at all?

The solution is to set a daily wage for chores and make payment every day. Doing so provides the immediate reward that is likely to improve your child's performance.

Quick Tip

A daily wage for chores—coupled with daily payment—not only makes it more likely chores will get done but reinforces your child's taking responsibility for doing so.

Let your child know exactly what your expectations are. Decide precisely what you want done and by when. Use a checklist that specifies all parts of a completed chore. If you want the table set each night by a certain time, say so. Try a system that reduces the wage when chore deadlines are not met. If he misses the last deadline and you have to do his chore, he pays you. For example, if the table is set by 5:00 P.M. with only one reminder, your son earns his daily chore allowance. If it gets done by 5:30, again with one reminder, he earns half pay. If it's not done until 6:00 P.M., it costs him nothing but he doesn't earn his daily pay. After 6:00, you set the table and he owes you. The reality is that you often wind up doing it anyway. Skip the argument and nagging and be paid for doing his chore.

Jan: After too many arguments over "you're not doing enough to help out," we drew up a list of all routine household tasks. This included everything—setting the dinner table, washing the dog weekly, paying monthly bills, laundry, grocery shopping, collecting and taking out the trash, drawing up a meal plan and grocery list, sweeping the sun porch, and more. In a family meeting, we divided the chores among all four of us. Then we decided which day each chore should be done, with some, like grocery shopping, on an ad hoc basis. Everything then went on a job chart posted on the refrigerator. (See page 219 to see what one of our job charts looks like.)

Now we know what we are supposed to do and when, so no one can say, "It isn't my night to walk the dog," or "I don't have to wash the dishes tonight." The chart is its own enforcer. We review it whenever hectic schedules warrant a change or I get frustrated by people not doing their jobs.

I know we require our kids to do more than many of their friends have to do. But I think the approach would work just as well for one or two chores as for our much longer list. The point

HOW TO GET CHORES DONE WITH MINIMAL HASSLE

1. Clarify exactly what you want done, and specify all steps needed for completion of the chore.

2. Determine deadline for completion.

3. Determine how many reminders he needs and their relationship to payment (e.g., only one reminder earns full pay; two reminders earns half pay, etc.).

4. Set wage and completion criteria. Consider different pay rates (full, half, no pay, he pays you) for differing levels of performance. (E.g.: full pay for completion by one deadline with one reminder; half pay for meeting a later deadline; no pay if done by an even later deadline; he pays you if chore is not done by final deadline.)

5. Use checklist to record completion of parts or all of chore.

6. Pay daily for work completed. If it works for both you and your child, log the amount owed on a chart on the refrigerator and pay the total on allowance night.

isn't how long the list is. Rather, it is teaching our children to take responsibility for their own lives.

Sharon: Because it is easier to remember things that happen every day, you will be more successful if your child's job is part of his daily routine. Since he can't even recall what days he has soccer practice or band, why do you think he will remember which day the trash goes out? Moreover, daily chores give him an opportunity to practice. Making it part of the daily routine and giving reinforcement with immediate payment increase the likelihood that your child will complete his chores with less support from you. For infrequent chores that will require more prompting, have him check a chore calendar every day.

As your child gets older, he should do more to help. If chores have been an issue, assume they will be even more so as your challenging child gets older. It is a mistake to ask more of a child who has not mastered what has been required of him in the past. Before you increase your expectations, be careful not to confuse age with maturity. As your child gets older, include him in the process of dividing up responsibilities and determining rewards and privileges. This is an excellent time to remind him that you will link his request for more freedom to his independent completion of household responsibilities. Then agree to make certain privileges contingent on his performance of chores. Documenting criteria for successful completion and whether he meets them saves a lot of argument later.

If a chore isn't getting done, ask yourself if it needs to be broken down into smaller parts. Is it too overwhelming as is? Does your child need assistance to know where to start? Will he be better able to complete the job if you break it into steps and list them? If so, make adjustments.

Jan: We use allowance to reinforce our kids doing chores, but especially those they are least interested in doing—such as their own laundry. It beats me why kids don't see any problem wearing dirty clothes over and over. We ceded to our kids the responsibility for doing their own laundry. The problem we've had is that it drags

JOB CHART

TASK	MON.	TUES.	WED.	THUR.	FRI.	SAT.	SUN.
Vacuum living areas		Theodore				Dad	Caroline
Set dinner table	Mom/Dad	Theodore	Mom/Dad	Mom/Dad	Theodore	Theodore	Theodore
Cook dinner			Caroline			Theodore	Theodore
Clear dinner table	Theodore	Theodore	Theodore	Theodore	Theodore	Mom	Caroline
Do dinner dishes	Caroline	Caroline/Dad	Dad	Caroline/Dad	Mom		Theodroe
Collect garbage							
Take garbage out							Dad
Clean bedrooms before noon						Caroline & Theodore	
Feed fish, A.M./P.M.	Mom	Mom	Mom	Mom	Mom	Mom	Mom
Feed and walk dog, A.M.	Caroline	Caroline	Caroline	Caroline	Caroline	Theodore	Theodore
Feed and walk dog, P.M.	Caroline	Theodore	Theodore	Caroline	Theodore	Theodore	Theodore
Tidy house			Everyone				
Wash dog			Caroline				
Laundry				Mom: Mom & Dad's clothes		Dad: sheets & towels	C & T do own clothes
Sweep kitchen		Theodore					Caroline

AS NEEDED:

Empty dishwasher:	Caroline and Dad dishes; Theodore silverware
Taxes:	Dad
Mow lawn:	Caroline ($5 front and back; subject to quality checks)
Plan meals:	Mom
Food shopping:	Dad big ones; Mom and Dad short trips
Cooking:	Mom and Dad; Caroline chooses and cooks meals for Wednesday (cooking entree on Sunday if possible); Theodore on Saturday

Clean fish tanks:	Mom
Put away groceries:	Everyone who's home
Water plants:	Mom
Sweep sun porch:	Mom
Pay bills:	Mom and Dad

out until after their bedtime, invariably leaving me to finish it. The solution was to build into their allowance an incentive for finishing their laundry by a certain time—5:00 Sunday afternoon. This has worked reasonably well. If they meet the deadline—with no (OK, minimal) reminders from us, they get the money. If they forget and don't get it done on time, or we have to bug them, no payment. We record it on the allowance chart if they earn the incentive.

Making Caroline and Theodore jointly responsible has been more problematic. After bickering for months over "you didn't switch the loads," or "you were supposed to fold that load and didn't," they agreed on a complicated division of labor. The arguments continued until they made one person fully responsible one week, the other the next week, which has worked fairly well.

BEHAVIOR ALLOWANCE

Sharon: Throughout the preceding chapters, I've emphasized giving your child incentives to change his behavior. Allowance can play an important role in that incentive plan. Making 40 to 50 percent of allowance contingent on meeting specific behavioral expectations gives a child a clear message about your priorities. Having half of his allowance riding on keeping his hands to himself signals to him how important that rule is to you. Using allowance to back up a guideline requiring that family members be addressed by their given names (no name-calling allowed) communicates your priority in a meaningful way to him. Daily pay if he meets your behavior expectations helps keep him on target. Moreover, it reduces the likelihood of your not paying him what he's earned if he screws up later in the week.

Jan: A substantial part of Theodore's allowance is contingent on behavior changes he's trying to make. We've included everything from turning off lights, flushing the toilet, taking his medication without reminders, and turning off the computer when time was up, to completing a "home alone" list. A "home alone" list is a short series of tasks we write on a yellow Post-it Note that

Theodore needs to accomplish while he's by himself in order to earn fifty cents. It can include chores, eating a snack or meal, completing parts of his homework, or taking his medication (which earns him another fifty cents, with a twenty-five cent fine for us if we forget to leave it out for him). "Home alone" lists help structure his time and keep Theodore focused on what he's supposed to be doing. Making part of his allowance contingent on behavior changes has been successful for many things; less so for others.

Theodore: I think the system of earning allowance for behavior change is very good because I can earn more allowance with it than without it and I get a reward for practicing doing things differently. Sometimes if I have plenty of money (like forty dollars), I won't try to earn the reward if it's something like ten cents because that's too little money to matter. It's not worth the effort to do whatever it is I'm supposed to do.

Jan: Because these are household guidelines, not just rules for Theodore, we also incorporated behavioral change expectations into Caroline's allowance. To say this has met with limited success is an understatement.

Caroline: It's not that I actually refuse to make the behavior change, it's just that the policy requires me to mark a chart for things that are part of my normal routine. For instance, I'd get ten cents for checking off each time I brushed my teeth. (This was when I wore braces and my parents wanted to make sure I brushed them well so my teeth didn't rot behind the braces.) Well, I brush my teeth regularly anyway. It's not like I was changing my behavior. I couldn't be bothered to check it off on the list. It just seemed like an excuse for me to have the same guidelines as Theodore so he wouldn't be able to say, "Why do I have to do this if Caroline doesn't?"

At first, because my parents wanted me to wear a watch, I could earn ten cents each day I wore it. Well, I didn't feel like wearing a watch, and ten cents wasn't enough money to inspire me to do so. They gave up. Last Christmas, however, I got a watch I really liked and I wear it every day, but it wasn't money that persuaded me.

Then there's the matter of earning twenty-five cents for each grade I show them. Here's something my parents actually want me to do, not just another thing on the chart. I just forget about my grades or leave the papers at school. I have numerous excuses for not bringing them home. I've nothing to hide because I get good grades anyway. I just don't feel like going out of my way to ensure that my parents see every grade—even though they want to.

To be honest, I've actively resisted this whole thing, though I could have earned a considerable amount of money by doing it. The entire business really annoys me.

Jan: Caroline's situation has perplexed us. We feel it's important to have one set of household rules, but have failed to develop a behavioral component for her that works. Even with her input, it hasn't worked. Either she suggests things, but then ignores them, or she refuses to come up with anything. Different incentives haven't worked either, unlike with Theodore. She's a responsible child who doesn't need reminders and incentives to behave well. But she's also a teenager and her ability to resist is greater than our need to insist. I still wish we could devise something that would make it worth her while to show us all her grades.

For Theodore, the behavior component is the largest part of his allowance. We constantly alter the list, depending on what is bugging us and what we want him to focus on changing. His most important incentives are chips for screen time and money. We keep track of both on his allowance chart and pay the total earned on Sunday nights. He collects chips in an old mayonnaise jar on the kitchen counter.

When a new issue arises, we revise the list and focus on the new item for a minimum of two weeks. Some things stay on the list longer because Theodore needs a lot of practice—like getting off the computer when time's up. He sets the kitchen timer and his watch alarm, then has to get off the computer before the timer goes off. This process works sporadically.

Theodore: I seldom get off the computer on time because my computer game is a whole lot more interesting than the reason I need to get off.

Would someone rather play on the computer or set the dinner table? Would someone rather play on the computer or do homework? Besides, my alarm usually goes off right when I'm in the middle of doing something good in the game.

Sharon: Theodore does need a lot of practice at turning off the computer on time because it goes against all his characteristics most affected by ADHD as well as very typical kid characteristics. He has to turn off a highly stimulating computer game right in the middle—not necessarily a natural stopping point—usually to do something much less interesting. No wonder it's so hard for him. However, obviously the incentive (fifty cents) isn't strong enough to make it worth his while. Jan and Jamie need to pick a more powerful incentive if they really want to change this behavior. At least they seem realistic about their slim chance at success.

Jan: Using allowance to reward behavioral change takes much tinkering to figure out what will work. What works one day won't necessarily work the next.

Below is one version of our allowance chart. We check the box to record when the behavior takes place. At the end of the week, we total everything and pay up. This is added to the "Value for Money Funds," for which Caroline gets considerably more than Theodore because she's three years older.

ALLOWANCE BONUSES
Sharon: Consider using bonuses to improve performance. Award a bonus when chores get done with no reminders or the week your child did his chores five days in a row. Use them for meeting behavioral expectations. Give a bonus for earning the maximum possible for behavior several days in a row or for an excellent week (or six of seven days) for both chores and behavior. Never demand perfection but reward it when your child achieves it.

Week of: _____

	Mon.	Tues.	Wed.	Thur.	Fri.	Sat.	Sun.
Caroline:							
25¢ we see homework list							
25¢ contacts out by 7 P.M.							
25¢ each grade we see							
$1.50 laundry w/o reminder by 5 P.M. Sun.							
Theodore:							
50¢ medication w/o reminder							
25¢ homework list fully filled out							
$1.50 laundry w/o reminder by 5 P.M. Sun.							
25¢ each, brush teeth A.M./P.M.							
50¢ computer off, no reminder							
50¢ home alone list completed							

TOTAL EARNED:

Pointer for Effective Parenting

If your child does better than expected, reward with a
bonus. If he does the best that anyone could expect,
reward with a bigger bonus. Don't demand perfection
but reward it when your child achieves it.

Summer Camp Fosters Independence

WHY IS MY KID AWFUL AT HOME BUT GOOD ELSEWHERE?

What really aggravates parents is how much worse their child's
behavior is at home than in almost any other setting. Teachers

report your child to be a joy and you wonder if they are thinking of the right child. Other parents tell you how helpful your daughter is whenever she visits. You've never seen this in your child.

It is very common for children to manage to do exactly what is expected when they are somewhere—anyplace—other than home. It shouldn't shock or even surprise you. After all, they only have to make the effort to behave well for a short time—which they can do. Besides, they know you'll still let them live at home if they don't measure up. They're not so sure whether the neighbor will invite them back. At a friend's home, the pressure to perform is short-lived and often more clearly appreciated because that parent is holding up your child's positive example to her errant child. Who could resist such accolades? Take heart: if your child can behave well at school or the neighbor's house, you must have done something right.

It's frustrating that your child won't or can't do at home whatever it is others report he can do. Teachers report that she sits for a half-hour lesson when she can't sit for five minutes at the dinner table. Parents tend to assume that their child *won't* do for them what he willingly does for others. It's not that simple.

Your child has learned that you will compensate for, or at least tolerate, his shortcomings. He's come to depend on your ensuring that things get done—through reminders, assistance, or doing it for him. This learned helplessness has no place at school. Teachers will not and cannot do things for him. By the time your child is in second or third grade, he's well aware that his teachers aren't going to function like parents. Trial and error has taught him that he is expected to follow directions and complete tasks without constant individual help. Moreover, he looks around and sees others accomplishing what they're supposed to do without incessant hand-holding.

At home, he doesn't have the benefit of peer pressure or example. What he needs is an environment where he can learn how to do without your help.

SUMMER CAMP: FREEDOM FOR YOU, INDEPENDENCE FOR YOUR CHILD

By the end of the school year, whether you are Mom or Dad, you're probably pretty tired of your job as homework supervisor and chauffeur. The prospect of having your child at home all day for three straight months may make your heart sink. As thrilled as your child is to be out of school, eventually those endless days of unstructured time become boring. You need a break. And your child needs some structure. How do you both get what you need? Summer camp, overnight or day.

Jan: Both Jamie and I spent wonderful summers at camp. Every June we send our kids to the camp I went to on Lake Michigan. Not only is camp fun after a long, demanding academic year, it gives Caroline and Theodore a chance to be on their own. At age six, they flew to see their grandparents for a week, then graduated to sleep-away camp at eight. Going off on their own has given them the confidence to function independently and cope with anything that arises.

Equally important, Jamie and I get a break from nine months of supervising homework and carting them to soccer, tennis, and basketball practice, and have time to spend with each other.

Caroline: I absolutely love camp because I relax, make new friends, see old ones, and have a lot of fun. It's also nice to get away from the stresses of school and family, and all the totally outrageous rules that impose on my freedom and independence at home. After all, I am a teenager. Don't I deserve a break from *them*?

Sharon: I'm a big fan of sleep-away summer camp for kids. I think most kids benefit from a break from Mom and Dad. Most parents enjoy, and benefit from, the freedom of having their kids away for a while. Camp is not just for typical kids. Challenging kids have as much or more to gain. If your child can perform well for short periods outside the home, think how much he would benefit from longer periods of practice. Summer camp makes that possible.

Camp potentially provides peer models, structured routines, and the opportunity to practice independence by following those routines. By doing the same tasks every day without the benefit (or the crutch) of your help, your child develops the habit of getting them done independently. Since his peers are doing the same, they act as role models for the skills he needs. Sometimes fellow campers act as the prompt, encouraging and laughing with or at your child to get him going. His counselors expect him to perform and will push harder than you might for him to meet their expectations. Many children rise to the occasion in part because they are so anxious to please their counselors and perform as their peers do.

Theodore: I find summer camp a really good place because I love the activities, especially soccer, archery, wood shop, and arts and crafts. Camp is also a place where I have more friends than I do at home.

Everything at camp is different from at home, but I have a set schedule every day. I know what I'm supposed to be doing and when I'm supposed to be doing it. I have two hours of free time every afternoon and enjoy rest hour after lunch when I can do something quiet. Also, I really like not having my parents bossing me around all the time, telling me what to do, how to do it, and when to do it.

Sharon: There are camp advisors who specialize in locating camps for special needs children. The associations and support groups for various disabilities maintain lists of camps, which they will send to you on request, and often publish those lists in newsletters.

Some kids would benefit more from a camp specifically for kids with special needs. Others, however, would do fine at a "regular" camp. If you choose to send your child to a "regular" camp, it is very important to first find out the camp's philosophy and approach to children with ADHD or other special needs. Check its literature, talk to the director(s), and see if it is included on camp lists provided by ADHD or other support groups. Whenever possible, talk to another parent whose child has a disability like your child's and see what their experience was at that camp. If your child's specific problem is not one that the camp has previously dealt with, it may not be a good match for your child—even if the camp is willing to take him.

As is the case with education, this experience is a partnership between you and the camp. It is important to disclose your child's condition so the camp can provide a healthy, positive social and learning environment for your child. For the same reason, camp is not the place for your child to take a "drug holiday." If he needs to do so, do that on your own time, not the camp's. If your child needs medication to function effectively on a daily basis, taking him off it while at camp may condemn him to having a miserable time. Moreover, it leaves the camp unable to figure out why your child is so difficult to deal with and having such a poor experience. Camp gives your child an opportunity to practice independence in a positive social environment. You want to maximize the likelihood of that happening, not reduce it by taking him off medication.

YOU MAY STILL HAVE TO BE YOUR CHILD'S ADVOCATE AT CAMP

Jan: Whereas all that's been necessary to ensure Caroline has a great summer at camp is to fill out the forms and send her off, it has taken far more effort with Theodore. Each year we write the camp a long letter. As with school, camp should be a partnership, so we've been candid about Theodore's ADHD and issues that might affect his experience. Although his first summer went well, some of his cabin mates teased and bullied him the second year. When he finally told me months after he got home, I was perturbed that his camp wasn't living up to its principle of treating everyone with respect. Theodore's counselors apparently hadn't halted the bullying, nor had camp leaders paid enough attention to his welfare. For that matter, I wasn't sure they had read our letter.

To prepare for Theodore's third summer, we wrote the camp director a strongly worded letter detailing our concerns about Theodore's previous summer and expressing our hope that the staff would ensure it didn't happen again. I followed up by telephone with the camp director.

Theodore: My third year at camp was much better than my second one because there were more kids in my cabin like me or who had interests like mine. For example, one friend was an extremely good chess player. I'm a big fan of chess so I got to play someone at my level. My leader also liked to play and so did almost everybody else in the cabin.

My counselor appeared to have more control over the kids and how they treated each other, which I really appreciated after the bad time my second year. Another reason I had a good summer was I became a good friend with someone who also has ADHD. That made it a lot easier because he knew how I felt and didn't tease me for having it.

Jan: Theodore's second year made me realize that sending off a letter wasn't enough—I had to actively enlist the camp leadership's cooperation. Consequently, they took greater care to train the staff to deal with more challenging kids like Theodore, paid closer attention to how he was doing, and had his counselor keep us apprised of his progress. The outcome was a great summer for him, happier parents, and a camp living up to its own philosophy.

It took a lot of effort to ensure that the camp would meet Theodore's needs, but we were more confident he would have a good summer. And we got a break from the strain of constant vigilance needed to raise Theodore.

Quick Tip

- -

Put your concerns in writing before sending your child to camp. Include a checklist of what has worked in the past. Follow up with a telephone call to ensure that appropriate camp staff (including your child's counselor) have read your letter.

Sharon: If you're hesitant about summer camp because of the cost, don't reject it out of hand. There are ways to reduce the cost. Shorter sessions (one or two weeks), scholarship programs, and camps sponsored by large groups such as Boy or Girl Scouts or the

YMCA can offer a less expensive, worthwhile learning experience. Whether a one-week program or a summer-long experience, it can prove invaluable. No-fee camp consultants have information on a variety of summer programs and can suggest camps according to your child's needs. A good place to start is with the American Camping Association (listed in the Resources section at the back of this book), which has names and descriptions of many accredited camps. You can get information on many camps—including those specializing in programs for challenging children—by finding their Web sites.

In your search, consider a day camp if cost is an issue. There are terrific day programs that cater to more active or challenging children; others are specifically oriented to children with special needs. It is a more economical way to expose them to the camping experience. Start early. Many camps have deadlines or limited enrollment that fills up early in the year. The time you invest in research can pay big dividends in positive learning experiences.

If your concern is whether your child (or you) can weather the separation, consider how he does on overnight visits to relatives' homes. If your child has never been away from you overnight, there's no time like the present. The sense of self and independence he may develop at camp are invaluable assets to take into adulthood.

COMING HOME: MAINTAINING SUMMER CAMP SUCCESS

No one wants the benefits from all the time, energy, and financial resources devoted to summer camp to be left there. You want that growth and independence to come home. If, however, you expect your child to return a new person, you (and he) will be sorely disappointed. Maintaining newly learned independence is difficult. After all, he's changed, but you haven't nor has the environment he's come back to. But change is possible. You are the key to incorporating that initiative and responsibility he developed over the summer into his life at home. Because different expectations and atmosphere at camp encouraged changes in your child, you must foster similar changes at home.

To help maintain his success, find out from camp personnel what your child has learned to do without any support. It might be he can make his bed by himself every morning. Maybe he's better able to manage his time or do more with fewer reminders. Or perhaps he's learned that if he counts to ten (or maybe three) when he gets mad, he's less likely to punch another kid.

Equally, if not more important, you must change your behavior. Communicate new expectations to your child. Include rewards or privileges he can earn if he continues to function independently at home. Be specific about how you will measure "independence." Use the process for behavior change laid out in chapters 5 and 6. Pick one or two things to focus on at a time. Choose an incentive that will make it worthwhile to do for himself what you did for him before—whether it is making his own sandwich or going to bed on time. Then select a visual reminder that will help him operate without your assistance.

STEPS FOR MAINTAINING CAMP SUCCESSES

1. Find out from the camp what your child has learned to do for himself.

2. Pick one or two things to focus on at home.

3. Choose an incentive that will make it worth his while to do on his own what you used to do for him.

4. Select visual reminders that will help him manage without your assistance.

Without careful thought and planning you may erode his confidence and newly found ability to act independently. If you fall back into old patterns of enabling learned helplessness, he will do the same. In doing so, you inadvertently communicate to your child that since you don't trust his ability to function without your assistance, there's no reason he should be confident he can.

Keep in mind, you don't want to always have to take care of your challenging child. At some point in the "sooner than you think" future, when he's on his own, you aren't going to be around to see that everything gets done. Your job is to prepare him. Start now. Make a list of daily tasks he should begin doing on his own, without your assistance. Select one and start working on it today.

10

Make New Friends but Keep the Old

Learning the Stuff Everyone Else Just Picks Up

ONE WISH

If I could only have one wish, I would wish to be liked by other kids. I would give almost anything so that other kids would just like me. That is the one thing that I have always wished for.

There are plenty of reasons why I would wish to be liked. One reason is that because no one likes me that singles me out and basically leaves me alone. The problem with being alone is that it makes me an easy target for teasing from anybody. I can't stand up for myself because I feel so overwhelmed. The main problem that I have when I get teased is that because I appear to be the only one that they can tease, that makes them so persistent. Every single time that I get teased, I so badly want to sock the person who is teasing me. But the problem is that they want me to react like that and if I do, I'm going to be in really big trouble.

Another reason that I would wish for people to like me is that I am always so sad. Every day at recess I always wander around feeling so alone in the world. I think about my life, my mind, my ways, and my world. I always think do I want to join other people and get teased early or stay alone and get teased later. I'm so confused and I have mixed feelings about how messed up my life is.

The final reason that I want to be liked is that I never have anyone to play with. Or to talk with. I have never had any friends and I long to know what it feels like to have friends who like me. Almost every single day I

wish that I was as big or bigger than the person teasing me. I always wish
for friends. I've had to endure this rugged road for seven years and if only
I had had friends along the way I would have been so happy.
—Theodore Reuter
Fifth-Grade Essay, Spring 1999

Jan: No aspect of Theodore's attention deficit disorder has been more heart-rending than the social isolation, teasing, and bullying he has experienced. Watching helplessly as friends evaporated in the early elementary grades left me bewildered. Why couldn't these kids see what a wonderful person Theodore was? Being smart was not cool—and Theodore was exceedingly bright. He was physically active, but you weren't "in" unless you started select/travel soccer in third grade and Theodore didn't until fifth grade. Being a strong tennis player and advancing rapidly through the tae kwon do levels brought no social status. As his doctor said, "There are no bragging rights with tae kwon do." Why wasn't there even one child for Theodore to connect with?

Observing his increasing social isolation as kids no longer invited him to birthday parties and stopped reciprocating his invitations to play was painful. They willingly came to our house, but seldom invited Theodore to theirs. Didn't the parents understand that invitations are supposed to be reciprocated—even if their kid didn't? Didn't they know how this made my son feel?

What broke my heart was realizing that Theodore was systematically being subjected to teasing and bullying. It started in the afterschool program. I made numerous attempts—sometimes calling in the principal—to try to change the environment there. Finally, I gave up and pulled Theodore out. I altered my work schedule to be home in the late afternoons until he was old enough to stay alone.

Usually teachers kept the harassment under control in the classroom, but the lack of playground supervision meant Theodore was fair game. He tried to avoid being hassled by walking around the far perimeter by himself, but wasn't always successful. Some kids went out of their way to target him. The slyness of the harassers knew no bounds.

One day the principal was supervising the playground after Theodore and I had reported a serious incident of harassment, and he had told her that the boys were again playing "Smear the Queer," which she had banned the previous year. When her back was turned, a group of "Smear the Queer" players surrounded him, demanding to know why he had blown the whistle. Theodore replied that it wasn't fun to have a bunch of kids pile on and pummel the kid designated as the "Queer." They told him they'd get him for it. Once I dragged the information out of him and took it to the principal, she ordered the boys to apologize. While this ended that particular harassment, it didn't win him any friends.

I agonized over what the right thing was to do. Should I stay out of it and let him suffer? Even if I could, no parent could sit idly by and watch their child in that much misery. Was there something I could tell Theodore to reduce his pain and humiliation? No words sufficed. I spent a lot of time trying to figure out whether the problem lay with Theodore or this group of kids. What was Theodore doing wrong?

Sharon: Parents have long-term goals for their children—health, happiness, and success in their choices of mate and career. For now, they want their children to be accepted and liked by their peers.

The child you find challenging may also challenge others socially until he is no longer included in peer activities. Many times part of the problem, as in Theodore's case, is that your child is poorly matched with his peer group. Sometimes a change of Scout troop or sports team can provide a better opportunity for your child to fit in. Even a change of school may need to be considered though this is not always an option. For most challenging kids, however, you also have to look at your child's behavior and determine what he or she is doing to impair relations with other kids.

Your talks and "running interference" sometimes can get him through the situation, but that won't last. And you can't be there every minute, every time. Because he doesn't know what to say, or what not to say—and he doesn't seem to learn—the result is peer rejection. Sometimes, it's not the peer but his parent who decides your child is not the right playmate. Few things are as painful as watching your child continually operate from the outside looking in, wanting so much to be part of the group.

WARNING SIGNS OF PROBLEMS IN PEER RELATIONS

Early on in your child's schooling, teachers may report that your child has poor play skills, an inability to share or relate to others. They may report aggressive behaviors. After all, Theodore's situation of being teased is just one side of the coin. Challenging children are as likely to be the aggressor as the victim. Initially, you rationalize, it's only this one incident or "boys will be boys." But you've seen it yourself when others come over to play, *if* they come to play. Even that happens less and less often.

When your child is with friends, he may be loud or bossy. Often, his high activity level grates on peers (or their parents). He seems to have no understanding of social protocol and little or no awareness of others' perspectives or feelings. He does what he wants, says what he thinks, and seems unable (or unwilling) to inhibit either. He shows little understanding of the need to share. Unable to adapt to others' ideas, he makes demands and decisions, and is incensed by other children's efforts to do the same. He may talk about his own agenda as if others share it, whether they do or not. When friends come to play, he may agree to do what they choose, but then rapidly tires of the activity. Going off on his own, he acts as if he has no responsibility to entertain. Too often he responds to reminders to stay with his friend or give others a turn with excuses or resistance.

Jan: After Theodore's diagnosis, as I learned how socially deficient some kids with ADHD can be, I began to identify the behaviors in Theodore that rubbed other kids the wrong way. I had long despaired of Theodore's failure to entertain kids when they came over. He would tire of doing something with his guest and retreat into playing with LEGOS. I once overheard another child say to him: "Theodore, I like to play Game Boy and build things with LEGOs just like you. But I don't like to do it for as long as you do. I want to do something else now." From Theodore's lack of response, I sadly realized he couldn't shift gears to "go with the flow" and find something both kids could do together. When he needed to withdraw, he would.

Theodore could also be bossy when playing board games. He would tell other kids what moves to make—a behavior that drives me nuts when I play with him. "Let me figure out my own moves!" I complain. Theodore wasn't so rude or overbearing that other kids blew up. But he didn't recognize when kids were becoming annoyed by his behavior.

Sharon: As your challenging child gets older, birthday party invitations may become scarce. Your child may complain that "nobody likes me" or "no one wants to play with me." He may report that other kids tease him. (Always verify this perception with teachers. If they haven't noticed, ask them to check it out.) Solicit the names of children your child plays with and whether your child or another initiates it. This may uncover possibilities for after-school play dates.

Children deficient in social skills—and many challenging kids are—often do poorly in team situations. They find it hard to follow the rules, share the ball and act as a teammate. Often they are picked last for a team. This humiliation can produce its own negative behaviors and many lasting bad memories. Before you continue to place them in team situations, remember they have no better skills than the last time they blundered at this. They've learned nothing new and are destined to repeat the same patterns of behavior. The previous situation resulted not from a bad day, a bad coach, or the wrong color uniform, but from your child's lack of skills. Despite your good intentions, you're risking his self-esteem, as he is headed for failure.

Instead, consider an activity that challenges him to develop his own expertise such as horseback riding, swimming, or martial arts like tae kwon do. These sports provide a group experience but are a measure of your child's individual performance. That relieves the pressure of a poor performance that may affect the whole team.

By later elementary years when children start making their own plans, your child may receive fewer invitations and not be included in Saturday activities or sleepovers. Invitations your child extends may go unreciprocated and his peer activities dwindle to participation with an organized team or Scouts.

By the time your child is a teen, he is acutely aware that he is left out. In adolescence, faced with the peer group's indisputable importance, if he does not have friends the isolation and loneliness are overwhelming. The result is often anger and bitter resentment hiding the anguish and hurt feelings. As a parent, you are powerless to affect the situation.

Once your child enters the upper grades, though academic pressures intensify, they may take a backseat to stress about his social isolation or rejection. When he was younger, your child may have been content with family activities or willing to entertain himself. Or he defined other kids as friends when they really weren't. Now, however, he is acutely aware of his loneliness. The almost unbearable longing to be part of a group—any group—results in enormous social pressure. Rather than the break lunch should provide, it's now a time to be endured—a visible reminder to all of your child's failure to establish social relationships. Time with friends is, for your child, time without friends.

Theodore: I like to be alone to do what I want by myself. I've learned from what happened in elementary school how to be independent and entertain myself without being in a bad mood because I didn't have anyone to play with. I can entertain myself more easily than I can with another kid. But I still wish that people would invite me to their house and to do things with them.

HOW DID HE GET THIS WAY?

Sharon: Your child's social difficulties are not your fault, and as his parent, you cannot fill the void or be his peer group. Many (though certainly not all) challenging children lack the social skills the rest of us picked up along the way. A few reminders were sufficient to learn to greet people when we enter a room. We just developed the give and take of conversation over time. Trial and error taught us that if Dad's face is red and he's pacing back and forth, it's probably not the right time to ask for a raise in allowance. No one sat down and told us how to read body language or how to pick up on nonverbal cues. We just "got it" over time. Your child hasn't and probably won't be able to unless he's taught how. If not, he will alienate his immediate peer group.

Many challenging children do not pick up the social do's and don'ts from watching or being around others. They have a genuine inability to read social signals. Often they have poor conversational skills. They have something to say—and have to say it *right then* because it seems all-important. They also tend to be poor listeners—in part because they're thinking about what to say next (a characteristic that is hardly limited to challenging children). Past experience, even social rejection, hasn't helped them develop better social skills.

IT'S NOT HOPELESS: STRUCTURE, PREDICTABILITY, AND LEARNING SOCIAL SKILLS ARE SOLUTIONS

Challenging children need structure imposed on their social interactions. Arrange for your child to interact with only one child at a time—not as part of a group. Have shorter and time-limited play periods with activities determined in advance. All day at a friend's house, sleepovers, and couples getting together for dinner while "the children play as we socialize" are recipes for disaster. To have a better chance at some social success, your child needs the structure of a specific activity to fill the time and the predictability of knowing exactly when time will be up.

Even more, your child needs the social skills he never picked up. He needs coaching on what to do and when and how to do it. Start with a social mentor. In the early years, it can be you. In later elementary years, that mentoring has to come from someone else because by preadolescence your influence as a teacher is waning. By then, he will learn social skills better through an extracurricular activity under the auspices of an older peer or coach.

What You Can (and Can't) Do to Help
with Social Skills

Instruction that takes place "in the moment" is more likely to make a difference. Not surprisingly, this limits your ability to influence your child's social development since such relationships usually develop elsewhere. However, some kind of social-skills training at home, at school, on the field—especially at the time of the activity—will be most effective.

Quick Tip

Use family interactions to model, teach, and reward good social skills.

INCREASING AWARENESS OF SOCIALLY APPROPRIATE BEHAVIORS

Before you decide on specific target behaviors, explore how much your child understands about social behaviors. Make a list that includes both socially acceptable and unacceptable behaviors, preferably in his words. See if he knows the difference between appropriate and inappropriate social behaviors and whether he recognizes which ones he does or doesn't do. You can't expect him to change a behavior he doesn't realize is unacceptable and he can't change one he is unaware that he does. Nor can you expect him to substitute an alternate behavior if he doesn't know one.

SAMPLE POSITIVE SOCIAL BEHAVIORS

- Keep hands and feet to self.

- Stay in the play area; stay with the group.

- Take turns.

> ### SAMPLE POSITIVE SOCIAL BEHAVIORS (CONTINUED)
>
> - Accept activity suggestion from others.
>
> - Offer others a choice of activities.
>
> - Allow others to have the first turn.
>
> - Play by the rules.
>
> - Talk quietly.
>
> - Allow others to talk without interruption.
>
> - Ask on-topic questions.
>
> - Stop activity when game is finished or when others suggest it is over.
>
> - Make empathetic statements.

Set up short visits to the park or playground where your child doesn't know the children. Pick one or two positive behaviors to watch for in other kids. Make it a game—whoever spots and describes it first, wins. Have your child look for a negative interaction, describe it, and relate what the children could have done differently. Then reinforce the lesson with a trip to his own playground or park as a reward and another opportunity to practice.

HOME-BASED REWARD PROGRAM

Ask your child to select one or two behaviors to practice over the next two weeks. Record them on a chart, cards, or erasable board. Post it for easy reference but not so conspicuously that it would embarrass him. Discuss what he wants to earn for using those new behaviors, especially around friends. Start by having him practice during games and play situations with you or his siblings. Having each sibling work on his own behavior reinforces the fact that all children have to meet family expectations and these efforts aren't to fix one broken child.

Quick Tip

- -

Having all siblings practice social skills conveys that everyone needs to meet expectations for appropriate behavior. This keeps your challenging child from feeling singled out as the one whose behavior needs to be fixed.

Although the behavior change may not last without reminders, practice, and feedback, it is worth the effort if it results in fewer negative incidents. Continued focus where he needs to use those skills (like at the Scout meeting) has the best chance of helping your child learn the necessary behaviors. Your goal

HOW TO HELP YOUR CHILD DEVELOP SOCIAL SKILLS

- Select one or two behaviors your child needs to do in a given social situation. Be specific.

- Discuss them with your child.

- Practice or role-play the specific behaviors.

- Give feedback—praise, a high sign, initial a card—when he uses the desired skill or behavior.

- Before he enters the situation, ask him what behaviors he should do (to see if he remembers from practicing or the last time).

- Discuss and reinforce his successes.

- Continue to focus on the same behaviors before going on to new ones.

- Give feedback for behaviors he's already practiced even while working on new ones.

is improvement, which is not the same as a cure. His success in one situation does not mean that he can now handle all social venues.

Practice Makes . . . Better

Your child's popularity is not enhanced by his insistence on doing things his way and changing the rules (even his own). Through structured practice, help him learn how to take turns and play by the rules.

PLAYING BY THE RULES

Choose a game and divide the time available into three increments: your time, your child's time, and "real rule" time. Use a timer for each interval, during which everyone has to play by that interval's rules. For your time, you make the rules. These may include an extra roll of the dice if you don't like the first one. Or you may choose to play the game as intended. Before the next interval starts, review the rules to be used during that time. If it is "Sara time," everyone plays by that child's rules until the bell rings. If it's "real rule" time, everyone has to play according to the printed rules. Meet any complaints or attempts to change the rules with "Is it 'Sara time' or 'real rule' time?" This exercise gives your child practice at taking turns for a time-limited period. The bell signals an end to your child's turn to decide how things are done. This structured practice demonstrates to your child the importance of reviewing the rules before starting a game, or any other activity, and staying with them unless all agree to change.

> *Quick Tip*
> --
> Teach your child always to clarify the rules of a game or activity before starting. Structured practice at "my rules, your rules, real rules" helps a child learn how to take turns and play by the rules.

LESS IS BETTER

Long, unstructured social situations are a fight, meltdown, or accident waiting to happen. Therefore, it is important to structure social activities, gradually increasing the time your child spends with other children. Longer periods that incorporate new activities should follow successful social experiences.

Theodore: I think that having kids spend too much time with me, like for a sleepover or all day, is hard. When kids come over, usually for the first few hours, I can get along well with them doing things we both want to do, but then I get bored. I know I should let them choose because they're the guest, but sometimes I get carried away in doing what I want instead of what they'd rather do. Having someone over for only two or three hours makes it much easier for me.

LIMITED LUNCH DATE

Sharon: Most kids like to eat—especially fast food. While I'm not endorsing fast-food's nutritional value, a trip to one of those places holds great promise as a positive social experience. Identify one or two behaviors your child should do during the outing. Be sure he understands that the next trip (or some other reward) depends on his using those behaviors this time. Invite your child's friend to join you for a meal at a fast-food restaurant. If your child is easily overstimulated, go at an off-peak hour for a late breakfast, early lunch, or dinner to avoid the crowds. Make sure both children understand the schedule in advance—meal only, no play. It's a good idea to have your child explain the outing's rules to his friend. That way you find out what he remembers and he takes some ownership of the process.

The next time, add on ten to fifteen minutes of play after the meal. Set a time limit (or timer) and reward your child for using the behaviors he practiced or discussed at home. If all goes well, the next trip can include fifteen minutes of play before and after the meal. Incorporate time at a park or neutral territory (neither child's home) before you invite a child to your house. Some children do better on neutral ground than at home. And some do better at a friend's house than at their own. Take these things into consideration as you increase the scope of the activities. Gradually add on time and vary the activity according to the level of success each time out.

Quick Tip

Inviting another child for a fast-food meal and gradually increasing playtime structured around it can help your child enhance his ability to interact in socially appropriate ways in time-limited situations.

STRUCTURED PLAY

Set up short periods of play for your child and a friend with a predetermined agenda. Less time with a specific agenda of activities increases the likelihood that your child will handle the situation successfully.

Have your child practice greetings, taking turns, and sharing toys. Assume the role of a real friend, then trade roles, with you taking the child's part and vice versa. Next, invite that friend over to play. Limit activities and playtime to reduce the chance that trouble will erupt. If you know your child can't play board games without blowing up or that wrestling matches invariably end in disaster, ban those activities for the visit. Instead, plan specific activities that are more side-by-side play than those requiring a lot of interaction or cooperation. Invite the other child to bake cookies, watch a rented movie, or do a craft project you set up and supervise. Have them choose between two activities that you know your child can handle. Go bowling, swimming, or to a movie.

Just before the friend arrives, have your child list the behaviors he has practiced and should use. Remind him of the rewards he can earn if he does so. When the visit is over, reward him if uses those behaviors. The reinforcement will be more effective if he gets the reward immediately after the other child departs. Structuring the time enhances the likelihood of leaving both children with a good feeling and a desire to do it again.

HELP YOUR CHILD FIND COMMON INTERESTS WITH OTHER KIDS

Encourage your child to enroll in high-interest and hands-on classes or clubs so he can meet kids with common interests. Team sports entail a lot of waiting around with group success dependent on individual cooperation and performance. Classes in art, pottery, photography, computer, and drama, or school chess and debate clubs, are more like parallel play where each child engages in something he enjoys doing. More physical endeavors include horseback riding and martial arts. Before- or after-school activities allow him to associate with children who can see him in a different light and may not know of his classroom behavior (or exploits). Other children's experiences with him are liable to be more positive when they share a common interest in your child's strength area. Moreover, in time-limited and structured activities, your child's social interaction is more likely to be successful.

Jan: By the time I applied what I knew about Theodore's need for structure and building on common interests, he had become so badly burned by his social isolation that he no longer wanted to invite anyone over. Now he shies away from reaching out to other kids—despite being in a new school environment where he is neither teased nor harassed, and has acquaintances, if not friends.

Theodore: Now that I'm in middle school, I've made friends, but I'm not close enough to them to invite them over. I'm so used to not being accepted by other kids that I'm afraid to reach out to new kids at school. I'm afraid that they'll reject me.

Back to Basics: Learning How to Make Friends and Get Along with Others

Sharon: Jan and Jamie are not the only parents who worry about their child's friendships. Marie had come to me for advice about her daughter's temper tantrums. Now, a year and a half later, she was back. She still wanted to discuss Amy, but it wasn't her temper she was worried about. It was her social life. Amy was so bossy with friends that, one by one, they were no longer available when she called. As Marie explained it, "Now Amy has no friends except me and I don't like her enough to be her one and only friend. In three weeks, it will be June, school will be out, and it will be just Amy and me. You have to help me."

While making friends comes naturally to many kids, some children—like Amy—have a talent for alienating them. It does no good to tell your child, as Marie informed Amy, that she'll have no friends if she keeps acting "that way" or ask how she would feel if someone treated her "like that." A lecture doesn't give her the skills she needs to better handle a social situation. Regardless of the cause (immaturity, lack of experience, or a specific disorder), your child needs coaching in the basics. This includes one or more of the following social skills:

1. Social entry skills (what to say when first joining a group or starting a conversation)

2. Conversation

3. Reading and responding to social cues

4. Sharing and taking turns

5. Conflict resolution

Jan: One of Theodore's most critical deficiencies was his inability to pick up on social cues. He interrupted because he was so eager to share whatever was on his mind that he didn't see the effect his behavior had on others. He never figured out that if a teacher told the class, "Pipe down!" it meant that if the noise continued, she'd get angry. As other kids matured, they became more responsive to nonverbal cues. He didn't because he never saw them.

SOCIAL ENTRY SKILLS

Sharon: It's not hard to recognize a child who lacks social entry skills. This child hovers at the edge of a group taking basketball shots making comments like "Oh, that's so easy. Anyone can make that shot." It doesn't occur to him to compliment the shooter, let alone to ask if he can join the group. If your child's social interactions break down right from the start, he may need you to show him how to greet others or call people by name. Teach him phrases to use when he enters a social situation. Develop a list of possible greetings. Have him select one or two and reinforce it each time he uses them in a social or family situation.

Jan: When he entered fourth grade, it was time for Theodore to get training in social skills. We'd dealt with medication and had restructured daily life by working with Sharon. Theodore had also gone away to camp that summer. Using the same process to find every other professional (get recommendations, talk to them until I found the one that felt "right"), we enrolled Theodore in a social-skills training program called Stepping Stones. It was time-consuming since it met weekly, with the parents in one room and the kids (all boys approximately his age) in another. We had to commit to the entire academic year and attend faithfully every week. The program leaders explained that missing sessions or leaving before the year was up were highly detrimental to the group dynamics.

Parents had to make the same commitment as the kids, though it was sad to see how few fathers—unlike Jamie—felt this was high enough priority to be there every week. We went over the same material as the kids so we could reinforce during the following week whatever they were working on.

An area the group worked on first addressed another of Theodore's social difficulties, which was not knowing how to join in and make a good first impression. One reason (which also affected relations with teachers) was his inability to make eye contact. The group did an exercise that helped him improve eye contact.

ASSIGNMENT FOR PRACTICING AND IMPROVING EYE CONTACT

1. Do you know the color of the following people's eyes?

   ■ Your mom?   Yes   No
   Her color is:

   ■ Your dad?   Yes   No
   His color is:

   ■ Your teacher?   Yes   No
   His or her color is:

   ■ A friend   Yes   No
   Name:
   Write the color here:

2. I notice that this child is looking at others in the eyes this week more than usual.

   ■ Parent: Yes   No
   ■ Teacher: Yes   No
   ■ Friend: Yes   No

Adapted from Stepping Stones Social Skills Training Program, In Step, P.C., Fairfax, VA, 1997.

The counselors gave Theodore and us copies of the weekly homework assignment. Following their advice, I made copies for Theodore's teachers and asked for their feedback. I seldom heard from them, and thus had little sense they were reinforcing him for practicing what he was learning. One week, however, one of his teachers related to me how Theodore had walked right up to her, looked her straight in the eyes, and said, "Hi." Because I'd given her the assignment, she knew he was doing his "eye contact" homework and checking out her eye color.

Learning to make eye contact has benefited Theodore at home as well as with teachers and peers. It's easier now to get and keep his attention. Consequently, the annoyance I felt when unsure if Theodore was listening has diminished markedly. Even if he does it just to humor me, I find that upswing of his head to meet my eyes reassuring.

CONVERSATION

Sharon: Many challenging children are unskilled at both starting and maintaining conversations. They don't know what to say and they certainly don't know what not to say. Communication for many challenging kids is more a pattern of statements than dialogue. They announce what they think without waiting to hear (or caring) what others have to say. For some, impulsivity causes them to state whatever comes into their heads. Others are so focused on their own agenda that no one else's needs or feelings occur to them. Lack of skills gets in the way of saying things that will enhance social interaction.

Jan: Theodore first needed to be taught how to start conversations. We worked with him on the following conversation do's and don'ts. Once he had begun to follow some of these, we practiced the art of deepening a conversation. That started to get us beyond the " 'How was your day at school?' 'Fine' " dinner table conversations.

DO's

DO Wait for a pause to begin to speak.
DO Ask appropriate questions.
DO Use a clear calm voice.
DO Make statements expressing interest in what the speaker is saying.

DO's (continued)

DO Look the other person in the eyes.

DO Stand one leg length away from the speaker.

DO Make active listening statements such as "Uh-huh,"
"Oh!" and "Mmmm."

DON'Ts

DON'T Hog the show.

DON'T Change the subject too quickly.

DON'T Look away when someone is talking.

DON'T Interrupt.

Adapted from Cathi Cohen, *Raise Your Child's Social I.Q.: Stepping Stones to People Skills for Kids* (Silver Spring, MD: Advantage Books, 2000. 1-888-238-8588.)

Sharon: Help your child develop a social script, including several lines he can practice to start conversations. Role-play using these new phrases. With older children and preadolescents, ask what information they would want to tell others about themselves. Then teach them how to ask questions to elicit such information from their peers. Help them distinguish between making suggestions and making demands. Suggest phrases that underscore a cooperative process. Stress the need to listen to what others say. Since your child's idea of conversation is that he talks, stopping to hear what others say is not part of his usual exchange. Teach your child how to become an active listener.

Jan: As a college professor, when I taught a unit on conflict resolution, I had my students do an exercise to enhance their active listening skills. Playing a similar "Reflective Listening Game" with Theodore helped everyone in the family become more respectful listeners. We used five minutes at dinnertime and while driving in the car to practice and reinforce this skill.

THE REFLECTIVE LISTENING GAME

1. You start a conversation such as: "How was your day at school?"

2. Your child responds by reflecting back what you said by putting it in his own words before answering: "You want to know how my day was? I had a good day at school until it was time for P.E. I was the last kid chosen for basketball teams."

3. You repeat in your own words what your child says before responding: "You said you had a good day until you were the last person chosen for basketball teams in P.E. I'm sorry to hear that. Has this happened before? Was it the teacher who was assigning kids or captains picking people for their teams?"

4. Most kids will just answer you with a long complaint about being picked last. Stop your child and ask him to reflect back what you said before he answers. He replies, "Oh, right, I'm supposed to say it back to you first. OK. You said you were sorry I was the last kid picked."

5. You then correct him and say, "No. I also wanted to know who was doing the choosing—the teacher or the captains."

6. Your child replies, "Right. You wanted to know who was doing the choosing. Well, it was Jeremy and Oliver."

Adapted from Cathi Cohen, *Raise Your Child's Social I.Q.: Stepping Stones to People Skills for Kids* (Silver Spring, MD: Advantage Books, 2000. 1-888-238-8588.)

READING AND RESPONDING TO SOCIAL CUES

Sharon: Your child's poor understanding of how to relate to others may be a function of his inability to read nonverbal cues. After all, you can't expect him to perform a set of behaviors he never even notices. If he seems unaware of others' feelings, he may be oblivious to the facial expressions, body language, and behaviors that signal them.

Read stories together and ask him to predict what will happen next. Tape television shows focused on young teens or elementary-aged children. When you sit together to watch it, pause the tape to:

1. Figure out what the characters are thinking or feeling by looking at their facial expressions and body language.

2. Identify both positive and negative social behaviors.

3. Predict what will be said next.

4. Predict the outcome.

5. Suggest alternative lines or expressions the characters might use to get the same point across.

Because it uses television, your child is likely to find this exercise more palatable than just discussion. You may need to guarantee that he can watch the show without interruptions after you finish.

SHARING AND TAKING TURNS

Often a child's view of sharing is that "You can have it when I'm tired of it or it's broken, whichever comes first." If your child always dictates the rules and decides who plays with what and for how long, then sharing and taking turns are not part of his social repertoire. If fights result when a sibling or peer picks up your child's toy even if just to examine it, then some guidelines and instruction are in order.

When friends come over, prepare your child by suggesting he set out three activities he would like to do and allow his friend to choose from them. Teach him the language for offering peers the first turn, including such phrases as "You go first." Using a reward program to reinforce letting others go first or taking turns helps shift the emphasis from winning or losing to developing your child's social skills so other kids will play with him.

Remove a few of the more "sacred" toys from the play area to reduce the chance your child will get upset if another child wants to play with them. Make it clear that if he doesn't want others to play with something, he will have to wait until later to play with it himself.

Quick Tip

Prevent blowups by removing favorite toys from the play area before friends come over. Remind your child that if he doesn't want to share something, he has to wait until later to play with it himself.

If your child suddenly becomes possessive about toys he lost interest in long ago, it's usually because someone else wants them. Prevent arguments by requiring that your child pick three toys or other special possessions he doesn't have to share. Have him mark these treasures with a colored dot (office sticker dots). These toys are off limits to everyone else; all others have to be shared.

Quick Tip

To keep toys or possessions from becoming hoarded treasures, allow your child to use colored dots to mark a limited number of them (three works well) as off limits. He has to share everything else.

Using a timer is an easy way to prevent arguments over how long "a turn" lasts. Teach your child to use words, not actions, to request the next turn.

Quick Tip

Timers are very useful to determine how long "a turn" lasts.

CONFLICT RESOLUTION

If your child plays by his own rules and attempts to control the play situation, then conflict is sure to arise. Teaching social skills can reduce conflicts but it doesn't teach your child how to deal with such situations.

Because conflict is inevitable in human relationships, children have to learn how to deal with disagreements. Rehearsing alternative responses and reinforcing your child's use of them helps him develop conflict resolution skills. Learning how to express his opinion is part of the process.

If your child's interactions tend to be volatile, stay nearby and intervene before things go too far. Listen for signs of overstimulation—when things get too loud or too physical—and step in. (Too quiet may not be good either. Always check if things get too quiet. If all is well, it's an opportunity to reinforce success.) Limit your child's exposure to situations that are likely to trigger conflicts. Competitive games, low-interest activities, and high-energy or aggressive peers can easily result in social disaster.

Jan: Learning conflict resolution skills was one of the most valuable aspects of Theodore's social-skills training. A problem solver by nature, he quickly mastered this area. One outcome of his year of social-skills training was that his school chose him to serve as a peer mediator the following year.

Since problem solving also comes naturally to me, I could reinforce Theodore's ability by practicing with him. Using the follow-ing "Steps for Problem Solving" when we disagreed helped me keep my cool. Eventually, Theodore got better at it than I am. Often I'd be venting or lecturing him only to hear him propose possible solutions. It's sobering to realize that your challenging child is better at constructively channeling an emotionally volatile situation into a productive effort to find a solution.

STEPS FOR PROBLEM SOLVING

1. What is the real problem?

2. What are all the possible solutions?

3. What are the consequences of each solution?

4. Develop a plan of action.

5. Then develop a back-up plan of action.

6. Implement the solution.

Adapted from Stepping Stones Social Skills Training Program, In Step, P.C., Fairfax, VA, 1997. See also: Myrna B. Shure with Theresa Foy Digeronimo, *Raising a Thinking Child: Help Your Young Child to Resolve Everyday Conflicts and Get Along with Others: The "I Can Problem Solve" Program* (New York: Pocket Books, 1996).

Applying these steps meant that we first had to sort out what the problem was—whether it was a conflict with us or someone else. Occasionally, Theodore would blow up over something trivial, but when pressed, reveal that he was really upset over something at school. I had to listen carefully to what he was saying and hear him out fully. I've learned to listen carefully to the whole story be-fore responding, then rephrase what I'm hearing to make sure it's what he means.

Second, I have to allow Theodore to propose alternative solu-tions. If I suggest something, Theodore's far less likely to think it's worthwhile than if he comes up with it himself.

Third, Theodore has to assess the strengths and weaknesses of alternative solutions. I help ensure he reviews them all and doesn't stop with the first one, as he tends to do. I also help him consider long-term as well as short-term consequences.

Finally, once he develops a plan, we often write it down. If it solves a conflict between us, writing it down prevents later misunderstandings and keeps him focused on what he needs to do.

Sometimes it's difficult not to take the process personally. If Theodore has a problem with someone else, and I can see how to fix it, but he doesn't choose my solution, I have to remind myself that I'm not responsible for solving his problems for him.

I'm better at praising him for beginning the conflict resolution process, but often forget to check to see how things are going. If his conflict is with someone outside our family, it's too easy to forget.

Theodore: I benefited from the peer mediation experience because I learned how to solve problems with other kids by coming to a compromise. I learned all the different ways to do problem solving and that usually if you help someone solve a problem, you should never tell anyone else about it because people like to keep these things private. I liked being a peer mediator because I was able to help kids resolve problems they had with other kids. I was able to walk away feeling I'd been able to help somebody.

BIRTHDAY PARTIES: A SPECIAL CHALLENGE FOR THE SOCIALLY DEFICIENT CHILD

Sharon: Birthday parties (your own child's or someone else's) can be a real debacle for challenging children no matter how much they want to go and how many times they promise they'll "behave." If you are hosting the party, have fewer children and structure all of the activities. Find creative ways to celebrate your child's birthday so it doesn't result in overstimulation and subsequent meltdown.

If your child is invited to someone else's party, prepare him by making sure he knows what will happen and in what sequence. Make sure he understands who blows out the candles and who gets the presents. Because parties are so stimulating, your child may need to take a prearranged break.

Be prepared with reinforcers for "following the party guidelines." Young children may be happy with earning a coupon for a cupcake with candle, so they can have a chance to blow out their own candle when they get home. Others may enjoy some "special time" or an extra story with Mom or Dad when they get home. Some may benefit from a quiet activity and individual attention right after all that stimulation and shared attention. In some cases, a trip to a batting cage or a local playground to "shoot hoops" may be just the reinforcer they need right after having to lower their own natural level of exuberance.

Jan: Children's birthday parties weren't good social outings for Theodore. Invariably other kids held parties at wildly overstimulating places that he loved but didn't do well at. Either he'd fall apart there and withdraw or come home a basket case. Luckily, since both of our kids have summer birthdays, for years we had their parties at the pool. The guests could blow off steam by swimming and were less likely to get in trouble. Plus, we had the lifeguards to keep things under some semblance of control. Usually I limited the number of kids to the birthday age—if Theodore was turning seven, then he could invite only seven kids. Later, we switched to smaller celebrations, such as inviting a couple of kids for a movie and dinner.

Quick Tip

When you host a birthday party, limit the number of kids to what your child can tolerate without excessive stimulation. Have the party in an environment that allows you to maintain control over their activity level.

Coping with Teasing and Bullying— Victim or Perpetrator

IF YOUR CHILD IS A BULLY

Sharon: The difficulty with teasing and bullying is that it's a matter of definition and degree. It's not always easy to define but you know it when you see it. Verbal threats and aggression, name calling, and ganging up on another child are clear-cut examples of bullying. Interaction that takes advantage of a child's weakness, mocks, or taunts, or otherwise pokes fun that results in a child's feelings being hurt, qualifies as teasing.

There must be negative consequences for children who bully or tease. You have to change this behavior in your child before it becomes habitual for him. Regardless of his reasons for doing it, your intervention is the same:

- Identify the inappropriate behavior

- Teach the behaviors you want him to use instead

- Reinforce it when he acts appropriately

- Apply negative consequences when he bullies anyone

Punishment may be loss of the privilege to play at a specific location or with certain friends. You might restrict him from the activity he was doing when the teasing or bullying occurred. You might require him to make amends to the victim through "friendly behaviors" or apologize by note or telephone. Do not accept explanations (which are no more than rationalizations) for the behavior. Make it clear that bullying and hurtful teasing are unacceptable to you.

If another parent reports that your child is bullying soneone, be sure to get as many details of his behavior as you can. After thanking the other parent for bringing it to your attention, make clear your intention to handle it. Don't minimize or excuse the behavior and don't shift the focus to the other child. (If the parent thought his child was in any way responsible, he'd offer that information.)

Do not state in detail all that you will do. For some, it is never enough.

Some children capitalize on their size to bully other kids. Let your child know that his size does not give him the right to intimidate or bully anyone. On the other hand, sometimes kids interpret the behavior of a child who is much larger than his peers as intimidating or aggressive even when it isn't meant to be. Adults may attribute negative motive to a large child's exuberance or clumsiness. After a while, such a child may assume the role others have assigned to him. If that happens, his behavior can become more purposeful.

If your child's size or age contributes to a perception that he is a bully or he has already been labeled as one, you may need to change his school or play setting. Children in a new setting who don't know him are less likely to prejudge him as a bully. If he is too rough with smaller children, it may help to have him around children of varying ages or older ones who behave more appropriately.

In some cases a child who is teased and bullied at home will become a bully outside of it. Whether he does so out of frustration and anger or because that's the behavior pattern he knows best is beside the point. Bullying is unacceptable regardless of the cause and he must pay the consequences. If, however, your child has become a bully because that's what he sees at home, the first step to change his behavior is halting that pattern of family interaction. If he sees one parent bullying the other or the children, the family needs outside help. If the problem is bullying among siblings, clearly state your expectations for change, reinforce appropriate behavior when it occurs, and punish hurtful teasing and bullying.

Never forget the power of your words. Your bullying may not be physical. Your child can interpret your attempts at humor as hurtful. When he mimics your sarcasm to his friends, they may perceive it as teasing. Your child does not necessarily have the judgment to determine when and in what situations humor is appropriate.

IF YOUR CHILD IS A VICTIM

Some children are perpetual victims. Something about them invites taunts and teasing. Many times, the child's response is what keeps it going. If ridicule provokes the desired response (often one that evokes more trouble), the teaser is emboldened to continue. Help your child identify what might induce others to harass him.

Discuss with your child the context in which these comments are made. An overly sensitive child may interpret impersonal statements as hurtful. Help him distinguish between unintentional slights and hurtful teasing. Stay neutral when he overreacts to innocuous comments. Too much attention in response to your child's overreactions conveys that it really is a serious problem.

For hurtful teasing, review the words that others use. Get your child to see that some insults are untrue. Others are just silly and make no sense. In some cases, the child who teases has no idea what he's talking about. Discussion helps your child realize how meaningless slights are, such as "Your father has no hair," when the teaser hasn't even met your family.

Help your child look at the other person's motives. If he understands that teasing may be another child's only way to feel good about himself, it might not make your child feel so badly. Review them often so the words don't bother him as much. If he hears things repeatedly, especially in a safe place or when said with humor, they lose their impact.

Quick Tip

Desensitize your child to common taunts by reviewing them often enough that the words don't sting as much. Hearing things repeatedly reduces their impact.

Suggest that your child keep a journal. He should enter teasing remarks and his response. He can rate the remark, from one to ten, on how damaging it was to his feelings or the rest of his day. Likewise, he can rate his response, from one to five. Did he handle the situation the way you had discussed? Did he like the way he ignored or responded to the teasing? Was the comeback one he felt comfortable using? Was it effective? Would he react that way the next time?

Practice better ways to respond—or not respond. Teaching him a simple phrase to use equips him to handle the situation without you. Though "sticks and stones" may work for some kids, your child should find a phrase that works for him. More than once I have suggested that a parent teach his child to yell, "I won't fight you and you can't make me." Or "I'm not getting suckered into a fight." Besides conveying a sense of constrained power, such phrases can alert nearby adults that trouble may be brewing. The adult who comes to investigate can get the story without your child seeming to tattle. Of course, teach your child to walk away quickly after making a proclamation like this. No sense sticking around for the final round.

Theodore: I think I was teased because I was smaller than other kids and was always talking fast. I dealt with it by usually just isolating myself and trying to stay away from the kids who were teasing me. It made me feel as if I was inferior to them. I'm not teased now because the kids in my middle school are more accepting of me. I don't think I've changed very much but I guess to other people it looks like I have because no one ever teases me anymore.

Jan: The teasing and bullying Theodore endured in elementary school was the worst by-product of his attention deficit disorder. For several years, I didn't intervene because I thought all kids needed to learn to cope with teasing. When I realized it had gone beyond teasing to bullying—first verbal, then physical—that's when I tried (in vain, for the most part) to find ways to halt it. I felt constantly frustrated that the school was unsuccessful at stopping it. Even now, I find it hard to fairly assess the actions of the teachers and school administrators because I am still angry about what Theodore endured. Everyone knew it was taking place, but given how sneaky some kids are, the verbal and physical assaults generally took place when adults weren't around to catch them at it.

It wasn't until fifth grade that Theodore had a teacher who would swiftly intervene whenever she got wind of anyone harassing Theodore. She was adamant that no one had the right to treat a classmate disrespectfully. He seldom complained, however, for fear of looking like a "teacher's pet" and making things worse.

TECHNIQUES FOR DEALING WITH TEASING

There are specific techniques that can be taught—and that a child can learn—to help him cope with teasing. Not every child will be able to utilize every technique, but when presented with a variety of ways to handle teasing, as Theodore was in his social-skills group, he can try out different ones until he finds something that works.

TECHNIQUES FOR DEALING WITH BEING TEASED

- Laugh it off.

- Walk away.

- "I am *out* of here. See ya!"

- Involve yourself in something else.

- Go with the flow:

  - *"Tell me something I haven't heard before!"*

- Ask a distracting question or make a distracting face:

  - *"Do you know the time?"*

- Find a friend to hook up with.

- Acknowledge mistakes and move on:

  - *"You're right! I blew it! Next time I won't do that!"*

TECHNIQUES FOR DEALING WITH BEING TEASED (CONTINUED)

- If physically threatened or constantly harassed, tell an adult.

- Articulate the obvious:
  - *"You're kicking my chair!"*

- If dealing with whispering or exclusion, confront quietly and firmly:
  - *"Do you have something you want to say to me directly?"* or
  - *"I have no intention of getting into a fight over this."*

- Smirk and say nothing.

- Perfect a dirty look.

- Miscellaneous comebacks
  - *"Are you enjoying yourself because I'm not?"*
  - *"Oh well, what can I say?"*
  - *"Hello!"*
  - *"That's a good one."*
  - *"Don't believe everything you read!"*
  - *"Get over it!"*
  - *"Whatever!"*
  - *"Yeah, right!"*
  - *"Really?"*

Adapted from Cathi Cohen, *Raise Your Child's Social I.Q.: Stepping Stones to People Skills for Kids* (Silver Spring, MD: Advantage Books, 2000. 1-888-238-8588.)

Theodore found it difficult to apply the "Techniques for Dealing with Being Teased" he learned in social-skills training. He never felt comfortable using the comebacks needed to turn it off, didn't have friends to go to, and was afraid to tell adults. He found it hard to laugh it off, "go with the flow," or walk away. His solution was to isolate himself and hope no one would pick on him.

Other kids in the group, however, reported success, especially in developing comebacks that worked for them. One child, when teased, learned to respond by saying, "Oh yeah? Who cares what you think?" Then he'd walk away.

It's unclear whether Theodore isn't teased anymore because the kids are older and have stopped picking on anyone who is even slightly different, or because he is better able to cope. Undoubtedly moving to a new school has helped. Moreover, his experience as a peer mediator gave him some social status, bolstered his self-esteem, and made him feel less vulnerable.

Additional Thoughts on Social Skills

Sharon: Sometimes your child's limited social skills are related to whatever it is that makes your child more challenging—whether that is ADHD or simply a fiery temperament. More than 50 percent of children with ADHD, like Theodore, are deficient in social skills. If your child's poor social skills are inherently related to a diagnosed disorder, his social functioning may lag behind what you'd expect from someone else his age. A child with sensory integration dysfunction may get too close to others when talking, barge into a group, or become too physical when playing. Poor social skills, by themselves, are not diagnostic, but a diagnosed disorder can help explain why all the discussion in the world along the lines of "You really should treat Bobby more nicely," will not result in meaningful change. Challenging children need to be taught the social skills that most of us just picked up. The approaches we've discussed can be effective whether the problem stems from immaturity, disorder, limited experience, or poorly developed skills.

YOUR DREAMS OR HIS?

Just because you feel your child is a jock or you want him to be one, doesn't make him a jock. Determine what your child is good at and his level of interest in doing it. Foster his strengths. Then find social situations to match. Help your child develop a peer group that shares his interests.

TOO MUCH TO DO, TOO LITTLE TIME

Too much overplanning and overscheduling can result in a child's decreased ability to establish and build strong social relationships. If the peer group changes by activity, he isn't able to engage in a variety of pastimes with one group of children. He can't work through differences and emerge with increased awareness of others' needs and preferences. And he won't experience the positive and negative effects of his own behavior.

SOCIAL-SKILLS GROUPS

Social-skills groups allow your child to experience success in a group situation and may give him the opportunity to assume a positive leadership role. He might even be the model for others. Although children learn new behaviors most effectively in the environment where they live and play, social-skills training groups in a therapist's office have their place. They provide feedback on your child's social behavior in a supervised setting. Often your child can hear from a group member what he would not hear in the heat of the moment from you or a friend outside the group. Your child will still need prompting and feedback outside the group as he tries new ways to handle social situations. The most meaningful benefits result from practicing what he learns with his peers in daily life.

The most successful social-skills training groups have some form of parental participation. You need to know what your child is learning so you can practice with him and reinforce his new skills at home. If possible, give the training information to teachers, coaches, and others who see and work with your child in a group situation. They can reinforce your child's new skills, which will enhance the likelihood that the training results in meaningful change.

To find a social-skills group, ask the other professionals your child has seen if they have recommendations, particularly counselors (including school counselors), therapists, social workers, psychologists, or psychiatrists. Also check with your pediatrician and with local mental health agencies, both public and private.

Unfortunately, teaching a child social skills doesn't necessarily mean peers are going to notice when he tries to use them. In fact, prepare him for their negative reaction. After all, it's probably taken years of poor interaction for your child's social life to be what it is now. It will take time—and maybe even getting your child into a fresh environment (new school, summer camp, or other activities) where he doesn't feel the constant struggle of trying to change others' perceptions of him.

Jan: We didn't see immediate progress when Theodore embarked on social-skills training. But we knew he was listening, learning, and storing away the knowledge for use later. Now he looks people in the eye more often and has become particularly adept at maintaining a conversation.

Theodore's classmates weren't receptive when he tried to interact in more socially appropriate ways, which disheartened him. They had labeled him and weren't going to change their minds.

Theodore: I've never been able to recognize when other kids are getting annoyed with my talking or anything. Also my talking fast would sometimes make kids not want to be friends because they couldn't understand me half of the time. Even after I went to Stepping Stones, I found that it was hard to make friends because I'd gotten timid. Now that I'm in a new school and have been able to start over, I'm more confident so I'm able to make friends more easily. I also find it easier to make friends at camp, where they haven't spent all year in class with me.

*   *   *   *

Sharon: Not all social isolation is indicative of problems. Your child may be one of the lucky ones who entertains himself and is content with quiet, independent activities. He may not require the amount of outside stimulation that you think is needed. The bottom line is to learn whether your child spends time alone by choice or because others are excluding him.

11

"We're All in This Together"

Restructuring Family Dynamics

Theodore: My family doesn't treat me like I'm some strange weirdo just because I have ADHD. Sometimes I feel my parents spend too much time on me trying to do things to help me and figure out ways to make my life easier. This helps me but I don't think they should be spending so much time doing it. When they do, it makes me feel as if I am someone who can't take care of myself. Other than that, I feel like I'm treated pretty much the same as they treat each other.

Sharon: Raising a child is the most emotional endeavor most people will ever take on. The books and parenting pundits say it must be done with consistency. Yet, with differing backgrounds and at times conflicting priorities, parents' approaches to parenting are likely to be very different.

Often a gap in parenting styles just makes a challenging situation more difficult. Most people's style of child rearing reflects that of their parents. They may do certain things because that's what their parents did. At the same time, they may do other things completely opposite, having vowed "never to do it that way because that is exactly what my mother did to me."

Moreover, my experience is that parents tend to react most strongly to those behaviors they did not like in themselves or others growing up around them. This can result in some serious discrepancies in what behaviors grab parents' attention. Dad may react strongly to something that Mom barely notices. Likewise,

Mom may repeatedly punish something that Dad sees as trivial, if he sees it at all. Mom, focusing on behavior that is of little importance to Dad, after a while will interpret his lack of response as personal rejection. "If you really cared about how I feel, you would support me in this," she says in arguments about their children's behavior. However, not only does the behavior not bother Dad, he's barely aware of it when it occurs. Years of such discord can be exceedingly tough on a marriage.

Add a challenging child to the mix and it's no wonder that marriages suffer. Parental disagreement on how to handle that child commonly leads to one adopting the role of the child's protector and the other that of disciplinarian. Not surprisingly, this just confuses the child more and becomes an additional obstacle to attaining any degree of consistency.

Jan: Jamie and I get along exceedingly well, with only an occasional fight or disagreement, usually over trivial matters. We have similar views on child rearing and almost never argue about money. We have two lovely children, a nice home, and a cute dog. My image of domestic bliss had only one discordant element—one of those lovely children had our household in chaos. Even after Theodore's diagnosis of attention deficit disorder, I clung to my image of our family as essentially functional—not completely messed up like all those other people who didn't know how to deal with their challenging child.

We are, in fact, a functional family. But that doesn't mean Jamie and I didn't have to deal with problematic aspects of our family dynamics and seriously rethink how we interacted with each other and our kids. We began to recognize that we had defined our roles as: Theodore the "Bad"; "Little Miss Perfect" Caroline; "Too Easily Frustrated, Chronic-Yeller" Mom; and "Easygoing but You'd Better Not Push Too Hard or You'll Regret It" Dad ("Because He Yells Even Louder than Mom"). Ouch.

Caroline, in her own way, can be as difficult as Theodore. And certainly to me, at times, she can be even more frustrating. Since she has no disorder other than adolescence, her occasional noncompliance was, to me, willful disobedience in ways I felt

Theodore's bad behavior generally wasn't. Sharon told us not to attribute negative motive or take bad behavior personally, but that's hard for me.

With Theodore's ADHD diagnosis came a new dimension to our previous roles: Theodore—the endearing, yet frustrating child with the disability that only I had read and studied enough to understand. This gave me the undisputed title of Defender of Theodore. Caroline—the budding adolescent who would not "get with the program," thus undermining my efforts to have the smoothly run, highly structured household so necessary for Theodore. Jamie—the one who, having not read enough and therefore being unable to fully understand Theodore's ADHD, tended to overreact to my chastising Caroline for what she did—became the Defender of (and Rationalizer for) Caroline.

Setting aside those roles and focusing just on the behavior helped us develop policies that covered both Caroline and Theodore. One set of guidelines meant they both earned the same punishment if they broke a rule and the same privilege if they did what they were supposed to do. At times, both kids fell short of doing what was required. Whereas Theodore had ADHD, Caroline had attitude. Sometimes we took a different approach for Theodore, but we eliminated our previous double standard by holding them to the same behavior expectations.

Sharon: Theodore isn't Caroline. This thought has occurred to Theodore, as well. Try as he might, certain things just don't come as easily to him as they do to Caroline. Jan and Jamie's response to Theodore isn't the same as their response to Caroline either. What works with Caroline doesn't with Theodore. That's a double whammy for him. When the parenting techniques that come naturally don't work, parents become frustrated and desperate for results. This message gets through to a child like Theodore who, try as he might, isn't getting it right. When he sees how readily his sister adapts, it certainly doesn't enhance his self-esteem. Compared to her, he knows he's a frustration to his parents.

Sibling Relations

When you are repeatedly challenged by one child's behavior, you reach a point where you'll do whatever it takes to prevent blowups. As a result, you avoid placing demands on the more difficult child, relying on his sibling to do more than his share of household chores and responsibilities. As you make necessary adjustments to meet the needs of the challenging child, the "easier" child becomes the unwilling victim of the schedule changes and curtailed activities. He must "go along" in an effort to keep the peace.

If you recognize this pattern, you need to redress the imbalance you've created. Start by rewarding your nonchallenging child for the additional demands you place on him. Without comparing children, award praise and privileges as extra-duty pay. This reinforces a child who well deserves it while setting a positive example for your more challenging child.

Watch out for roles that communicate favoritism. If your child complains or you feel there's an imbalance, take action to change that perception. Figure out ways in which you have taken on "defender versus disciplinarian" roles. Discuss methods for changing your behavior, such as doing fun activities with the child for whom you are the "disciplinarian." Consider ways in which you and your partner can switch roles.

Make sure you spend time alone with your less challenging child on a regular basis. Special, private time with Mom or Dad demonstrates your feelings in a way that no reward or privilege can. Moreover, it gives that child the opportunity to share his frustrations. Be accepting of these feelings. Don't minimize or judge his thoughts on the struggles of sharing space with someone as difficult as his sibling can be. Remember how defensive you become when you vent about the trials of living with your challenging child and others minimize your plight.

If doing things together as a family is too difficult, opt instead for excursions with one child at a time. The result is liable to be a better experience for both of you. You are more likely to get through the activity without major meltdown, each child has his own time, and you can be reminded of the qualities you like in your children.

> ### Quick Tip
> --
> Short outings with one child at a time often are more successful than excursions with the entire family. They minimize the likelihood of meltdowns and give you time alone with each child.

THE FLASHLIGHT EFFECT

The child who challenges creates what I call the "flashlight effect." By drawing the bulk of the parents' attention with his behavior, the spotlight on the challenging child means that the other kids escape scrutiny entirely or get away with far more than they would otherwise. Parents often don't notice what their other children are doing—or their behavior looks so much more benign, they don't bother to address it. As the challenging child's behavior improves and the flashlight effect is removed, the shadows in the dark corners lift. The dichotomy between "Little Miss Perfect" and the "bad" child is no longer so sharp. When you change the rules or apply them to the "perfect" child too, it can breed resentment in the child accustomed to less scrutiny.

Jan: I understood the flashlight effect once we developed one set of rules that applied to Caroline as well as Theodore. She was accustomed to being "Little Miss Perfect" as compared to "Bad" Theodore. She was also used to getting away with things because of our focus on Theodore's disruptive behavior. Escaping our scrutiny served her well, though there is no question that she also suffered from our inattention. A single set of rules, combined with Theodore's improved behavior, meant we had more time to focus on her. We had more time to spend with her—and more attention to focus on her behavior—which suddenly didn't look so perfect anymore.

Caroline: After having spent so much time being seen as an angel, it was tough to suddenly realize that not only was I not an angel, I was in fact imperfect. That's hard to accept for someone who for so long has only received praise.

Changing Family Dynamics

"MIND YOUR BUSINESS, NOT HIS!"

Sharon: The first step to changing family dynamics is to clarify roles. Parents parent. Siblings don't parent siblings. Since this is a common problem where the less challenging child tells the challenging child what to do, make it a rule to "Mind *your* business, not his."

> ### Pointer for Effective Parenting
> --
> Make this a mantra: "Mind your business, not his."
> This policy reduces the "competitive tattling" of all children, challenging or not.

Jan: Our kids are tired of hearing "Mind your business, not his," because we repeat it endlessly, particularly at dinner. It quiets the offender quickly. Though the quick fix has been enough so far, if necessary, we could add bonuses for days we can go without needing the reminder. Until then, this Band-Aid minimizes the problem.

Sharon: Step two is to put the responsibility back onto your child for doing what he or she is supposed to do. Parents are not in charge of getting the challenging child dressed in the morning—

that's your child's role. Establish clear guidelines and rules to convey your expectations to him.

Step three is to be true to your other roles in life. Before you were anyone's mother or father, you were, likely, someone's wife, husband, or partner. That person continues to have expectations of you as a partner in life, not just a coparent. Your parenting relationship is enhanced if your life partnership is fulfilling.

What most often gets lost in the process of raising children is your individuality. Being somebody's mother or father too often takes precedence over who you are as an individual. The increased stress of raising a challenging child depletes your reserves, draining you in a way that no other responsibility does. If you don't *make* time for yourself, there will be nothing left to give to your children.

THE FAMILY MEETING

Family meetings provide a forum for structured discussion where everyone can have his say. Just as your child has to learn how to solve problems in his social relationships, so, too, families need to learn how to resolve differences. Family meetings structure communication by providing an effective mechanism for solving problems as well as exchanging ideas on things like vacation destinations.

Most family issues, both positive and negative, get resolved on the spot—often in the heat of the moment. One result is that families make decisions in reaction to negative events with little time to consider what the outcomes might be. By structuring what gets said and how it is expressed, family meetings allow highly emotional issues to be discussed more calmly and rationally.

Develop an agenda for a family meeting by posting a blank form, titled "Family Meeting Agenda," in the kitchen or another central point each week. Everyone—not just Mom and Dad—can add to it. Doing so gives everyone a sense that they have input into what happens at family meetings.

Use the posted form as a mechanism for responding to your child's request for a privilege or something he wants to do, which of course he wants decided right then. You can say, "That's a great idea (or 'that's something we can consider'). Write it on the agenda."

This keeps you honest, too. Too often, what your children have heard is "We'll see," or "I'll talk about it with your father/mother and get back to you later." Later never arrives. Consequently, they badger you senseless until you give them an answer, preferably the one they want to hear. Turn it off by telling your child to put his request on the agenda.

Another effective response to intense badgering is "I need time to talk to your mother/father. If you need an answer right now, the answer will be 'No.' " Pause, then ask: "Do you want me to answer you right now?" If he does, say no. The frequency of badgering will rapidly diminish.

Quick Tip

Halt intense badgering by telling your child to put his request on the family meeting agenda. Alternatively, say: "I need time to talk to your mother/father. If you want an answer now, it will be 'No.' Do you want me to answer now?"

A written agenda for the family meeting, compiled ahead of time, informs everyone about what will be discussed and helps keep discussion on track. Review it before the meetings to ensure the topics are subject to group discussion and decision. Some things, such as issues of health, safety, or behaviors that violate the law, are not.

Initially, include the same items in the agenda. Discuss chores, privileges, and behavior at each meeting before you discuss new items. One of the most important guidelines is that each person can only discuss his own behavior. Siblings may not comment on each other's behavior. Instead, each child reports on his own progress, which is less threatening because it becomes routine.

Often, especially when you start holding family meetings, participation can be a problem. Some family members may not want to take the time. Some don't want to come together as a group (experience has taught them this is not going to be fun) and some can't make it all the way through the meeting without getting upset. Conclude each family meeting with a fun, child-oriented activity such as ordering pizza, watching a video, making sundaes, or playing a board game, with participation conditional on joining in the meeting.

A common pitfall of family meetings is that some members tend to be overparticipators while others are underparticipators. An effective method for controlling that is to hand out pieces of colored paper or paper clips, with a different color for each person. Poker chips, pickup sticks, etc. also work. Give everyone one or two clips for each agenda item. Every time you speak, you give up a clip. When you are out of clips, you are out of comments. If you use at least 80 percent of your clips, and stay to the end, you're eligible to participate in the postmeeting activity. (Adolescents may need a different incentive. By this age, just getting them to stay through the meeting is a coup.)

Establish guidelines for what constitutes appropriate clip use. You can set different requirements depending on your children's individual needs. If one child tends to make editorial rather than constructive comments, make "positive suggestions" the criteria for the reward activity. Require the underparticipator to use a certain number of clips to be eligible.

The same guidelines apply to parents. Parental domination of family meetings (a not uncommon occurrence) violates the pur-

FAMILY MEETINGS

PURPOSE

A regularly scheduled time for the whole family to establish guidelines, discuss behavior, solve problems, make decisions, and plan for vacations and special events.

PROCEDURES

- Set a regularly scheduled time to hold family meetings every week.

- Rotate the role of chairperson weekly. Even the youngest gets to chair meetings.

- Rotate the role of secretary. Younger children can use a tape recorder.

- Prepare a written agenda for each meeting. Post blank agenda form on refrigerator or other central point so everyone can add to it. Make sure topics are appropriate for family discussion.

- Put topics not covered at the previous meeting at the top of the next meeting's agenda.

- Keep written minutes to document decisions.

- Enforce a time limit for topics to ensure meetings do not exceed 20–25 minutes with younger children, 30–40 minutes with adolescents.

- Make sure all members have a chance to offer ideas/comments. Encourage brainstorming solutions.

- Use good communication skills.

- For under- or overparticipators, use paper clips (one color per person) to monitor participation. One clip for each comment. When you're out of clips, you're out of comments. Require underparticipators to use a certain number of clips to be eligible for the reward activity.

- Plans and decisions made at one meeting stay in effect until the next meeting.

- Conclude every meeting with a fun family activity (i.e., ordering a pizza, playing a board game, watching a movie).

pose and your child's confidence that his voice counts as much as yours. Often the worst scenes result from a parent dominating a discussion so that a child feels he'll never be heard.

Jan: We found family meetings useful for discussing many issues, though they tended to run too long and cover too little. We sometimes had difficulties with the mechanics and following the rules. Using pickup sticks ensured everyone had an opportunity to talk, which curbed our parental tendency to dominate discussions.

Usually, we had full agendas and a twenty-to-thirty-minute limit seemed too short. Finding solutions takes time. Even when we used family meetings to discuss vacation destinations, we couldn't do that quickly. Invariably, we'd go over the time limit, the kids would get restless, and we'd have to decide whether to keep going or stop, leaving important matters unresolved. Now we use meetings for the issues that require a more structured discussion. Increasingly, we have focused family meetings on matters affecting everyone, such as reallocating chores and tasks not being done.

Theodore: I thought that family meetings were a very effective way of figuring out anything we thought that we should change or fix. They were well organized because we each would get a couple of pickup sticks and that would be the number of times we would be allowed to talk. It was good that we traded jobs each week for running the meetings and writing things down, because we didn't argue over whose turn it was.

They also worked because we had a piece of paper on the refrigerator. If anything came up during the week that we wanted to talk about, we'd put it on the list and talk about it at the meeting.

Also, they worked because after each one, we would all do something together, like play a game, watch a movie, or do something. That was important because we weren't able to do things together as a family often enough.

Caroline: Family meetings are helpful because they allow everyone to have a say in such things as the distribution of chores and what we're going to do over the weekend. Sometimes they go on for too long because people aren't willing to compromise.

The Inevitable Power Struggles— Every Family Has Them

Sharon: Family meetings, household structure, behavior programs, and contracts are all designed to reduce the frequency of inevitable power struggles between parents and their children—challenging or not. Although every family, at one time or another, faces this problem, some are more subject to it than others. Those families need to take extra measures to avoid the blowouts, reduce their intensity, and resolve them when they occur.

AVOIDING POWER STRUGGLES

The most effective approach to power struggles is to not have them. You can avoid many by following a few general principles:

- *Ignore minor misbehavior.* Pick your battles carefully. Constant criticism breeds hostile and resentful children. And it doesn't improve their behavior. It's true what they say about "not sweating the small stuff."

- *Don't badger.* Tormenting and belittling your child in any way only increases anger and animosity. Say what you have to say without judging his character.

- *Avoid nagging, lecturing, and arguing.* They don't work. The past is past. Let it go. Your child isn't listening to your words of wisdom—much less your sermon—anyway. So stop. If your child tries to argue, state your position calmly and walk away. It takes two to argue, so don't participate.

- *Get out of the moment.* Try to see the situation in terms of the big picture. Ask yourself if this one point is worth the toll the argument may take on your relationship. Will an intractable approach further your child's understanding of the point you are trying to make? Can whatever you have to say wait until later? With your emotion, can you express yourself in a constructive way?

*   *   *

Another way to reduce the frequency of power struggles is to have a plan for early recognition and intervention. First, gather input from everyone, including your child, so you can list on paper the situations or issues that trigger power struggles. Next, develop a structure for handling them. What is the policy for last-minute requests to have a friend spend the night? What, if any, are the circumstances under which you will advance allowance? Think about these situations and plan for them ahead of time—not when your child is in your face (and you're in his). Once you have determined procedures, discuss them with your child (and the rest of the family). Let everyone know what the outcomes will be when these situations are resolved smoothly and when they're not.

STRATEGIES FOR AGREEING TO DISAGREE

Agree on ways for you and your child to disagree. Think about how he can express anger, frustration, or disappointment without automatically triggering a negative response from you. Your child will feel all these emotions at some point. Notice what he already does that are acceptable ways to express his feelings. Suggest methods for him to declare "I think this is a really bad idea," without you immediately becoming defensive. Rather than yelling, he can go to his room, even slam the door and write out what his concerns are. Acknowledge that as long as he is able to state that your idea is dumb (as opposed to you being dumb), the discussion can continue. Agree to a signal that communicates "Stop now, before you go too far" that both parent and child can use when bad is about to get worse. Use a gripe list that is posted in the kitchen where your child can record his concerns and know that it will be discussed that very evening. There is no chance of raising a child without him disagreeing with you. If you haven't figured out an acceptable way for him to do so, he will continue to step over "the (undefined) line" and you will always be telling him what he did wrong.

Watch for signs that your child is on the brink of meltdown. Head off the big blowup when you see behaviors that signal he's about to lose it. Calling for a break increases the likelihood that you'll keep yourself under control and substantially reduces the chance that you will have one of those knockdown, drag-out, no-holds-barred power struggles.

A break in different rooms gives both you and your child time to calm down. Moreover, it gives you a chance to reevaluate how important your position really is. Are you blowing things out of proportion? Is the point you are trying to make really so critical? Should you rethink your position? Sometimes you need to find a way to back down. Other times, reevaluation allows you to reconfirm your position's importance, whether or not your child can see its merits.

A break also gives you the opportunity to think through exactly what outcome you want. What's realistic? Boiled down to basics, it may be that you simply want him to follow your direction. Or there may be a specific behavior you want him to stop. He doesn't have to be thrilled about it. If you expect compliance with no negative attitude, you expect too much. A break gives you time to ask yourself whether the argument is a result of your need to have him accept the outcome happily.

HANDLING A POWER STRUGGLE

Power struggles can take place over anything. What distinguishes them from ordinary disputes is the extent to which each side becomes entrenched, determined not to yield. Often, both lose perspective. What gets said is unproductive and can, in fact, be hurtful and counterproductive. Whichever side prevails, the outcome is not worth the destructive process. You must learn how to deal with power struggles when your kids are young, because when they become teenagers, battles of this magnitude put great stress on a changing relationship.

No magic phrase will turn around a situation when you're engaged in a power struggle. No pearl of your wisdom will change your child's mind. Emotions are already so high that even if you did know the right words, your child wouldn't hear them. You delude yourself if you think that by continuing to talk, your child will see the light and concede. He feels that as long as you stay in the room, he still has a chance to get you to see his point of view. Neither of you is listening to the other.

You should remember three things about power struggles:

1. *No one wins a power struggle.* Even if you get your way or your child ends up with exactly what he wanted, there is no winner. The emotional fallout, the residual feelings one or both of you have, do not go away easily—if at all. More often, they fester and reemerge unexpectedly at another time.

2. *If you think you may be engaged in a power struggle, you are.* You can feel it in your body. Your stomach may be tied in knots or your jaw clenched. Whatever it is, pay attention to it. It's telling you that you are headed for or already involved in something you want to avoid at all costs. The only way out is to do something different.

3. *Because there can be no winner, the only solution is to disengage.* Walk away. Get out.

TAKING A BREAK: HOW TO DISENGAGE FROM AND RESUME DISCUSSIONS

Taking a break is an effective tool for disengaging when tensions increase and discussion turns into argument. Establishing procedures ahead of time for doing so—including how you'll proceed when you resume—lets everyone know what to expect. Discussion is less volatile when there has been time to gain perspective and cooler heads prevail.

Make it clear that whether the discussion resumes (thus giving your child the opportunity to be heard) depends on his limiting argumentative behaviors and sticking to the plan. When you return, bring paper and pencil to record your child's concerns. Be prepared to listen and to praise improvement in your child's method of expressing his concerns. If he states his position in a different way or his wording is less contentious, the tone not as argumentative, praise your child before responding. Improvement is progress and progress is success.

Allow him to talk uninterrupted, as long as he limits himself to stating his concerns. Name calling and disrespectful language ends the discussion. But be realistic. Expect some attitude and be prepared for that tone that makes your blood boil.

When explaining the process make it clear what, if any, decisions will be made on the spot. Your policy may be that the current conversation affects future situations but won't change the one now under discussion. Or you may take the information you have recorded into consideration and return with possible alternatives in an hour. This makes it clear that nothing will happen this

PROCEDURES FOR TAKING A BREAK

1. Anyone can call for a break.

2. Determine signals you'll use to communicate the need for a break, such as a hand signal across the throat indicating "Cut!"

3. Decide ahead of time how long a break will last (e.g., fifteen minutes, thirty minutes, etc.).

4. Determine the place and length of time for follow-up discussion (e.g., at the kitchen table for no more than fifteen minutes).

5. Set a timer and take notes when you resume discussion.

6. Each party must listen without interruption.

7. A raised voice or name calling ends the discussion.

8. Decide ahead of time what the policy is for decisions resulting from the discussion. For example, no decision or change will occur at that time; decisions affect only future situations; or you will consider the matter and make a decision later.

minute. Whatever the procedures, you need to review them more than once or participants will return to old habits.

Keep in mind your child is learning from you how to handle disputes. If you blow your stack at the first sign of his disagreement, he's not likely to develop much skill at conflict resolution. Finally, at the end of any exchange, what message do you want to leave with him? Certainly not "win at any cost."

Some children seem to enjoy arguing. These future lawyers are prepared to keep up the argument at all costs. When you try to leave the room, they will dog your steps and follow you. Be sure to include contingencies for these behaviors when you develop procedures for handling power struggles. They need to know the downside of perpetuating unproductive arguments. Children who

STEPS TO REDUCE POWER STRUGGLES

1. Make a list of potentially volatile topics and situations.

2. Decide on ways to handle these situations, including rewards and punishments.

3. Agree on strategies to disagree, including ways to handle power struggles.

4. Watch for signs that your child is headed for a meltdown.

5. Develop a plan to respond to meltdowns and power struggles. Explain it to everyone in the family.

6. Stick to the plan.

7. When a power struggle starts, DISENGAGE.

8. Use the procedures for taking a break from contentious discussions (see p. 283), including the plan for resuming discussion.

relish a fight often lose sight of the original point. Once the discussion escalates, all they care about is winning. If your child is like this, it is important to stick to a plan for disengaging from the situation.

Jan: Like Theodore, I can be argumentative at times and when I'm not careful, an argument can escalate into a power struggle. Sometimes it's over truly silly stuff such as when I insist that Caroline not wear those clunky shoes because they're "inappropriate" or Theodore wear a long-sleeved shirt because I'm cold. Often my kids will concede, but when they don't—or I'm already cranky—the need to have my way can escalate until my position gets locked in. Not surprisingly, that can result in a corresponding response in my child. While the struggle may subside, without resolution, it can devolve into a silent contest of wills.

I am trying hard to recognize when to back off on unimportant things. As we negotiate the teenage minefield, I know I must choose my battles carefully and willingly relinquish the control I am losing anyway. After all, my goal is to raise my kids to be independent.

Caroline: I can be pretty stubborn but most of the time I feel that fights really aren't worth it and just go with the flow. A lot of times, though, if a fight begins, I want to be the one who has the last word.

Jan: Caroline usually does get the last word.

I am better than I used to be about disengaging from unproductive arguments. The real champion, however, is Theodore. He is more likely to recognize when we're not getting anywhere and he wants to take a break. Currently, if he starts to feel himself getting upset, calls for a five-minute break, and goes to his room, he gets a reward when the time's up. When he calls for a break and departs, leaving me fuming and *not* ready to disengage, I sheepishly realize that he's being the more mature one.

Take Care of Number One: Preserving Your Mental Health

Sharon: It is hard to live with and rear a challenging child. The constant stress of just trying to cope with—much less do right by—such a trying child can overwhelm anyone. When a parent's well-being is in question, it is much more difficult to make the distinction between a challenging child and a parent who is challenged. The exhausted, overwhelmed, clinically depressed parent may overreact to typical child behavior. With fewer positive interactions and continual punishment, the task of parenting becomes even more overwhelming. A pattern of punitive parenting adversely affects your child's behavior, which will, over time, become more challenging. The demands of raising this child put you at greater risk for both psychiatric and medical disorders.

Furthermore, a family with a challenging child may become isolated. Often this child's behavior results in fewer invitations for the parent and child to be with others. With fewer opportunities to share stories and commiserate with others, parents feel increasingly alone in their plight. Moreover, they are often embarrassed by their child's behavior and so afraid of what he will do in a group situation that they turn down the few opportunities that do come their way. This puts a parent at greater risk for emotional difficulties.

Finally, a psychiatric disorder that runs in the family may be the basis for some of the most challenging behavior in children. The parent who suffers from this same disorder, if untreated, is ill equipped to deal effectively with the child's behavior.

A warm, nurturing, accepting parent-child relationship is so important to a positive outcome for challenging children. A stressed, overwhelmed, exhausted parent is not a good candidate for providing this environment. If you recognize yourself anywhere in these descriptions, reach out for help. Talk to a friend or family member. Seek professional guidance. Do things to nurture yourself.

Pointer for Effective Parenting

- -

If you are overwhelmed by the stress of rearing your challenging child, *do something good for yourself. If you are constantly overwhelmed or depressed, GET HELP.*

The Extended Family: Enlisting Support and Fending Off Unwanted Advice

Be prepared for the onslaught of advice you will receive as you struggle to raise your challenging child. Educate yourself. Read as much as you can so you are better prepared to address their concerns (and your own). See the Resources section for recommended titles. You will not feel confident explaining an approach to parenting, much less sticking to it, if you do not understand it yourself.

Your parents may offer advice because they believe they are more experienced at parenting than you are. This is true. For better or worse, they raised you and do have experience you don't. Because they have a personal stake in how their grandchildren turn out, they may be receptive to new insights and information that other highly critical, judgmental relatives are not. It is difficult, however, for parents to accept education from their own children because they find it hard to see you in any light other than as their child.

Information from recognized professionals is often more palatable. Presenting it as a recommended approach to parenting that they can read on their own enables them to review the material without it appearing as a rejection of their suggestions and the way they raised you. If they can also use the same approaches when your child is with them, it will provide the structure he needs during his visits. This consistency teaches him that those closest to him share the same expectations for his behavior.

A best-case scenario includes the support of extended family and friends for your new approaches to your challenging child. However, that isn't always going to happen. In fact, you're more likely to get unsolicited advice and criticism. Learn how to fend off these comments. You can do little about the critics. They have already come to a conclusion and nothing you say is likely to change their minds.

Too often, well-meaning relatives have told you that if they only had your child for two weeks he wouldn't behave this way. The reality is that sometime during that stay, your all-knowing, concerned, well-meaning relatives are highly likely to experience the full range of your child's behavior. And, they are unlikely to be able to "fix" it. However, when anybody—any living, breathing, trustworthy person—suggests taking your challenging child for any period of time, *let him*. You need the break.

12

Striving to Maintain Calm

Taking It One Day at a Time

Theodore: Mornings now are a lot smoother. There's a lot less yelling. I think it's partly because I get up at 6:40 (or at least I try to) and take a hot shower before I do anything else—even before I make my bed. Also now that I have a morning list, I know what I need to do. With the morning list I can earn an incentive—money, chips for screen time, or whatever—and we have set times for when I have to get part of my list done to earn part of the incentive. That way I don't waste time until five minutes before I have to leave and then rush around trying to get everything done. If my morning goes well, I feel I'll have a good day.

Jan: I groggily awoke this morning to the sound of Theodore's piercing alarm clock shrieking at 6:40 A.M. Half awake, I heard his bedroom door open, his feet pad across the hall to the bathroom, then the sound of the shower going full blast. Confident he was up and about, I dozed off until my radio went on at 7:10. I lingered in bed for ten minutes, then wandered out to the kitchen, turned on the teakettle, and drifted into the breakfast room, where Theodore was dressed and quietly reading a book while he polished off a bowl of cereal and several muffins. I mumbled, "Good morning, Theodore," before I headed back to my room to get dressed. When the teakettle whistled, I ambled back into the kitchen, poured hot water through my tea strainer, contentedly cut my grapefruit, and spied Theodore's empty cereal bowl. The dog was sleeping in the corner of the kitchen; obviously Caroline had fed and walked her. As I sat down to eat, I heard the electric tooth-brush buzzing in the background. When it stopped, I called out; "Theodore, clean up your breakfast dishes." A few minutes later, Theodore reappeared, teeth brushed, and whisked his bowl off the table, depositing it in the dishwasher. He disappeared again, book in hand. At 7:30, Jamie arrived home, having dropped Caroline off at her school bus. He, too, settled down to eat, ensconced behind the sports page.

At 7:45, Theodore reappeared, tucked his morning list into the jar on the counter, and extracted his lunch box from the refrigera-tor. "Don't forget to put the cold pack in," I reminded him as I loaded my dishes into the dishwasher. Draining my mug, I headed for the coat closet. As I pulled on my coat, Theodore was stuffing a pair of shorts into his backpack, in preparation for this after-noon's tennis team tryouts. "OK, Theodore, let's go." At 7:50, right on time, we headed to the car. As I drove him to school, we chatted about his prospects for making the tennis team.

As I write, I think back on what getting out the door in the morning was like three years ago, before Theodore was diagnosed with attention deficit disorder. Not all mornings are as quiet and calm as this one. But, for the most part, the frantic rushing around, the yelling at Theodore to hurry up, the mad scramble to locate shoes and coat, assemble lunch, and get out the door on time are in the past. Why is it so different?

Theodore now has an obnoxious alarm clock that could awaken the dead. It's connected to a "bed shaker," so even if he could tune out the shrieks of the alarm, he can't ignore the vibra-tion under his pillow. Soaking in the shower finishes the process of waking him up—all without us having said a word to him. He tosses his clothes on, yanks up the quilt on his bed, and heads for the kitchen. There, before he eats, he takes his medication from the bottle I set out on the counter the night before and pops it into his mouth. Then he scrounges for breakfast and munches away—sur-reptitiously reading either a book or the newspaper if we've re-moved the book as a distraction. His lunch box resides in the refrigerator, filled the night before; his backpack, shoes, and coat were piled by the front door last night. Breakfast over, he cleans up his dishes (sometimes with a reminder) and brushes his teeth (also sometimes with a reminder). He hasn't looked at his morning list because he now knows all the steps, but he sticks it into the jar and is ready to go.

What's changed? Theodore now has a structured morning routine, with the tasks reduced to an absolute minimum, and certain ones shifted to the night before. When he's done them all, the completed list goes in a jar on the kitchen counter. Theodore earns one chip for screen time for getting himself out of bed by 7:00 A.M. and two chips for finishing the list by 7:40.

New tools (alarm clock and bed shaker) help him get up in the morning; he showers upon awaking, and I set out his medication ahead of time. Most important, we have made *Theodore*—not Jan or Jamie—responsible for getting himself up, dressed, and out the door in the morning.

Theodore's morning routine is structured, predictable, includes a visual reminder to keep him focused, and earns him chips for screen time when he completes everything on time.

STRUCTURE & PREDICTABILITY
+ VISUAL REMINDERS & INCENTIVES
= A CALMER HOUSEHOLD

Maintaining Calm

Sharon: A household that is calm is a work in progress. The more challenging the children, the more challenged you are as parents, the more work it will take. If you get only one thing from our book, it's the idea that a calmer household is not achieved overnight and maintaining it is not a one-step process. To maintain a calm (or calmer) household, you must work on it one day at a time. Everything that happens is another opportunity to see what works and what needs revision.

Like you, challenging children want to do the right thing. But if they knew how, they'd already be doing it. Their world is a confusing place. More to the point, the world we expect them to live in is a confusing place. Our expectations for them are constantly changing and they aren't always able to make sense of them. Their frustration surfaces as negative behavior. Often they negotiate, argue, and manipulate in an attempt to gain control because it's scary not to have any control, just as it is scary for a child to have too much control. Some of the children parents find most challenging are just reeling from an inability to make sense of their world. Parents contribute to the problem—even create it—by failing to make their child's world predictable. These children need a structure that makes their world predictable.

Establishing family routines and making your child's world predictable are the most essential steps to achieving a calmer household. When your child knows the sequence of events he is to follow and understands what is expected of him, he can better predict what the outcome will be. All of us, but challenging children in particular, benefit from this structure. With it, your child will be more comfortable, less reactive, and less volatile.

PERSISTENCE MEANS STAYING THE COURSE

Once you've established household routines, it takes persistence and communication to keep things on a somewhat even keel. Don't let small disruptions scuttle the routines you set up. Don't give in to the heat of the moment and make decisions you may later regret. Recognize that the trend of progress is more important than the moment of regression when your child slips up.

COMMUNICATION: A TWO-WAY STREET

It takes communication to establish and maintain routines. Don't just check a calendar to come up with a schedule. Parents need to talk to each other. The burdensome feeling of shouldering all of the responsibility is sometimes a function of poor (or no) communication between spouses. Your partner may not realize that you are looking for a specific kind of support. He feels he makes many contributions to the parenting process. If that version of support is not what you're looking for you'll overlook his efforts and continue to feel like a one-man army. Sometimes, just talking alleviates the sense that you are solely responsible and reminds everyone of the need to share responsibility. Divvying up some of the daily child-rearing tasks can make the job less burdensome. Discuss each person's role when there are multiple time constraints before you commit to being everywhere at once.

It's not just your partner you have to confer with. Talk to your child. Set limits on what he may undertake before he announces he wants to play on two teams. Make him aware of the big picture—the family schedule—before he focuses on his own agenda to the exclusion of others'. Clarify your expectations if he has an after-school activity the day before a project is due.

Communication is a two-way street. For your child to become comfortable with priorities and time constraints, he must be included in the process of determining them. Be receptive to your child's input when developing routines. Whenever possible, ask for his ideas on ways to prioritize when there are competing activities. Show him a list with essential ones starred and ask him to check off one additional activity you can fit into the day.

To maintain calm, communication goes beyond crafting and adjusting routines. When parents—or kids—slip up, the remedy is communication. Just as parents get to remonstrate when tasks aren't completed, kids get to complain when their allowances aren't paid on time or when one child has to do more chores because another is evading them.

KEEP YOUR EXPECTATIONS REALISTIC—AND THINK AHEAD

Children's behavior frequently falls short of their parents' expectations. When that happens, your response will determine whether your child learns from the incident or continues to repeat the behavior. What you do before these situations arise is critical to the long-range outcome. Make sure your expectations are reasonable. Swift, severe punishment may interrupt the behavior but it won't teach your child what to do differently in the future. Working out an alternative strategy with your child and setting rewards for its use has a better chance of producing positive change in the long run.

PRIORITIZE WHAT TO WORK ON—AND ADAPT SOLUTIONS TO YOUR NEEDS

Focus on one (or two) issues at a time —whatever is nearest and dearest to your own boiling point. If you change too many things at once, you'll drive your child and yourself nuts. Structure and reinforcement change behavior, not lecture and punishment. Most important, take any of the approaches we've suggested and make them your own. Only you can figure out exactly what works for you, your family, and your child.

Jan: Because the problem felt minor, my friend Katie didn't want to set up an elaborate system to get her daughter to do small chores. So she adapted one of our suggestions as the Lily List. She asks Lily once to put her backpack away, set the table, etc., then writes the task on the Lily List. No TV as long as there is anything on the list, which is posted on the refrigerator. She doesn't use it for "finish your science project" but for the thirty-second to five-minute chores that, left undone, drive her nuts. This simple but effective system works for her and Lily.

CONSISTENCY

Sharon: Maintaining consistency is a little like nailing Jell-O to the wall. The enormous effort required to provide the structure and predictability your challenging child needs is exhausting. It's not easy to keep track of all those things you're supposed to be doing. And just when you think you've got it all in place, something throws a monkey wrench in it.

As your child develops and matures, his needs change. Generally, if you see things start to fall apart, go back and see if you haven't changed or abandoned procedures that once were effective. If you stay with the principles that worked in the past—the structure and routines, supported by visual cues and positive reinforcement—the result will be as close as anyone can come to consistency.

ADJUST, REVISE, AND FINE-TUNE

You constantly need to review, reassess, and reevaluate whatever you put into place. Often it is necessary to fine-tune rules or procedures. What works today to get your kid to walk the dog is probably not going to work three to six months from now. Interests change; maturity affects what matters. What works for the freshly diagnosed ADHD eight-year-old won't work for a sixteen-year-old adolescent who longs for every privilege, including the car, but wishes to have nothing to do with the family. The shift from one stage to the next comes without warning. Overnight you are faced with a new situation and have to develop Plan B. Having an array of tools, a command of approaches, and the confidence of knowing what to do will help reassure you that you *can* get things back on track.

Jan: It has not been easy for us to maintain consistency in dealing with Theodore. We have so many structures, routines, and incentives to remember—probably too many! Our kitchen is full of the evidence of the techniques we use. An old mayonnaise jar by the toaster is stuffed full of family fines. An empty powdered bouillon jar on the counter holds the paper clips Theodore's earned for screen time. Spare paper clips reside in their box next to the flour canister. A heap of used copies of Theodore's morning list litter the windowsill. Caroline's blue walk-the-dog ribbon (no longer used, but never put away) is looped over the cabinet handle. The refrigerator door is patchworked with our "visual cues"—the yellow list for the backpack, the green weekly allowance chart, and the pink chore list. Most prominent is "Job Rules," banged out on the computer by me in a fit of irritation, all in bold capital letters, ticking off rules for chores neglected. To it, in clashing red and blue ink, Caroline and Theodore have scrawled a running commentary:

"*$2 fine if Car/T goes into the other's room and takes something.*"

"*Theodore may <u>NEVER</u> again play Roller Coaster Tycoon.*"

"*Caroline may <u>NEVER</u> ever again play Age of Empires II or*

MechWarrior 3 even for eternity and if she touches them or uses any part of them in any way, C pays T $2."

It isn't only the kitchen that's cluttered with visual reminders. Our bathrooms all have signs taped to the mirrors, scrawled in bold red letters proclaiming: "10 CENTS FOR FLUSHED TOILET."

This plethora of visual cues has become part of the background to me, but that's not the case when guests arrive. The night I had my students over for dinner, one of them emerged from the powder room and handed me a dime. A little perplexed, she announced, "Here's my 10 cents. I flushed the toilet."

I am tired of eternal vigilance and chronic tinkering with incentives, routines, and procedures. I am weary of checking that Theodore's turned off his light by his bedtime every night—and then having to remember to dock him fifteen minutes the next night when he forgets. Did I put Theodore's paper clips in the jar for getting up and completing his morning list today? Did I set out his medication in the bottle on the kitchen counter last night? "Jamie, why did you let Theodore have screen time tonight? He didn't earn any clips this morning, so he's not allowed to use any for screen time tonight. . . . Sorry, I forgot to tell you."

I wish, I wish, I wish that for once, we could just put something in place and then *forget about it* while it works effectively until Theodore goes off to college. Usually it helps if I think about where we were a year ago (or two, or three).

ONE DAY AT A TIME

Sharon: You just have to make it through one day at a time. Think about the small successes. Focus on the importance of what you are achieving. If you stop and think about the long years facing you, you'll give up in frustration. Just keep telling yourself that all you have to get through is today. Getting it right today helps you know what to do tomorrow. A good week is a success, even if it doesn't last. It's hard work, but the payoff will be a happier, more productive, less disruptive child.

GET STARTED

It's not your fault that you have a challenging child. Nor is it your child's fault. But it is you who have to change to make the difference in your child because he's not capable of changing on his own. There is a lot you can do. But you have to get started. You

---

PRINCIPLES FOR A CALMER HOUSEHOLD

- *Decide what it is you want your child to do, in specific terms.*

- *Discuss those expectations with him.*

- *Set up a system of cues and reminders that he can see, so he doesn't have to rely on you telling him what to do.*

- *Reinforce him when he gets it right.* Incentives work because they make it worth your child's while to change his behavior. It takes a lot less energy to be positive than punitive.

- *Be reasonable in your expectations.* It's a gradual process. Recognize improvement. He's not going to get it right every time, every day. If the negative behavior happens less often, doesn't last as long, and, when it does occur, isn't as severe, there has been improvement.

- *Notice trends.* Don't be defeated or sidetracked by backsliding, which is inevitable. Improvement is success and reason enough for celebration.

- *If you want to see the behavior happen again, pay attention to it.* When you walk into a room, ask yourself what's going right and comment on it. Tell yourself, if there's no blood and no flames, something is going right. Praise your child for it.

can stay stuck in a "Why me?" "What did I do to deserve this?" "What did I do wrong?" mode or get over it and start mobilizing your resources. Altering what happens in your own house has the best chance of changing how your child behaves. Your efforts are still your child's greatest prospect for success.

Paying Attention to the Positive

If I could recommend only one thing to help you begin the process of change with your challenging child, it is to emphasize the positive. If I could get parents to pay as much attention to the positive as they insist on paying to the negative, everyone would be a whole lot happier. With a challenging child, that isn't easy. But for your sake, and that of your child, it is essential. If the right moment never seems to come or words fail you, there are alternatives.

Have fun with your child—for no reason at all. Don't wait for a birthday or special event. Find something to do that will make you both laugh. Make the time to get away from the stresses of homework, a messy room, and bad manners to go to a playground, shoot hoops, play miniature golf, have a water battle, feed the ducks, make a cake together, or go to have a makeup lesson at a department store. Do whatever it takes to have some one-to-one time with each of your children. You need to get back in touch with the happy side of your child—and yourself.

I worked with a couple who was terribly concerned about their daughter's general well-being. Her behavior was part of the problem, but their chief concern was that she was uncommunicative—distant and sullen. After several sessions with both parents, it was clear that they did not know how to reach their daughter. They weren't sure how to talk to her. The mother talked around every issue while the father said nothing.

I suggested they spend an hour selecting greeting cards that communicated sentiments they thought were important. Each week they were to find at least one opportunity to leave a card for their daughter. They were to write a personal note that explained what prompted them to consider the moment an opportune time and leave it for Marianne. Though they left more than a dozen cards, there was no real change in her communication.

Several months later Marianne's father called and told me that she had phoned from her friend's house asking that someone look in her drawer for a sweater she'd forgotten. When her father did so, he was thunderstruck to find Marianne had saved every card they had left for her.

Sometimes, the written word can speak for you when you can't find the words to say. It can remind your child that you aren't always yelling at him, that despite all the problems, the fights, and the battles, you really do love him. Someday when you can't manage to say something nice to your child, try writing down how much you appreciate him for the qualities that make him special. The written word can document feelings long after the spoken word has been forgotten.

*   *   *

Theodore: My life is a lot better now than it was before I was diagnosed with attention deficit disorder. Using the stuff in this book has made life much easier. Sometimes it took a while for me to see why we were doing something. Sometimes it took longer for it to work and some things didn't work until we changed them to operate a little differently. But almost everything in this book has helped me a lot.

Life in our house is now a lot calmer than before. We'll probably never be entirely free of yelling and screaming, just like medication won't cure my ADHD—but it can help treat it. Our book is like that. It won't make your house free of all problems (or all the yelling), but it will make life a lot easier and calmer for everyone in your family.

It's been hard for me to get along in life. Sometimes I found it difficult to share my personal life in this book because I've always been embarrassed about it. I've always said to myself, "Why can't I be a normal kid like everybody else?" Now I know there are other kids like me. If I can help even one of them know that life can be better, then it will be worth it. I hope this book helps you too.

SOLUTION FINDER

REFERENCES

Barkley, Russell A. *ADHD and the Nature of Self-Control*. New York: Guilford Press, 1997.

———. *Taking Charge of ADHD: The Complete, Authoritative Guide for Parents*. Revised ed. New York: Guilford Press, 2000.

Becker, Wesley, Siegfried Engelmann, and Don Thomas. *Teachers: A Course in Applied Psychology*. Chicago: Science Research Associates, 1971.

Becker, Wesley, ed. "An Empirical Basis for Change in Education" and "Reducing Behavior Problems: An Operant Conditioning Guide for Teachers" in Becker, Wesley, Siegfried Engelmann, and Don Thomas. *Teachers: A Course in Applied Psychology*. Chicago: Science Research Associates, 1971, pp. 129–65.

Castellanos, F. Xavier, and Karen J. Miller. "Attention Deficit Hyperactivity Disorders." *Pediatrics in Review* 19, no. 11 (1998): 373–84.

Cohen, Cathi. *Raise Your Child's Social I.Q.: Stepping Stones to People Skills for Kids*. Silver Spring, MD: Advantage Books, 2000.

Madsen, C. H. Jr., W. C. Becker, and D. R. Thomas. "Rules, Praise and Ignoring: Elements of Elementary Classroom Control." *Journal of Applied Behavior Analysis* (1968): 1, 139–150.

Phelan, Thomas W. *1-2-3 Magic: Effective Discipline for Children 2–12*. Glen Ellyn, IL: Child Management Inc., 1995.

Robin, Arthur L., and Sharon L. Foster. *Negotiating Parent-Adolescent Conflict: A Behavioral Family Systems Approach*. New York: Guilford Publications, 1989.

Seligman, Martin E. P. *Learned Optimism: How to Change Your Mind and Your Life*. Reissue edition with new introduction. New York: Pocket Books, 1998.

Wilens, Timothy E., M.D. *Straight Talk about Psychiatric Medications for Kids*. New York: Guilford Press, 1999.

RESOURCES

For Parents

Some of the following may be out of print. For such books, try your local library or Internet sites specializing in out-of-print books, such as *www.abebooks.com* and *www.alibris.com*.

Asher, Steven R., and John D. Coie, eds. *Peer Rejection in Childhood.* Cambridge, England: Cambridge University Press, 1990.

Attwood, Tony. *Asperger's Syndrome: A Guide for Parents and Professionals.* London: Jessica Kingsley Publishers, 1997.

Ayres, A. Jean. *Sensory Integration and the Child.* Los Angeles: Western Psychological Services, 1987.

Barkley, Russell A. *Taking Charge of ADHD: The Complete, Authoritative Guide for Parents.* Revised ed. New York: Guilford Press, 2000.

Barkley, Russell A., and Christine M. Benton. *Your Defiant Child: Eight Steps to Better Behavior.* New York: Guilford Press, 1998.

Beekman, Susan, and Jeanne Holmes. *Battles, Hassles, Tantrums and Tears: Strategies for Coping with Conflict and Making Peace at Home.* New York: Hearst Books, 1993.

Blume, Judy. *Letters to Judy: What Kids Wish They Could Tell You.* New York: Pocket Books, 1987.

Brooks, Robert, and Sam Goldstein. *Raising Resilient Children: Fostering Strength, Hope and Optimism in Your Child.* New York: Contemporary Books, 2001.

Carlson, Trudy. *Depression in the Young: What We Can Do to Help Them.* Duluth, MN: Benline Press, 1998.

———. *The Life of a Bipolar Child: What Every Parent and Professional Needs to Know.* Duluth, MN: Benline Press, 2000.

Cohen, Cathi. *Raise Your Child's Social I.Q.: Stepping Stones to People Skills for Kids.* Silver Spring, MD: Advantage Books, 2000.

Cohen, Shirley. *Targeting Autism: What We Know, Don't Know, and Can Do to Help Young Children with Autism and Related Disorders.* Berkeley, CA: University of California Press, 1998.

Cytryn, Leon, and Donald H. McKnew. *Growing Up Sad: Childhood Depression and Its Treatment.* Chicago: W. W. Norton, 1998.

Faber, Adele, and Elaine Mazlish. *How to Talk So Kids Will Listen and Listen So Kids Will Talk.* New York: Avon Books, 1980.

Fassler, David G., and Lynne S. Dumas. *"Help Me, I'm Sad": Recognizing, Treating, and Preventing Childhood and Adolescent Depression.* New York: Penguin, 1998.

Fling, Echo R. *Eating an Artichoke: A Mother's Perspective on Asperger Syndrome.* London: Jessica Kingsley Publishers, 2000.

Forgatch, Marion S., and Gerald R. Patterson. *Parents and Adolescents Living Together, Part 2: Family Problem Solving.* Eugene, OR: Castalia, 1989.

Freed, Jeffrey, and Laurie Parsons. *Right-Brained Children in a Left-Brained World: Unlocking the Potential of Your ADD Child.* New York: Simon and Schuster, 1977.

Garber, Stephen W., Marianne Daniels Garber, and Robyn Freedman Spizman. *Good Behavior: Over 1200 Sensible Solutions to Your Child's Problems from Birth to Age Twelve.* New York: Villard Books, 1987. Also *Good Behavior Made Easy Handbook,* 1995.

Goldstein, Sam, and Nancy Mather. *Overcoming Underachieving: An Action Guide to Helping Your Child Succeed in School.* New York: John Wiley and Sons, 1998.

Greene, Ross W. *The Explosive Child: A New Approach for Understanding and Parenting Easily Frustrated, "Chronically Inflexible" Children.* New York: HarperCollins, 1998.

Greenspan, Stanley, with Jacqueline Salmon. *Playground Politics: Understanding the Emotional Life of Your School-Age Child.* Reading, MA: Perseus Books, 1993.

Haerle, Tracy, ed. *Children with Tourette Syndrome: A Parent's Guide.* The Special Needs Collection. Bethesda, MD: Woodbine House, 1992.

Hallowell, Edward. *When You Worry about the Child You Love. Emotional and Learning Problems in Children.* New York: Simon and Schuster, 1996.

Hallowell, Edward M., and John J. Ratey. *Driven to Distraction: Recognizing and Coping with Attention Deficit Disorder from Childhood through Adulthood.* New York: Simon and Schuster, 1995. Also *Answers to Distraction.* New York: Bantam Books, 1996.

Harris, Sandra L. *Siblings of Children with Autism: A Guide for Families.* Bethesda, MD: Woodbine House, 1994.

Hartmann, Thom. *Attention Deficit Disorder: A Different Perception.* Revised edition. Grass Valley, CA: Underwood Books, 1997.

Ingersoll, Barbara D., and Sam Goldstein. *Attention Deficit Disorder and Learning Disabilities: Realities, Myths and Controversial Treatments.* New York: Main Street Books, 1993.

———. *Lonely, Sad and Angry: A Parent's Guide to Depression in Children and Adolescents.* New York: Main Street Books, 1996.

Jones, Clare B. *Sourcebook for Children with Attention Deficit Disorder: A Management Guide for Early Childhood Professionals and Parents.* Tucson, AZ: Communication Skill Builders, 1991.

Joslin, Karen Renshaw. *Positive Parenting from A to Z.* New York: Fawcett Books, 1994.

Katz, Mark. *On Playing a Poor Hand Well: Insights from the Lives of Those Who Have Overcome Childhood Risks and Adversities.* Chicago; W. W. Norton, 1997.

Kilcarr, Patrick J., and Patricia O. Quinn. *Voices from Fatherhood: Fathers, Sons and ADHD.* New York: Brunner/Mazel, 1997.

Koplewicz, Harold S. *It's Nobody's Fault: New Hope and Help for Difficult Children and Their Parents.* New York: Times Books, 1996.

Kranowitz, Carol Stock. *The Out-of-Sync Child: Recognizing and Coping with Sensory Integration Dysfunction.* New York: Perigee, 1998.

Kurcinka, Mary Sheedy. *Raising Your Spirited Child: A Guide for Parents Whose Child Is More Intense, Sensitive, Perceptive, Persistent, Energetic.* New York: HarperPerennial, 1992. Also *Raising Your Spirited Child Workbook,* 1998.

Levine, Mel. *Educational Care: A System for Understanding and Helping Children with Learning Problems at Home and in School.* Cambridge, MA: Educators Publishing Service, 1994.

MacKenzie, Robert J. *Setting Limits: How to Raise Responsible, Independent Children by Providing CLEAR Boundaries.* Rocklin, CA: Prima, 1998.

Miller, Jeffrey A. *The Childhood Depression Sourcebook.* Lincolnwood, IL: Lowell House, NTC/Contemporary, 1999.

Myles, Brenda Smith, and Jack Southwick. *Asperger's Syndrome and Difficult Moments: Practical Solutions for Tantrums, Rage and Meltdowns.* Shawnee Mission, KS: Autism Asperger, 1999.

Novello, Joseph R. *What to Do until the Grownup Arrives: The Art and*

Science of Raising Teenagers. Kirkland, WA: Hogrefe and Huber, 1991.

Nowicki, Stephen Jr., and Marshall P. Duke. *Helping the Child Who Doesn't Fit In.* Atlanta, GA: Peachtree, 1992.

Papolos, Demitri, and Janice Papolos. *The Bipolar Child: The Definitive and Reassuring Guide to Childhood's Most Misunderstood Disorder.* New York: Broadway Books, 1999.

Parker, Harvey C. *Put Yourself in Their Shoes: Understanding Teenagers with Attention Deficit Hyperactivity Disorder.* Plantation, FL: Specialty Press, 1999.

Phelan, Thomas W. *1-2-3 Magic: Effective Discipline for Children 2–12.* Glen Ellyn, IL: Child Management, 1995. Available in Spanish as *1-2-3 Magia: Disciplina Efectiva para Ninos de 2 a 12, 1997.*

————. *Surviving Your Adolescents: How to Manage and Let Go of Your 13–18 Year Olds.* Glen Ellyn, IL: Child Management, 1998.

Powers, Michael D. *Children with Autism: A Parents' Guide.* The Special Needs Collection. Bethesda, MD: Woodbine House, 2000.

Pruitt, David B., ed. *Your Child: What Every Parent Needs to Know about Childhood Development from Birth to Preadolescence.* American Academy of Child and Adolescent Psychiatry. New York: Harper Reference, 1998.

Rapoport, Judith L. *The Boy Who Couldn't Stop Washing: The Experience and Treatment of Obsessive-Compulsive Disorder.* New York: Penguin Books, 1991.

Robin, Arthur L., and Sharon L. Foster. *Negotiating Parent-Adolescent Conflict: A Behavioral Family-Systems Approach.* Guilford Family Therapy Series. New York: Guilford Publications, 1989.

Shure, Myrna B., with Theresa Foy Digeronimo. *Raising a Thinking Child: Help Your Young Child to Resolve Everyday Conflicts and Get Along with Others: The "I Can Problem Solve" Program.* New York: Pocket Books, 1996.

Silver, Larry B. *The Misunderstood Child: Understanding and Coping with Your Child's Learning Disabilities.* Third ed., revised and updated. New York: Times Books, 1998.

Smith, Sally L. *No Easy Answers: The Learning Disabled Child at Home and at School.* New York: Bantam Books, 1979.

————. *Succeeding against the Odds: Strategies and Insights from the Learning Disabled.* Los Angeles: Jeremy P. Tarcher, 1991.

Turecki, Stanley. *The Emotional Problems of Normal Children.* New York: Bantam Books, 1994.

Wilens, Timothy E., M.D. *Straight Talk about Psychiatric Medications for Kids.* New York: Guilford Press, 1999.

Wolf, Anthony E. *Get Out of My Life, but First Could You Drive Me and Cheryl to the Mall?: A Parent's Guide to the New Teenager.* New York: Noonday Press, 1992.

Zeigler Dendy, Chris A. *Teenagers with ADD: A Parents' Guide.* Bethesda, MD: Woodbine House, 1995.

Zentall, Sydney S., and Sam Goldstein. *Seven Steps to Homework Success: A Family Guide for Solving Common Homework Problems.* Plantation, FL: Specialty Press, 1999.

For Educators

Brooks, Robert. *The Self-Esteem Teacher.* Circle Pines, MN: American Guidance Service, 1991.

Cumine, Val, Julia Leach, and Gill Stevenson. *Asperger Syndrome: A Practical Guide for Teachers.* London: David Fulton Publishers, 1998.

Curwin, Richard, and Allen Mendler. *Discipline with Dignity.* Second ed. Reston, VA: Association for Supervision and Curriculum Development, 1999.

Goldstein, Sam, with Lauren Braswell, et. al. *Understanding and Managing Children's Classroom Behavior.* Wiley Series on Personality Processes. New York: John Wiley and Sons, 1995.

Karlin, Muriel Schoe, and Regina Berger. *Discipline and the Disruptive Child: A Practical Guide for Elementary Teachers.* Englewood Cliffs, NJ: Parker, 1992.

Levin, James, and John M. Shanken-Kaye. *The Self-Control Classroom: Understanding and Managing the Disruptive Behavior of All Students, Including Those with ADHD.* Dubuque, IA: Kendall/Hunt, 1998.

Mannix, Darlene. *Life Skills Activities for Special Children.* West Nyack, NY: Center for Applied Research in Education, 1992.

———. *Social Skills Activities for Special Children.* West Nyack, NY: Center for Applied Research in Education, 1993.

Rief, Sandra F., and Julie A. Heimburge. *How to Reach and Teach All Students in the Inclusive Classroom.* West Nyack, NY: Center for Applied Research in Education, 1996.

Shapiro, Edward S., and Christine L. Cole, *Behavior Change in the Classroom: Self-Management Interventions.* The Guilford School Practitioner. New York: Guilford Press, 1994.

Swift, Marshall S., and George Spivack. *Alternative Teaching Strategies: Helping Behaviorally Troubled Children Achieve: A Guide for Teachers and Psychologists.* Champaign, IL: Research Press, 1975.

Wagner, Sheila. *Inclusive Programming for Elementary Students with Autism.* Atlanta: Emory Autism Resource Center, 1998.

Wong, Harry, and Rosemary Wong. *How to Be an Effective Teacher: The First Days of School.* Mountain View, CA: Harry K. Wong Publications, 1998.

For Children

Brown, Laurene Krasny, and Marc Brown. *Dinosaurs Divorce: A Guide for Changing Families.* Boston: Joy Street Books, 1986.

Brunger, Bruce A., and Cathy Reimers. *The Buzz and Pixie Activity Coloring Book: An Entertaining Way to Help Young Children Understand Their Behavior.* Plantation, FL: Specialty Press, 1999.

Buehrens, Adam. *Hi, I'm Adam: A Child's Book about Tourette Syndrome.* Duarte, CA: Hope Press, 1990.

Davis, Leslie, and Sandi Sirotowitz, with Harvey C. Parker. *Study Strategies Made Easy: A Practical Plan for School Success.* Plantation, FL: Specialty Press, 1996. (Also in video.)

Garland, E. Jane. *Depression Is the Pits, but I'm Getting Better: A Guide for Adolescents.* Bethesda, MD: Magination Press, 1998.

Gehret, Jeanne. *I'm Somebody Too.* Fairport, NY: Verbal Images Press, 1996.

Gordon, Michael. *I Would if I Could: A Teenager's Guide to ADHD/Hyperactivity.* Dewitt, NY: GSI Publications, 1992.

———. *Jumpin' Johnny Get Back to Work! A Child's Guide to ADHD/Hyperactivity.* Dewitt, NY: GSI Publications, 1991. (Also in Spanish as *Juan el Brincon de Nuevo a Tu Trabajo! Guia para el Nino con ADHD/Hyperactivity* and in video.)

———. *My Brother's a World-Class Pain: A Sibling's Guide to ADHD/Hyperactivity.* DeWitt, NY: GSI Publications, 1992.

Ingersoll, Barbara D. *Distant Drums, Different Drummers: A Guide for Young People with ADHD.* Bethesda, MD: Cape Publications, 1995.

Levine, Mel [vinD.]. *All Kinds of Minds: A Young Person's Book about Learning Abilities and Learning Disorders.* Cambridge, MA: Educators Publishing Service, 1992.

——— *Keeping a Head in School: A Student's Book about Learning Abilities and Learning Disorders.* Cambridge, MA: Educators Publishing Service, 1991.

McCutcheon, Richard. *Get Off My Brain: Survival Guide for Lazy Students*. Minneapolis, MN: Free Spirit Publishing, 1998.

Moser, Adolph. *Don't Feed the Monster on Tuesdays!: The Children's Self-Esteem Book*. Emotional Impact Series. Kansas City, MO: Landmark Editions, 1991.

———. *Don't Pop Your Cork on Mondays!: The Children's Anti-Stress Book*. Emotional Impact Series. Kansas City, MO: Landmark Editions, 1988.

———. *Don't Rant and Rave on Wednesdays!: The Children's Anger-Control Book*. Emotional Impact Series. Kansas City, MO: Landmark Editions, 1994.

———. *Don't Tell a Whopper on Fridays!: The Children's Truth-Control Book*. Emotional Impact Series. Kansas City, MO: Landmark Editions, 1999.

Quinn, Patricia O. *Adolescents and ADD: Gaining the Advantage*. New York: Magination Press, 1995.

Quinn, Patricia O., and Judith Stern. *Putting on the Brakes: Young People's Guide to Understanding Attention Deficit Hyperactivity Disorder (ADHD)*. New York: Magination Press, 1991. (Also *The "Putting on the Brakes" Activity Book For Young People with ADHD*, 1993, and *The Best of "Brakes": An Activity Book for Kids with ADD*, 2000.)

Romain, Trevor. *Bullies Are a Pain in the Brain*. Minneapolis, MN: Free Spirit Publishing, 1997.

———. *Cliques, Phonies and Other Baloney*. Minneapolis, MN: Free Spirit Publishing, 1998.

Schnurr, Rosina G. *Asperger's Huh? A Child's Perspective*. Gloucester, Ontario: Anisor Publishing, 1999.

Sharmat, Marjorie Weinman. *Bartholomew the Bossy*. New York: Macmillan Publishing, 1984.

Sternberg, Kate. *Mama's Morning*. Bethesda, MD: Advantage Books, 1997.

Videos

Brooks, Robert. *Look What You've Done! Learning Disabilities and Self-Esteem: Stories of Hope and Resilience*. Alexandria, VA: PBS Video, 1997. (Separate teacher and parent versions.)

Goldstein, Sam. *Why Isn't My Child Happy?: A Video Guide about Childhood Depression*. Salt Lake City, UT: Neurology, Learning and Behavior Center, 1994.

Goldstein, Sam, and Michael Goldstein. *Educating Inattentive Children*. Salt Lake City, UT: Neurology, Learning and Behavior Center, 1990.

Lavoie, Richard. *How Difficult Can This Be? The F.A.T. City Workshop*. Alexandria, VA: PBS Video, 1989.

———. *When the Chips Are Down: Learning Disabilities and Discipline Strategies for Improving Children's Behavior*. Alexandria, VA: PBS Video, 1997.

Robin, Arthur L., and Sharon K. Weiss. *Managing Oppositional Youth: Effective Practical Strategies for Managing the Behavior of Hard to Manage Kids and Teens!* Detroit: Specialty Press Videos, 1997.

Schubiner, Howard. *ADHD in Adolescents: Our Point of View*. Detroit, MI: Children's Hospital of Michigan, 1995.

Organizations

American Speech-Language-Hearing Association. 10801 Rockville Pike, Rockville, MD 20852. (800) 638-8255. *www.asha.org*. For 24 hours a day, 7 days a week automated information: ASHA Line: (888) 321-ASHA. ASHA Action Center: (800) 498-2071; fax: (877) 541-5035; e-mail: actioncenter@asha.org (first point of contact); also nsslha@asha.org

Center for Development and Learning (CDL). 208 S. Tyler Street, Suite A, Covington, LA 70433. (504) 893-7777. *www.cdl.org*

Children and Adults with Attention Deficit Disorder (CHADD). 8181 Professional Place, Suite 201, Landover, MD 20785. (800) 233-4050 and (301) 306-7070; fax: (301) 306-7090; www.chadd.org; e-mail: national@chadd.org (Contact local chapter, which can be located on the Web site, for information.)

Council for Exceptional Children (CEC). 1920 Association Drive, Reston, VA 20191-1589. (888) CEC-SPED (232-7733) or (703) 620-3660. TTY (text only): (703) 264-9446; Fax: (703) 264-9494; *www.cec.org*; e-mail (constituent services): *service@cec.sped.org*
- Division for Learning Disabilities (DLD): www.dldcec.org
- Canadian CEC: 1010 Polytek Court, Unit 36, Gloucester, ON, Canada K1J 9J2 (613) 747-9226; Fax: (613) 745-9282; *www.igs.net/fimpccec/*; e-mail: ccec@igs.net.
- International CEC: Division of International Special Education and Services (DISES) www.wmich.edu/sped/dises.html

Educational Resources Information Center (ERIC). ERIC Clearinghouse on Disabilities and Gifted Education. 1920 Association Drive, Reston,

VA 20191-1589. (888) CEC-SPED (232-7733) or (703) 620-3660; *http://ericec.org*

Learning Disabilities Association of America (LDA). 4156 Library Road, Pittsburgh, PA 15234. (412) 341-1515. www.ldantl.org

- Learning Disabilities Association of Canada. 323 Chapel Street, Ottawa, Ontario, Canada. K1N 7Z2 (613) 238-5721; Fax: (613) 235-5391; *www.ldac-taac.ca.*; e-mail: *information@ldac-taac.ca.*

National Alliance for the Mentally Ill. Colonial Place Three, 2107 Wilson Boulevard, Suite 300, Arlington, VA 22201-3042. (800) 950-NAMI (6264); TDD: (703) 516-7227; front desk: (703) 524-7600; fax: (703) 524-9094; *www.nami.org*

National Alliance for the Mentally Ill—Children and Adolescent Network. 703-524-7600

National Information Center for Children and Youth with Disabilities (NICHCY). P.O. Box 1492, Washington, DC 20013. (800) 695-0285 (voice/TTY) or (202) 884-8200 (voice/TTY); fax: (202) 884-8441; *www.nichcy.org*; e-mail: *nichcy@aed.org*

Other Resources

ADD Warehouse (publishers and distributors of resources on attention deficit disorder and related problems). 300 Northwest Seventieth Avenue, Suite 102, Plantation, FL 33317. For catalog, call: (800) 233-9273; (954) 792-8944; fax: (954) 792-8545; *www.addwarehouse.com*

American Camping Association (resource for summer camps). 5000 State Road 67 North, Martinsville, IN 46151. (765) 342-8456; fax: (745) 342-2065. Extensive e-mail list on Web site: *www.acacamps.org*. For bookstore catalog, call (800) 428-CAMP. e-mail: *bookstore@aca-camps.org*

American School Directory (lists all K–12 schools in the U.S., organized by state). *www.asd.com*

INDEX

Page numbers in *italic* indicate figures; those in bold indicate tables.

Janet E. Heininger, Ph.D.

Dr. Janet E. Heininger is currently making a documentary film, *Memorializing America's Past: National Monuments and National Identity*, about what monuments tell us about the difficulty of agreeing on who we are and what we value as Americans, as well as how we prefer to view the past and how we want future generations to remember it. Prior to that, she was a consultant for strategic planning and long-term growth to the president of an international student exchange nonprofit, Youth for Understanding. She was Assistant Professor of International Politics and Diplomacy in the Washington Semester Program at American University from 1993 to 1998 and faculty chair from 1994 to 1996. She was also a member of the faculty of American University's School of International Service. Jan is the author of *Peacekeeping in Transition: The United Nations in Cambodia*, funded and published by the Twentieth Century Fund in November 1994, as well as other articles and book chapters. She is working on another book, *China Unveiled: Chinese Exceptionalism and Americans' Images of China*.

Jan spent seven years on Capital Hill and four years in the State Department. From 1986 to 1991, she worked for Sen. Robert C. Byrd when he was Senate Majority and Minority Leader, then Chairman of the Senate Appropriations Committee. She also served as Senator Byrd's Legislative Director. She covered regional foreign policy issues and foreign aid appropriations subcommittee issues. She then served as Administrative Assistant for Rep. Barbara B. Kennelly, Chief Deputy Majority Whip in the House of

Representatives. In that position, she also covered foreign policy issues.

In the State Department, Jan served as the Senior Analyst for International Organizations in the Office of Global Issues in the Bureau of Intelligence and Research, an analyst of internal Chinese political developments and in the State Department's Office of the Historian.

Jan has a Ph.D. in twentieth century and U.S. diplomatic history from the University of Wisconsin–Madison (1981). Her minor was in East Asian Studies. She also received an M.A. from the University of Wisconsin in American history (1976) and a B.A. from Oberlin College (1974).

She is the mother of two children, Caroline Heininger Reuter, fifteen, and Theodore Heininger Reuter, twelve. She and her husband live in Arlington, Virginia, with their children, a Lakeland terrier named Murphy, and too many saltwater fish.

Sharon K. Weiss, M.Ed.

Sharon Weiss is a behavioral consultant in private practice in northern Virginia. Her areas of expertise include parent and staff training in behavior management, specific skill training, and crisis intervention. She has worked as a teacher of special-needs children and a program coordinator and supervisor of behavioral intervention programs for behavior disordered children. A highly sought after speaker, Sharon is known for presenting practical, useful information in a humorous way. She speaks nationally and internationally on topics such as parenting and behavior management in both the home and educational settings. She consults to private and public schools nationally, has been on the faculty for courses for the American Academy of Pediatrics, has taught college-level courses on behavior and provides technical assistance to area professionals.

She has been featured on radio and cable television programs and in the video *Managing Oppositional Youth*, which she also coauthored.

The primary focus of her practice is not child therapy, but parent and professional training. It's the nuts and bolts of general behavior management, structure, and discipline.

Sharon's background is in psychology, with graduate work in Special Education of the emotionally disturbed, an internship in crisis intervention, and postgraduate work in counseling.